MW00463949

Government for the Future: Reflection and Vision for Tomorrow's Leaders

Government for the Future: Reflection and Vision for Tomorrow's Leaders

EDITED BY

MARK A. ABRAMSON

DANIEL J. CHENOK

JOHN M. KAMENSKY

ROWMAN & LITTLEFIELD PUBLISHERS, INC.
Lanham • Boulder • New York • London

ROWMAN & LITTLEFIELD PUBLISHERS, INC.

Published in the United States of America
by Rowman & Littlefield Publishers, Inc.
A wholly owned subsidiary of The Rowman & Littlefield Publishing Group, Inc.
4501 Forbes Boulevard, Suite 200, Lanham, Maryland 20706
www.rowmanlittlefield.com

Unit A, Whitacre Mews, 26-34 Stannary Street, London SE11 4AB

Copyright © 2018 by IBM Center for the Business of Government

All rights reserved. No part of this publication may be reproduced,
stored in a retrieval system, or transmitted in any form or by any
means, electronic, mechanical, photocopying, recording, or otherwise,
without the prior permission of the publisher.

British Library Cataloguing in Publication Information Available

Library of Congress Cataloging-in-Publication Information has been requested

ISBN 978-1-5381-2169-6 (cloth : alk. paper)
ISBN 978-1-5381-2170-2 (paper : alk. paper)
ISBN 978-1-5381-2171-9 (electronic)

Printed in the United States of America

♾™ The paper used in this publication meets the minimum requirements of American
National Standard for Information Sciences—Permanence of Paper for Printed Library
Materials, ANSI/NISO Z39.48-1992.

TABLE OF CONTENTS

CHAPTER ONE

Introduction: Looking Back to Look Forward

Mark A. Abramson
Jonathan D. Breul
Daniel J. Chenok

INTRODUCTION:
LOOKING BACK TO LOOK FORWARD

Mark A. Abramson, Jonathan D. Breul, and Daniel J. Chenok

At any given moment in time, governments in the United States and around the globe carry out key missions in service of their citizens, learn from and engage with partners in other sectors, and act as cost-effective stewards of public resources. The countless positive daily actions of government leaders go largely unrecognized amidst a constant focus on the highly visible but far smaller set of challenges and problems faced by the public sector. However, stepping back to view progress over a span of decades reveals evidence of the sum total of this continuous evolution in government management—as well as providing perspective on the future of public service.

It is from this longer-term perspective about the performance and potential for government that the IBM Center for The Business of Government wrote *Government for the Future: Reflection and Vision for Tomorrow's Leaders*. Since 1998, the IBM Center has published research from more than 400 outside contributors—largely from academia, as well as nonprofits and journalists. Collectively, these contributors created a body of knowledge about best practices and lessons learned for government improvement. In addition, the IBM Center has developed a record of public sector challenges and opportunities through more than 500 interviews with government leaders on its radio show, the "Business of Government Hour." In *Government for the Future*, we draw from this rich repository of content to reflect on major drivers of public sector progress over the past two decades.

More importantly, reflection on this content provides a foundation to paint a vision of what government management may look like two decades hence. As described below, we have built on this foundation to bring together a set of viewpoints about the public sector in 2040, through a set of collaborative brainstorming sessions and a crowdsourcing of ideas about future scenarios. This vision of tomorrow's government is framed through essays from experts that lay out a roadmap for how to maximize benefits and minimize risks, with potential innovations ranging from the workplace of the future to the advancement of space exploration.

The IBM Center has been privileged to contribute cutting-edge research that led to practical, actionable recommendations for government executives during the last twenty years, and to have collaborated with like-minded organizations to improve government performance. With *Government for the Future*, we look continue this collaboration among government, academia, nonprofits, and industry through the next twenty years.

History of the IBM Center
for The Business of Government

In June 1998, a group of leaders in the consulting firm PricewaterhouseCoopers created a new organization: The PricewaterhouseCoopers Endowment for The Business of Government. The Endowment's goal was simple: to encourage academic research on topics of import for government managers, and to increase understanding about what works in government. To encourage this research, a small grants program provided research stipends to experts, based on a competitive review of proposals submitted in response to a semiannual announcement with research priorities for the coming year. With the IBM acquisition of PwC Consulting in 2002, the Endowment moved to IBM and was renamed the IBM Center for The Business of Government.

Since its creation, the IBM Center has awarded stipends to more than 400 researchers across the world, who have produced nearly 350 reports and essays—and counting. In addition, the Center has produced 23 books and many special reports, and hosted hundreds of radio interviews and dozens of events with government, industry, academic, and nonprofit experts.

The Center's mission has remained the same throughout our twenty years: to stimulate research and facilitate discussion of new approaches for improving the effectiveness of government at the federal, state, local, and international levels. We strive to assist public sector leaders and managers in addressing real-world problems through practical ideas and original thinking to improve government management. We hope that the Center's efforts have raised awareness about the importance of good management to an effective government that makes a positive difference in the world.

A GUIDE TO READING
GOVERNMENT FOR THE FUTURE

Consistent with our objective of painting a future vision through reflection on past progress, this book consists of two sections:

- **Part I: Reflections on 20 Years of Management Progress**
  Part I examines six significant and enduring management trends of the past twenty years:
    - Going Digital
    - Using Data
    - Managing Performance
    - "Liking" Social Media
    - Becoming Collaborative
    - Assessing Risk

These six enduring trends were identified through analysis of content in past IBM Center reports, as well as insights about key government reforms gained from a survey of current and past government executives and leading academics.

- **Part II: Visions of Government in 2040**
  Part II looks twenty years ahead and consists of two sections:
  - **Perspectives on the Future:** During Fall 2017, the Center sponsored a Challenge Grant Competition through which individuals proposed a vision for government in 2040. Based on a review of nearly 100 submissions, we selected five proposals to be expanded into chapters.

  - **Envisioning the Road Ahead:** During Spring 2018, the Center hosted four small group "envisioning" sessions. Each session brought experts, academics, and government practitioners together to examine the road ahead to 2040 in the following areas:
    » The Future of Work
    » The Future of Artificial Intelligence
    » The Future of Citizen Engagement
    » The Future of Data and Analytics

    Four of these experts—Darrell West, David Bray, Hollie Gilman, and Shelley Metzenbaum—each prepared a chapter describing their visions on the above topics, based on both the envisioning session in which they participated and their own extensive research conducted throughout their careers.

In conducting research for this book, we found the academic literature on innovation very helpful, and adopted an innovation adoption model to frame the chapters in Part I. For example, we tracked cutting-edge management innovations early in their implementation—such as the use of blogs, Twitter, and wikis in government—and assessed their growth and institutionalization over time. This provided a useful vantage from which to view the evolution of management initiatives. Each of the Part I chapters include discussions of the following stages in the lifecycle of each of the six enduring management trends, each of which is the product of multiple management initiatives.

- **Early action:** This phase is generally categorized by extensive experimentation. A new management initiative is deployed, usually on a pilot basis, by entrepreneurial agencies that volunteer to serve as early innovators and adopters. As would be expected, this phase is characterized by successes to build on and failures to learn from. In many instances, agencies benefited from the experience of the early adopters.
- **Expansion:** Based on successes during the first stage and increased attention given to a new initiative, the second phase is characterized by increased adoption. More agencies implement the new innovation, and more learning takes place—a "let a thousand flowers bloom" attitude

often prevails. During this phase, individuals from different agencies collaborate through formal or informal communities of practice to share knowledge. For each of the management trends described in Part I, challenges and barriers are identified during the expansion phase—based on agency experiences with new management initiatives—as well as pathways to overcome or mitigate such obstacles.

- **Institutionalization:** The following actions, or some combinations of these actions, are usually taken during the institutionalization phase of an initiative: passage of new legislation, integration into annual budget planning, issuance of new regulations and guidance documents, and development of norms and processes that sustain the initiative. These activities lead to consistent practices across government, and to a governance framework that provides ongoing leadership and direction. The governance framework frequently includes new structures, such as interagency committees and councils, and new positions, such as chief risk officers and chief data officers.

Identification of Major Management Trends Over the Past Twenty Years

In Fall 2017, the IBM Center surveyed a broad cross-section of government managers and academic experts to identify management initiatives that had the greatest impact on government operations over the past twenty years. We developed the survey by reviewing the IBM Center's nearly 350 reports to identify about 150 key management activities implemented over the last twenty years (we focused on specific initiatives and not on broad efforts such as Reinventing Government, the President's Management Agenda, or individual management statutes). We then grouped that list into 50 management initiatives, and asked respondents to assess the impact of each initiative.

Informed by the survey results, we identified six major management trends that were rated as having the highest impact on government operations over the past two decades:

- **Technology:** In looking back over the past twenty years, one survey respondent said, "Technology has been the prime driver." Specific technologies ranked as having the highest impact included mobile computing and cloud computing, both discussed in Chapter Two.

- **Data:** Initiatives in this area include big data, data analytics, data visualization, and dashboards—all of which have been enabled by technology. Data is discussed in Chapter Three.

- **Performance management:** The evolution of the supply of performance management information, and creating a demand for its use, was enabled by linkages with technology and data initiatives that drove performance management progress. Performance management is discussed in Chapter Four.

- **Social media-related:** Today, the impact of social media has been evident at all levels of government and has become a major communication tool by and for agencies. For example, at the federal level, the number of "likes" of the National Aeronautics and Space Administration's Facebook page increased from 7,000 in 2009 to 20 million in 2018. Social media is discussed in Chapter Five.

- **Collaboration:** The last twenty years have seen a substantial increase in different types of collaboration, such as public-private partnerships, cross-agency collaboration, and inter-governmental collaboration. Collaboration is discussed in Chapter Six.

- **Risk management:** The last twenty years also saw an increase in the importance of managing a wide range of risks—cyber risks, financial risks, environmental risks, and more. Risk is discussed in Chapter Seven.

KEY LESSONS LEARNED FROM IMPLEMENTING MANAGEMENT REFORMS

What does the implementation of management reform in these six areas over the past twenty years teach current and future government leaders about how to proceed with management reforms in the future? Several common themes emerge from our analysis of the management trends in Part I.

Lesson One: Management reform is not for the faint-hearted. Management reform requires major commitment and staying power. In short, it is not for the timid or those with short time horizons. It takes a well-executed implementation plan and sustained commitment from the top.

Lesson Two: In launching management initiatives, government leaders should target key goals and not overload the "system" with too much reform concurrently. Some management initiatives in our survey were rated as having low impact. We believe that these ratings were most likely based on either poor implementation of the initiative or lack of "staying power" on the part of government leaders. One survey respondent noted, "Many innovations seem to be mostly a 'flavor of the day' effort." Another respondent summed up this phenomenon well, "There have been many attempts at real reform and improvement, but they always end up with too many at a time." In contrast, successful change leaders in government are selective about which management initiatives they decide to launch.

Lesson Three: Successful management initiatives require much time and effort, and a focus on implementation. While less successful initiatives launched over the last 20 years may have been sound conceptually, many suffered from poor execution. One survey respondent told us, "There have been lots of good ideas, but they rarely have been implemented effectively." Another respondent noted, "While government is working better as a result of many management initiatives, much more focus and effort is still needed." In evaluating the impact of initiatives, government leaders must assess implementation—including training as well as timing.

Lesson Four: Effective leadership makes management initiatives succeed. While it has become a cliché, leadership from the top drives success in launching a management initiative. This comes from an effective combination of career and political leaders. Several survey respondents commented on the turnover of political appointees as a challenge in successfully implementing management reform. In preparing this book, we clearly saw the value of leaders communicating the importance of management reform and devoting a significant portion of their time to overseeing implementation.

LOOKING TOWARD THE FUTURE

Based on lessons learned from the past work by the IBM Center, our Challenge Grant essays, and our envisioning sessions, an outline of a vision of what government might look like in 2040 came into focus. We see two sets of developments evolving. First, technology will drive the redeployment of resources—people, dollars, and organizational structures. Second, as a consequence of these technology changes, the way people work and interact will change, and this will reframe how government works—including service delivery, citizen involvement, and different business models.

We envision three technology-based agents of change for government in coming years:

- **Artificial and augmented intelligence (AI) will drive new realities.** Advances in the use of AI will change roles, both within government and between government and citizens. Darrell West, in Chapter Thirteen, says that with AI "workers will be able to navigate mundane tasks quickly and efficiently," and AI will take on more repetitive administrative work in operational areas like human resources, grants, acquisition, financial management, and benefits processing. As a result, this "will free workers from the mountain of paperwork currently required" and allow them to spend time in different ways.

  In Chapter Fourteen, David Bray elaborates further: "Much of the benefits to government will come from a people-centered approach of pairing humans with machine learning to amplify human strengths via augmented intelligence. Such a people-centered approach means the success of public service in the future depends on identifying beneficial ways to augment the extracted human abilities of networked, cross-sector teams—who want to improve the delivery of public services—with digital assistants and learning machines to amplify the team's strength, mitigate any possible blind spots, and increase the capabilities of the team as a whole."

- **Data will drive progress.** The increased availability and use of data will reframe how government managers use knowledge and insight to analyze performance, make decisions, and deliver services. For example, in Chapter Ten, Lori Gordon envisions a new managerial class of data managers. These data managers, writes Gordon, "will oversee a virtual government workforce comprised of teams that aggregate data in digital workspaces and process it almost instantaneously via the eighth-generation wireless networks."

    In Chapter Sixteen, Shelley Metzenbaum writes that the key to the increased use of data will be to use it to empower front-line workers. She envisions that, by 2040, "Government will have identified the front-line workers focusing on the government's priority mission objectives, and given them ready access to the information they need to do their jobs well and continue to improve."

- **Government services will become platform-based.** By 2040, observes Sukumar Rao in Chapter Eleven, "government could be described as a platform for the production and delivery of a range of services and activities that can be mixed and matched." In this scenario, government will be more of a facilitator, creating the conditions for platforms that could be built in the private and nonprofit sectors collaborating with the public sector. Services will be based on digital platforms using principles such as Agile, modular in nature, and rooted in peer networks of partners or communities of interest. In fact, government may move from being organized around agencies and programs to a network of services focused on sets of results.

    Indeed, at the city level, the authors of Chapter Twelve – Marc Ott, Lee Feldman, and Tad McGalliard – write that city managers in 2040 will leverage such platforms to lead "an interconnected community of sensors, automation, data, IoT, and artificially intelligent technologies that will enable them to visualize issues and challenges in ways that today's managers cannot."

Moreover, the visions of our authors suggest that these technology drivers will have three broader impacts on the government of the future:

- **Government will be more citizen-driven.** Government in 2040 will be more citizen-focused, with people leveraging technology and data to interact with their government. Rao sees the role of a citizen to be one of "leader and co-producer." There will be greater citizen involvement in co-creating policy and co-producing more citizen-centric personalized services.

    For example, Rao writes, "Design and delivery of services will be focused on finding solutions for citizen problems and needs, and based on events and activities in a citizen's life journey. Services will increasingly span all levels of government...and will become more seamless and transparent to users." And Gordon writes: "technology is the best lens through which [government] can understand its constituency," by creating a customized service management function not constrained by traditional agency boundaries.

- **Government will become more network-based.** Gordon boldly envisions that, "by 2040, the federal government will disband its traditional agency structure and will establish networked teams to perform government work." And, in Chapter Eight, W. Henry Lambright projects how a public-private network can catalyze a twenty-year journey that brings humanity to Mars.

   West sees the role of government workers evolving within a network-based environment as a result of technology changes. West says: "Flatter, more open, and more collaborative organizations reduce the number of mid-level managers [and] empower front-line workers."

- **Volunteer participation with government will increase.** Citizens will have more time to spend on volunteer activities in 2040—either as retirees or as members of a 2040 workforce that benefits from technology reducing the need to work as many hours. A big question will then be how to engage citizens with their government. Advances in behavioral science may be used to incentivize greater volunteer participation around project-based tasks, which may blur the lines between government employees and citizen volunteers.

   Hollie Gilman, in Chapter Fifteen, writes: "The longer-term future presents an opportunity to set up institutionalized structures of engagement across local, state, and federal levels of government—creating a 'civic layer.'" This civic layer would allow citizens to earn "civic points" for engagement across a range of activities. And in Chapter Nine, Lora Frecks writes that "By 2040, government employees will regularly produce public services side-by-side with volunteers. Community members will be frequent and active volunteer participants in the work of government. Volunteers will provide both labor and input in the form of ideas, feedback, and opinions."

This positive view of a government for the future can be realized by leaders who continue to reflect on lessons from the past. We hope that the perspectives provided throughout this book help increase the likelihood that this vision can turn into tomorrow's reality.

Mark A. Abramson served as the founding and first executive director of the *IBM Center for The Business of Government from 1998 to 2007. Jonathan D. Breul* served as executive director from 2007 to 2012. *Daniel J. Chenok* has served as executive director from 2012 to the present.

PART I: REFLECTIONS ON 20 YEARS OF MANAGEMENT PROGRESS

CHAPTER TWO

Going Digital

Daniel J. Chenok

Highlights

- Technology has played a critical role in the delivery of government programs and the conduct of government operations. The evolution toward a "digital government" has improved services, reduced costs, and enhanced security through efforts that have progressed over the past two decades.

- Digital government promotes the introduction of emerging technologies, agile development, a skilled workforce, and flexible investment strategies.

- Law, policy, strategy, organizational, and governance frameworks have laid the foundation for continued improvements in adopting commercial best practices to implement digital government.

GOING DIGITAL

By Daniel J. Chenok

The New York City Fire Department uses a computer-driven Risk-Based Inspection System that leverages digital technology to predict where fires might break out in different parts of the city. This system runs on an algorithm combining data from five agencies and uses artificial intelligence to develop a list of potential high-risk buildings, initially based on 60 indicators. The current version of this system is ten times more powerful than the first version launched in 2010. In 2015, the department started developing a third version to combine data from 17 agencies to predict potential suspect buildings based on 7,500 factors. This example shows how digital change has helped improve government amidst growing complexity.[1]

INTRODUCTION

Today's digital economy has evolved significantly since the eras of mechanical and analog electronic technology. This evolution began in the late 1950s with the advent of mainframe computing as a standard practice for leading businesses, accelerated in the late 1970s with the introduction of personal computers, and continues to the present day in the form of emerging technologies that include cloud computing and artificial intelligence. Beginning in the 1990s, the internet brought about a revolution in how citizens and businesses access, share, and retain information over open networks. These digital steps forward have led to significant changes in how information technology (IT) impacts society, the economy, and government.

What is Digital Government?

Just as the private sector has adapted digital technologies and ways of doing business to serve its customers, government has grown in its digital capacity over the past twenty years. The initial adoption of internet applications for government services two decades ago led agencies to incorporate these technologies in placing information on the web. Early agency websites were followed by the development of applications that enabled secure transactions for citizens and businesses—ranging from student loans to financial filings.

Digital Government Defined

Jane Fountain, Director of the National Center for Digital Government at the University of Massachusetts, Amherst and author of multiple IBM Center for The Business of Government publications, defines digital government as "governance affected by internet use and other information technologies (IT). Digital government is typically defined as the production and delivery of information and services inside government and between government and the public using a range of information and communication technologies. The public includes individuals, interest groups, and organizations, including nonprofit, nongovernmental organizations, firms, and consortia. The definition used here also includes e-democracy, that is, civic engagement and public deliberation using digital technologies."[2]

Today, governments can leverage open networks in the cloud, where individuals work together over the internet in a secure environment to communicate and develop new ideas and applications. Given advances such as artificial intelligence and the "internet of things," mechanisms exist to collect, distribute, and access vast amounts of data in various formats from many sources to help government leaders make decisions that deliver on missions and programs. Moreover, digital transformation has disrupted how government operates—how agencies do work, tackle problems, and meet expectations. Key examples of digital information include:

- Digital government places the user experience front and center. It has ushered in new ways to improve how citizens interact with government, leveraging cross-disciplinary approaches such as design thinking—a structured, interactive method to facilitate innovation among stakeholders. It also affects the government employee experience in ways that can improve service to the citizen; employees who use mobile devices to perform their roles across the country can serve their communities more rapidly, productively, and efficiently.
- Digital processes change the skills needed in today's government workforce—technologies like artificial intelligence (AI) and advanced robotics enable automation of manual tasks. These technologies require new expertise and new ways of working to deliver mission outcomes that meet or exceed user expectations.
- Digital technologies have facilitated the application of virtual and augmented reality in government. Federal agencies have begun working with virtual reality, such as NASA for data visualization and the Department of Veterans Affairs to treat post-traumatic stress disorder.

The U.S. Federal Chief Information Officer (CIO) Council's 2016 *State of Federal IT Report*, prepared under the direction of federal CIO Tony Scott, found that digital technologies now significantly impact every federal agency and employee.[3] The adoption of emerging technologies has begun to improve internal collaboration, human resources and procurement operations, resulting in a shift away from legacy systems and a push towards transparency and open data. This evolution has been amplified by the impact of technology to improve government collaboration with external partners—agency leaders can now leverage new innovations, like blockchain to work with business partners in a network that provides speed and security for their digital interactions.

Organization of Chapter: The Evolution of Digital Government

Progress in this arena has moved through three major phases along the journey of the past 20 years, as shown in the chart "Evolution of Digital Government: 1998-2018."

*   **Early action:** As the position of agency-level chief information officers was authorized under a landmark IT management statute in 1996 (the Clinger-Cohen Act), the growing importance of IT in implementing agency missions led CIOs to develop business cases that showed return on IT investments in the form of mission achievement and cost management. The mission-critical nature of IT also pointed agencies to start integrating security and privacy into planning and implementation. At the same time, the internet first entered wide use in the public sector as agencies took their large volume of written public information and made it widely available on the web. Early cross-government applications, such as the FirstGov web portal, introduced the notion that government could use technology at a wide scale to improve citizen service.
*   **Expansion:** The advent of e-government was accelerated by a U.S. federal initiative that established citizen-facing IT projects, shared services for back-office operations and cross-agency architectural standards to drive significant progress. This acceleration was codified in the E-Government Act of 2002, which authorized a presidentially appointed government-wide leader of IT under whose direction agencies continued to advance IT policy and programs, and drive IT security and privacy. Such activity led to the use of open data and open government as ways to continue integrating innovation with citizen service and program outcomes, fueled by enabling technologies like cloud and mobile computing.
*   **Institutionalization:** Agency IT progress pointed to the need for strategy, policy, and law to support an updated framework for bringing new talent into government, while strengthening the authorities of CIOs working as leaders of technological change with other mission and mission-support executives to drive outcomes. The highly visible challenges and resolution efforts associated with the roll-out of healthcare.gov in 2013 led the Office of Management and Budget (OMB) and the General Services Administration (GSA) to drive commercial best practice into government through "digital services" teams, innovation officers, and chief technol-

ogy officers. Congress stepped forward with two statutes that advanced governance and funding frameworks. The government has continued to move forward through several 2018 Cross-Agency Priority goals, placing IT modernization as Goal 1 in the President's Management Agenda in a way that is closely linked to data strategy as Goal 2 and workforce improvement as Goal 3. The tie between IT, data, and workforce is especially important given the large volume and variety of digital data now available to agency teams, who can leverage analytics technologies to derive insights from the data that enable them to improve citizen service and performance (see Chapter Three and Chapter Four for more detail).

Evolution of Digital Government: 1998-2018

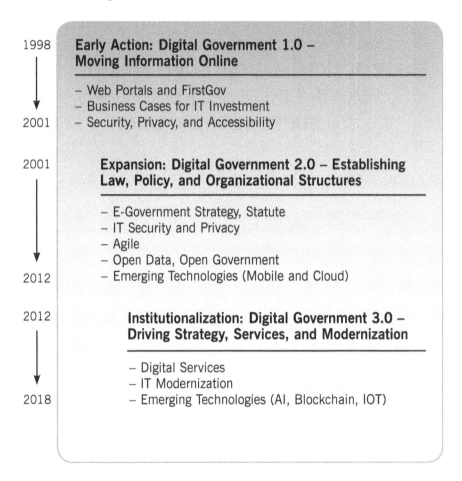

1998

Early Action: Digital Government 1.0 – Moving Information Online

– Web Portals and FirstGov
– Business Cases for IT Investment
2001 – Security, Privacy, and Accessibility

2001

Expansion: Digital Government 2.0 – Establishing Law, Policy, and Organizational Structures

– E-Government Strategy, Statute
– IT Security and Privacy
– Agile
– Open Data, Open Government
2012 – Emerging Technologies (Mobile and Cloud)

2012

Institutionalization: Digital Government 3.0 – Driving Strategy, Services, and Modernization

– Digital Services
– IT Modernization
2018 – Emerging Technologies (AI, Blockchain, IOT)

To continue advancing digital government, agencies must invest in modern technologies that support secure and scalable applications. Identifying and prioritizing efforts for investment, integrating these priorities into agency and federal budget planning cycles, and applying appropriate measures to track the success of key efforts will drive progress. Critical to effective investment in digital modernization is understanding the existing barriers to capturing savings over time from those investments, and identifying means to overcome these barriers. Investing in emerging technologies that can help government will inform where and how private sector entities may most effectively support digital transformation to improve performance and reduce cost.

The remainder of this chapter presents more detail about these three phases. The chapter concludes with lessons learned and observations about what's on the horizon as government relies on emerging technologies to drive continued performance improvement.

EARLY ACTION: DIGITAL GOVERNMENT 1.0— MOVING INFORMATION ONLINE TO SUPPORT THE MISSION

Policy Foundations

The roots of digital government actually took hold well before 1998. Toward the end of the Carter administration, with the increased use of IT systems to collect federal information and deliver services, Congress focused on improving oversight of federal IT, and ultimately enacted the Paperwork Reduction Act of 1980 (see the box highlighting key the statutory milestones that drove the early years of digital government). OMB then worked with senior agency IT officials to oversee information management for well over a decade, reviewing implementation challenges with major IT systems—including "Presidential Priority Systems" in the 1980s and "SWAT" teams in the early 1990s. With the advent of the internet in the mid 1990s, government agencies followed a private sector trend and began to create CIOs to manage information as a strategic asset in the context of rapidly evolving technologies. Key national IT issues that arose in the 1990s remain on the agenda for digital government today, including the government's approach to the internet, electronic commerce, encryption, and website policies. During this time frame, the National Performance Review led numerous experiments and pilot programs to adapt commercial innovation in these areas for government.

Statutory Foundations of Digital Government

1974: The Privacy Act[4] established a Code of Fair Information Practice that governs the collection, maintenance, use, and dissemination of personally identifiable information about individuals maintained in systems of records by federal agencies.

1980: The Paperwork Reduction Act[5] gave OMB authority over agency IT and information policy and management, using the term "information resources management" (IRM) to describe such activity.

1987: The Computer Security Act[6] was intended to improve the security and privacy of sensitive information in federal computer systems and to establish minimally acceptable security practices for such systems. It required the creation of computer security plans, and appropriate training of system users or owners where the systems would display, process or store sensitive information.

1996: The Clinger Cohen Act[7] authorized a CIO at each agency who had responsibility for IT leadership, and led to an Executive Order that created the Federal CIO Council.

First Digital Steps
Web Portals

By 1998, most agencies in government had created websites that enabled internet access for citizens and business. As agencies expanded the amount of information on the web, it became apparent that the public would have an easier time understanding and accessing government data by establishing a "portal" that would tie together different websites within and across agencies, following private sector advances in the use of portals to link common information for consumers. State governments made early progress on portals, as discussed in the 2001 report by Jon and Diana Burley Gant and Craig Johnson, *State Web Portals: Delivering and Financing E-Service*—portals allowed states "to use the internet and web-based technologies to extend government services online, allow citizens to interact more directly with government, employ customer-centric services, and transform the provision of traditional government services."[8]

FirstGov

As 2000 approached, federal agencies had created over 30,000 different sites, with loose coordination from OMB for policy and GSA which led a federal webmasters working group. GSA developed an early experiment to pilot a federal portal, initially referred to as "webgov." At the same time, internet companies were developing search capability well before the founding of Google several years later. An early search engine industry leader, Inktomi, offered to index all government information on the web and make it searchable by the public—a proposal made by Inktomi CEO Eric Brewer to President Bill Clinton at the 1998 Davos Conference. The administration supported Brewer's idea and launched an initiative to expand webgov and develop "FirstGov"—the government's first cross-agency web portal linked to this new search capability. The effort served as the first major interagency technology effort, with leadership from OMB and the National Performance Review, and governance and funding from multiple deputy secretaries who served as a Board of Directors. FirstGov was launched in September 2000. Since then, it has evolved significantly in terms of functionality, was rebranded as www.usa.gov, and has expanded as a resource for government and the public. The site is still managed successfully by GSA.

Business Cases for IT Investment

As is the case today, new technology initiatives like FirstGov were constrained by legacy systems and performance issues with in-house IT operations. The Internal Revenue Service, the Office of Personnel Management, and a range of other agencies were managing large, complex, mainframe-based systems that delivered key mission services and programs—but had no common standards or metrics by which to measure that performance. To help manage this growing complexity of technology-mission intersection, OMB developed a common template for agencies to justify the investment and track progress in IT investments over time, based on commercial best practice and consistent with federal law in the implementation of the policy. This template was implemented as a budget requirement in the late 1990s, referred to as the "Exhibit 300," and significantly expanded in the early 2000s. Although the title and specifics around this requirement have evolved, agencies still track progress and submit a business case for their IT investments to OMB.

Security and Privacy

A key element of these business cases, and of success in agency IT delivery generally, revolved around computer security and privacy challenges that remain present for government today. The Privacy Act of 1974 and the Computer Security Act of 1987 provided initial statutory focus for agency leaders to address these imperatives. Genie Stowers' 2001 report, *The State of Federal Websites,* addressed legal and policy issues that remain challenges today: "to ensure security, provide security against hackers, and protect citizens' privacy."[9]

In 1998, Congress updated the Computer Security Act to increase its focus on data protection; around the same time, agencies developed secure data transaction strategies through the introduction of digital signatures. Through efforts led by GSA and the Federal CIO Council, agencies leveraged digital signature and emerging encryption technologies to strengthen how the public exchanged information with government, providing key protections to help agencies address "issues of privacy and security as they increase access to information and delivery of services electronically," as noted in the 2001 report by Janine Hiller and France Belanger, *Privacy Strategies for Electronic Government*.[10] The digital signature programs were managed by GSA based on expert guidance from the National Institute of Standards and Technology (NIST) and overseen by agency CIOs and OMB, progress outlined by Stephen Holden's 2004 report *Understanding Electronic Signatures*.[11] These programs have evolved in maturity, but policies in this area remain in place today.

Accessibility

As more government programs and services moved online, the need to ensure digital access for populations who faced challenges with access to technology became a paramount objective—to ensure that all citizens could share in the benefits of this change. In 1998, Congress amended the Rehabilitation Act of 1973 to require federal agencies to make IT accessible to people with disabilities. Section 508 of this law[12] applies to all federal agencies when they develop, procure, maintain, or use electronic and information technology. Under Section 508, agencies must give disabled employees and members of the public access to information that is comparable to the access available to others. The implementation of this law continues twenty years later, with renewed focus on adapting digital technology being led by GSA and the Access Board (a small agency charged with Section 508 policy oversight).

Case Study: Student Financial Aid Modernization

An early example of agency movement to digital government that addressed all of these issues, and which remains instructive today, was the reform of the Department of Education's Student Financial Aid systems. The Department had already introduced a web option to apply for Federal Aid, launching this as one of the first online government applications in 1996—but Education's back-end systems remained beset with legacy performance issues. Working with National Performance Review and OMB's Office of Federal Procurement Policy, the Department awarded a contract that allowed its industry partner to make investments and be repaid from the savings that those investments brought by streamlined operations—a concept known as "share-in-savings." This incentive structure enabled the industry partner to work in collaboration with the government to develop a modernization and integration roadmap. It also set the foundation for additional statutory authorizations of share-in-savings, as well as current consideration of funding models that support modernization and share risks and rewards between government and contractors.

EXPANSION: DIGITAL GOVERNMENT 2.0— ESTABLISHING LAW, POLICY, AND ORGANIZATIONAL STRUCTURES TO LEVERAGE EMERGING TECHNOLOGY

As government began to recognize the power that emerging digital technologies offered to help improve productivity and mission effectiveness while reducing costs, the need for leadership in driving change became apparent. This manifested itself in the form of federal law, policy, and strategy that enabled new technologies to improve mission and back-office operations, while also ensuring protections for cybersecurity and privacy.

Organizational Advances: The OMB Office of E-Government and the E-Government Act

OMB sought to elevate the focus on IT across the government in the early 2000s, in response to calls from the IT industry and Congress for a government-wide Chief Information Officer. The Bush Administration created a political appointee position in OMB dedicated to technology with the title of "Associate Director for E-Government and IT" in 2001. This official, Mark Forman, established a governance structure to bring commercial best practices to the federal government, lead implementation of IT and security law and policy, and formulate President's Management Agenda initiatives related to acquisition and use of IT. This led to a multi-faceted IT transformation initiative focused on managing IT as an investment and a set of cross-agency initiatives and policies, shifting OMB's role in federal IT from one largely focused on policy and general oversight to one that also drove specific government-wide initiatives designed to gain effectiveness with a focus on citizen services, and gain efficiencies by reducing duplicative systems—a role that continues today.

At the same time, Congress introduced bipartisan legislation to authorize this enhanced oversight role in IT. The E-Government Act of 2002[13] codified many of the policies and initiatives of the new E-Gov office. The Act designated the head of the new E-Gov office as the "Administrator for E-Government and Information Technology"—this position was the de facto federal CIO, and as discussed below would later receive that designation formally as well. Mark Forman became the first Administrator

The E-Government Act also reauthorized an expansion of prior security statutes, renamed as the Federal Information Security Management Act (FISMA). Other provisions enhanced agency responsibilities and OMB authorities in numerous related areas, including privacy, records management, digital signatures, and citizen services. Finally, the Act authorized a fund for E-Government initiatives, administered by GSA and building on previous funding mechanisms that provided OMB with authority to direct spending on innovation. The budget approach used for the E-Gov Fund has since been revised and used for other purposes, and in 2017 was given impetus from a new statute (see the discussion of the Modernizing Government Technology Act later in this chapter).

The E-Gov office also expanded its role across areas related to IT activity in the agencies, raising attention to oversight and review of key agency systems and elevating resolution of significant issues through program reviews led by the OMB Deputy Director for Management. Other areas of increased attention that would be addressed by the E-Gov office included shared services across government back office functions, authentication of identities by federal employees and contractors in using government IT systems, greater focus on cybersecurity for civilian agencies, and coordination of IT security with the Intelligence Community.

The E-Gov Strategy

A key advance in the digital evolution of the federal government involved a three-part strategy led by the E-Gov office, which was incorporated into the first President's Management Agenda (PMA) in 2001.

Project Quicksilver

Under the first part of this strategy, OMB worked with the President's Management Council and the Federal CIO Council to develop a set of 25 cross-agency initiatives that improved service to four portfolio groups: citizens, businesses, state and local governments, and government employees. These initiatives, which resulted from an E-Government Strategy Study often referred to as "Quicksilver," were the product of a team of government innovators who followed a method for driving technology change in the private sector. The study team conducted interviews across all federal agencies and led public outreach efforts to solicit ideas for improved service to all constituencies— from small businesses to grant recipients to national park visitors. The team developed more than 50 project candidates organized into the four portfolios noted above and worked with the President's Management Council to select the 25 final projects based on review of high-level business cases. These projects were led by interagency teams, driven by a lead agency and involving multiple partners, who leveraged digital technology and related processes to develop public-facing, user-friendly websites or consolidated systems that improved access to and service from agencies. Many of the initial E-Gov websites remain in operation today as models of digital government, ranging from Regulations.Gov (the subject of a 2013 report by Cynthia Farina, *Rulemaking 2.0: Understanding and Getting Better Public Participation)*[14] to IRS E-File (the subject of a 2006 report by Stephen Holden, *A Model for Increasing Innovation Adoption: Lessons Learned from the IRS e-file Program)*[15] to Disasterassistance.gov.

This citizen focus was intended to build trust in government through technology that enhanced citizen participation. As noted in the 2004 report led by Marc Holzer, James Melitski, Seung-Yong Rho and Richard Schwester, *Restoring Trust in Government: The Potential of Digital Citizen Participation,*[16] "Technology has created new tools for allowing citizens to more meaningfully participate in a dialogue with their fellow citizens and their government. In an increasing number of cases, these tools have been successfully employed and are improving the quality of public decisions." Trust among government and industry was similarly enhanced by greater efficiencies delivered through advanced procurement reforms introduced by OMB in the 1990s, and implemented through GSA by several e-procurement initiatives that improved business interactions with government. The federal government also learned from and was influenced by the e-procurement experiences of state governments and international governments, as outlined in a 2001 report by M. Jae Moon, *State Government E-Procurement in the Information Age: Issues, Practices, and Trends,* and Mita Marra *Innovation in E-Procurement: The Italian Experience* in a 2002 report.[17]

Federal Enterprise Architecture

The second part of the E-Gov Strategy sought to modernize the technology that supported public-facing applications and data systems through "enterprise architecture," a discipline that had driven commercial reforms in the financial and other sectors. Although the Clinger-Cohen Act created the requirement for a government wide architecture, this was never associated with a mechanism to measure and drive better return on IT investment. OMB created a "Chief Architect" position to drive this work forward—a position that still sits within the Office of the Federal CIO—and worked with federal CIOs to develop a Federal Enterprise Architecture (FEA). The FEA served as a blueprint for IT modernization at multiple layers: technology infrastructure, software applications, data, business processes, and performance information. Each layer was outlined through a reference model that set out common standards and approaches. In parallel, OMB aligned every federal IT investment with the architecture to identify redundant systems across agencies. The FEA has since been integrated into agency architectures and serves as a foundation for specific architectural initiatives like the recent Human Resources Integrated Business Framework that the Office of Personnel Management is using to drive common personnel approaches.

Shared Service Lines of Business

The third part of this strategy, begun under Mark Forman and significantly expanded by the next E-Gov Administrator, Karen Evans, involved the integration of common business functions, referred to as "lines of business" (LOBs) that brought together common back-end services across agencies. Similar to the governance of the Quicksilver initiatives, the LOBs were driven by lead agencies who developed standard processes that other user agencies could adapt. The initial LOBs focused on financial management, human resources, grants management, case management, and health IT—commencing progress that continued into 2018, with shared services now led by GSA's Unified Shared Services Management Office. This office has considerably advanced on the work of these early LOBs, especially in the financial and human resources space.

Integrating Digital Government and Cybersecurity

The tragic events of 9/11 changed the world, including government. At an organizational level, both the integration of civilian mission agencies into the new Department of Homeland Security (DHS) and the coordination of intelligence agencies under the Directorate of National Intelligence have helped enhance how government agencies work to protect the nation. In the Government IT space, the focus on cybersecurity significantly expanded post 9/11 as well, with Karen Evans leading cross-agency cybersecurity work alongside DHS, National Institute of Standards and Technology (NIST), and the Federal CIO Council—all working closely with intelligence community efforts. These federal efforts were aided by FISMA, discussed previously in this chapter (FISMA was reauthorized in 2014[18] and remains the primary cybersecurity law for agencies to follow).

Organizational Drivers for Cybersecurity

The need to build cybersecurity into the fabric of digital government continued to become more evident throughout the first decade of the 2000s. This focus expanded with the 2009 establishment of a National Coordinator for Cybersecurity in the White House, as well as OMB's later designation of a separate "Cyber Unit" in the Office of E-Government for policy and delegation to DHS for operations. These and similar organizational enhancements at DHS and NIST were accompanied by policies that required greater agency focus on cyber across the range of IT and mission programs. This digital policy infrastructure remains largely in place today.

Identity Management

As more government online transactions required greater protections for security and privacy, the need to bolster identity management policies and processes became a major priority. In the aftermath of 9/11, this objective moved forward significantly through a presidential policy mandating a digital ID credential for government employees and contractors—the Personnel Identity Validation (PIV) card required by Homeland Security Presidential Directive 12.[19] This Directive increased the government's priority on digital signature and secure authentication activity that had been introduced in the late 1990s, and expanded by the Quicksilver "E-authentication" initiative. PIV cards are now the standard for all physical (and a significant amount of IT) access to government resources. Identity policy evolved into the 2011 National Strategy for Trusted Identities in Cyberspace[20] and into a 2018 effort at upgrading identity management efforts led by OMB.[21]

Technology, Innovation, and Government Reform

The Obama administration built on the significant preceding activity to focus on open government, citizen participation, and cloud implementation. This work commenced with a tech-focused agenda in the 2008 Presidential Transition. As Beth Noveck and Stefaan Verhulst wrote in their 2016 report, *Encouraging and Sustaining Innovation in Government*: "the transition team set up the first ever presidential transition website to inform and engage the American people in the process of planning the first 100 days of the new administration.... The transition also notably included the first ever committee to design and plan a technology strategy for the first 100 days of the Obama administration called the Technology Innovation and Government Reform (TIGR) team."[22] This team drafted an Open Government directive that the president signed as one of his first actions after taking office, on Jan. 21, 2009.[23]

The administration then appointed the first Chief Technology Officer (2009) and later the first Chief Data Scientist (2015) in the U.S. Government, both of whom were positioned in the White House Office of Science and Technology Policy. Also, the E-Gov Administrator at OMB was given the additional title of federal CIO, which became and remains the primary title for the position today.

Advances in digital government were spurred on by the adoption of agile techniques in agencies. The government began a shift away from large-scale and long-term systems development that can take years before the first functionality is available for testing. A more innovative approach commenced with agile, a commercial best practice for software development relying on short, iterative "sprints," releasing new functionality in increments, and gathering user feedback using design thinking principles. This effort was first chronicled in a 2013 report by Phillipe Kruchten and Paul Gorans, *A Guide to*

Critical Success Factors in Agile Delivery.[24] Agile approaches have remained key tenets behind the work of new innovation and digital services offices described below.

Two Technologies that Drove Digital Government Expansion

The evolution of two specific technologies demonstrates how digital evolution brought about significant change in government: mobile computing and cloud computing.

Mobile Computing

Mobile computing transformed how people interact with technology, through a broad range of devices (from cell phones and tablets to watches and wearables) that enable communication anytime and anywhere over open networks. Mobile "apps" that improve how people interact in the private sector have also been adopted by government. There are two broad types of government apps:

- **Enterprise-focused apps:** mainly for internal use within a public organization. They are accessible to employees and operate within secure firewalls established by the agency.
- **Citizen-oriented apps:** intended for external use. They are accessible to anyone who seeks to use government services.

Mobile government has brought significant benefits to agency operations, including:

- Cost reduction
- Efficiency
- Transformation/modernization of public sector organizations
- Added convenience and flexibility
- Better services to the citizens
- Ability to reach a larger number of people through mobile devices than would be possible using wired internet only

The federal government has taken steps to drive mobility forward, led by GSA's Digital Government Division that promotes mobile-oriented testing, registry, and related solutions. For example:

- "Making MobileGov" was a multi-media project created by the cross agency MobileGov Community of Practice to help federal agencies discover, discuss, and design a citizen-centric path to mobile government services and information. Begun during the summer of 2011, this project served three strategic goals: educate, develop resources to accelerate mobile efforts, and build a Mobile Gov Community.[25]

- A state-level model can be found in "Gov2Go in Arkansas", recognized by the National Association of State CIOs as a leading "personal government assistant" app.[26]

However, while the foundations for mobile government have been put into place, the uptake in the use of mobile applications in government remains a work in progress. The report *Using Mobile Apps in Government* by Sukumar Ganpati found that as of 2014, only 3 percent of people interacted with federal agencies via digital apps, and only 17 percent of federal agencies had a digital app.[27] Advances have been made since, but room for progress remains.

Cloud Computing

Cloud computing has transformed businesses across industries, shifting how IT is delivered by hosting infrastructure and applications remotely at lower cost. A 2008 IBM Center report by David Wyld, *Moving to the Cloud: An Introduction to Cloud Computing in Government*, provided one of the first definitions of what was then a new term for distributed computing and has seen massive growth since: cloud computing is "delivered over the internet, on demand, from a remote location, rather than residing on one's own desktop, laptop, mobile device, or even on an organization's servers...to deliver applications, computing power, and storage."[28]

The private sector has built many applications that leverage cloud computing's cost and efficiency benefits. After a slow initial rate of cloud adoption, governments have also accelerated progress—though financial constraints and the continued reliance on older legacy systems to deliver services have limited agency deployment of cloud-based solutions.

While a major benefit of cloud computing involves containing costs through shared services and infrastructures, cloud adoption is also helping government agencies to improve operational flexibility despite a continued reliance on back-end legacy systems. Cloud computing has allowed the deployment of more current services with elastic capacity, helping government programs to respond to changing business conditions. Additionally, cloud computing has allowed agencies to increase agility in responding to new challenges and opportunities, accelerating expansion of digital government. For example, if critical websites get hacked, cloud applications can allow agencies to quickly rewrite the controlling software; cloud can also speed access to track real-time data for mission applications like air traffic control.

The federal government launched two programs to foster consistent implementation and compliance for cloud computing, which facilitated its expansion across agencies: CloudFirst and FedRAMP.

- **CloudFirst.** The government instituted its CloudFirst policy in 2010 to accelerate the pace of cloud adoption.[29] This policy promoted service management, innovation, and adoption of emerging technologies. According to the policy, "focus will shift from the technology itself to the core competencies and mission of the agency."[30] As a result, many agencies can now support their mission-critical operations with agile and innovative cloud deployments that incorporate mobile, social, and analytics technologies. However, they also have to take stringent compliance and security measures to protect their systems from internal and external threats.

- **Federal Risk and Authorization Management Program (FedRAMP).** FedRAMP, introduced in 2011, is designed to standardize security services and streamline assessments so that each cloud service considered by federal agencies is evaluated once, at the government-wide level.[31] FedRAMP is intended to avoid duplication of effort across agencies, saving time by supporting initial security evaluation and allowing continuous monitoring of cloud security. FedRAMP continues to address issues of slow processes that have been the subject of some critiques in agencies' ability to keep pace with commercial practices for cloud computing.

Crucial IT and business advances have been enabled by cloud applications in government. For example:[32]

- **IT consolidation:** Government agencies have realized the benefits of consolidating redundant or unnecessary IT assets to increase operational efficiencies. They are reducing the cost of IT ownership by integrating systems through the cloud. Similarly, data center consolidation, an effort that spans multiple administrations, is helping to reduce hardware costs and also to drastically reduce energy consumption.
- **Shared services:** More government agencies have moved towards sharing IT services to reduce costs and to improve business process efficiencies. Some key federal programs have leveraged shared cloud-based infrastructure and software solutions, as well as security capabilities like continuous diagnostics monitoring and threat detection.
- **Citizen services:** Cloud-based technology improves delivery of a variety of public applications, such as allowing citizens to monitor their energy and water consumption, check the status of their service requests to government programs (e.g., benefit and loan applications), and access their medical records.

A number of federal agencies, including the Departments of Defense, Justice, Agriculture, and Education, were early cloud adopters, setting the trend and direction for others to follow in expanding their use of the cloud. Many agencies started with email—GSA was the first federal agency to adopt cloud-based email back in 2010; the National Oceanic and Atmospheric Administration followed a year later, migrating employees and contractors; and the Department of Justice began migrating its email accounts in December 2016. The main drivers for cloud email adoption included money savings, enhanced data sharing capabilities, and improved collaboration.

State and local governments have also made significant progress in moving to the cloud. For example, the 2013 report by Shannon Tufts and Meredith Weiss, *Cloudy with a Chance of Success*, showed how North Carolina put in place five successful public sector cloud computing contracts.[33] Paul Wormeli's 2012 report, *Mitigating Risks in the Application of Cloud Computing in Law Enforcement,* discussed challenges and opportunities for public safety professionals to leverage the cloud in improving their productivity, and effectiveness in protecting and serving the public.[34]

Identifying Challenges to Institutionalization

Overall, federal agencies are still in the expansion phase for digital tools in general. Ganapati's 2016 report on mobile government, cited above, found that the top barriers for incorporating digital tools are:
- Limited or declining IT budgets
- Security and privacy concerns
- Lack of digital skills in the agency
- Limitations of legacy systems
- Cultural resistance
- Unclear long-term vision

In addition to these barriers, two longer-term challenges face agencies as they seek to institutionalize digital practices:
- **Governance:** Technology now permeates all aspects of organizational activity, whether in industry or government. Agency CIOs are a central— but by no means the only—player in technology adoption to improve mission performance; a range of other key stakeholders includes chief financial officers, procurement executives, customer experience and design experts, program managers, industry partners, oversight offices, and ultimately system users in the public. Absent a delineation of roles and responsibilities, consistent metrics, and a clear decision framework, digital advancement can be stymied if different elements spin out of control. A governance framework can help to bring these pieces together; related to governance is the challenge of "orchestration," which calls for integrating technology management with a skilled workforce, user experience, and service delivery to foster significant productivity improvements.
- **Investment Tools:** Government agencies often have difficulties obtaining capital investment dollars to upgrade and modernize systems. Technological innovation most often comes from the private sector, and government has struggled with limited experience using an investment model that allows agencies to leverage commercial innovation while minimizing substantial upfront investment costs; the student aid modernization case study discussed earlier in this chapter has proven to be the exception rather than the rule. Government faces a challenge of incentivizing investment in the private sector that public agencies then pay for through

operational budget savings over time. In response, through a service model where the private sector provides the technology, agencies can also build those costs into long-term contracts. Such "share in savings" or "gain sharing" models are often used by industry in moving to commercial providers for shared services management and operations, to improve service and reduce costs. As discussed below, the Modernizing Government Technology Act now authorizes flexible funding arrangements in government for investing across years with a savings payback requirement.

INSTITUTIONALIZATION: DIGITAL GOVERNMENT 3.0—DRIVING STRATEGY, SERVICES, AND MODERNIZATION

As digital technology took hold throughout the economy in the last decade, new business models flourished that rely on mobile, cloud, and now emerging technologies like artificial intelligence and blockchain, to enable reinvention of how users find information and receive services. As with each wave of the digital journey over the past 20 years, government has followed suit. At the federal level, this movement has been facilitated by strategic, organizational, and statutory drivers across the past decade.

Developing A Digital Strategy

The 2012 Digital Government Strategy, released by OMB with implementation led by GSA's Office of Citizen Services and Innovative Technologies, laid out a broad digital plan to harness information technology in federal agencies.[35] This strategy integrated and updated a set of IT-related actions that had been introduced under a "25-point plan" for IT reform championed by federal CIO Vivek Kundra in 2010.[36] The Strategy was premised on four principles:
- Create an information-centric government that focuses on open data and content
- Establish a shared platform within and across agencies
- Take a customer-centric approach in presenting data
- Build required security and privacy measures up front

The Strategy set out broad goals for the institutionalization of digital government:
- Enable the American people and an increasingly mobile workforce to access high-quality digital government information and services anywhere, anytime, on any device.

- Ensure that as the government adjusts to this new digital world, agencies seize the opportunity to procure and manage devices, applications, and data in smart, secure, and affordable ways.
- Unlock the power of government data to spur innovation and improve the quality of services for the public.

Creating Digital Services and Innovation Offices

A number of new organizational structures have increased capacity and sustainability for digital government over the past decade. These include the Presidential Innovation Fellows, GSA's 18F office, agency innovation offices, and the U.S. Digital Service.

Presidential Innovation Fellows

The Digital Strategy's principles had already begun to be practiced through a new program designed to bring private sector technology talent into government: the Presidential Innovation Fellows.[37] Introduced by the federal chief technology officer in 2012, as Noveck and Verhulst write in their *Sustaining Innovation* report, the Fellows program "connects innovators from the business, nonprofit, and academic sectors with government departments. Together, they work to produce innovative, short-term projects to improve government efficiency. The program has evolved from one that parachutes new people into the White House to one that pairs innovators with civil servants to help implement change."[38]

GSA's 18F

The original Presidential Innovation Fellows model envisioned shorter details with government, followed by a return to the private sector. As Fellows moved into agencies, many found that they wanted to remain in the government for a longer tenure because of the impact they saw that digital transformation could have on key missions for the American people. To provide a home for Fellows who remained and a venue for other technology experts to join the government, GSA established an innovation office called "18F" in 2014 (so titled because GSA's DC headquarters are at 18th and F STs NW). 18F[39] brought in a high-tech start-up culture to government, aiming "to provide cutting-edge support for our federal partners that reduces cost and improves service."[40]

Agency Innovation Offices

As the Fellows and 18F began to use digital services to help a growing number of agencies modernize their applications, several agencies established their own innovation offices, led by the Department of Health and Human

Services. In a 2014 report by Rachel Burstein and Alyssa Black, *A Guide to Making Innovation Offices Work,* the authors identified key characteristics of federal innovation offices, comparing and contrasting them with state, local, and global counterparts to draw key lessons, such as: "moving forward with setting up a center of gravity for innovation should follow a careful assessment of the mission of the new office, financial resources available, and support from key partners."[41]

U.S. Digital Service

Even as government was transforming to institutionalize digital innovation, a core federal program suffered a major setback: the flawed release of the healthcare.gov website, which was the public's main channel to access health insurance exchanges in 2013. This website was critically linked to the success of the implementation of the Affordable Care Act. The website's operational problems resulted from numerous challenges identified above, including:

- a lack of governance across stakeholders
- limited use of agile techniques to deliver incremental functionality
- contract-related constraints on leveraging commercial innovation

In responding to these and other challenges, the administration brought on a "rescue team" of private sector technology and business experts who used digital best practices to fix issues with the website and its underlying IT systems. The success of this effort led the administration to conclude that replicating this approach would be a benefit to modernizing other large and complex technology systems—resulting in the 2014 establishment of the U.S. Digital Service (USDS) in OMB, driven by numerous IT leaders including federal CIO Steve VanRoekel.[42]

USDS drew on lessons learned from a similar office in the United Kingdom, the Global Delivery Service, to address challenges throughout government by using digital technology. As Ines Mergel wrote in her 2017 report, *Digital Service Teams: Challenges and Recommendations for Government,* USDS and other digital service teams "typically operate outside existing agency IT organizational structures and recruit IT talent directly from the private sector. They are given a mandate to rapidly implement change initiatives using commercially-developed tools and processes such as human-centered design and agile innovation management techniques—which are standard practice in the private sector, but have been infrequently adopted in the public sector."[43] Mergel's report also pointed out the challenges of integrating across new digital service and existing agency IT teams, including the different roles and cultures involving change agents relative to those involving the delivery of government operations at scale. This healthy tension can be made into a benefit through clearly defining responsibilities across the IT development lifecycle, communicating in a transparent manner as prototype digital applications migrate to a subsequent delivery phase, and approaching collaborative activities with mutual respect.

USDS summarized key digital service principles and recommended actions in its 2014 "Digital Services Playbook,"[44] which has since been used by agencies and industry partners to guide digital projects throughout government. Many of these elements focus on frequent interaction with users through agile development as well as "design thinking," an approach to innovation where groups of users collaborate in real time to innovate on new ideas and develop code; government and industry now even co-create together in a variety of "design studios."

Legislation Catches Up: FITARA and MGT

Government use of digital technology over the past two decades had been accomplished primarily through two statutes, the Clinger-Cohen Act of 1996 and the E-Government Act of 2002. Following the significant attention to the positive outcomes that technology could bring, as well as the risks that accompanied technology failures, Congress recognized the need to update frameworks that authorized agency activity, including CIO authorities to drive change and implement funding flexibility and respond to ever-increasing cybersecurity risks and threats. Two new laws have helped the government to lock in and drive forward progress in digital transformation.

New Approaches to CIOs and Governance: The Federal IT and Acquisition Reform Act of 2014 (FITARA)

FITARA[45] changed how federal agencies acquire and manage IT. A central purpose of FITARA was to give greater authority to agency CIOs in directing IT spending, procurement, and activity across their enterprises, with the goal of enhancing effectiveness. Under this statute, the CIO is accountable for the performance of all IT projects in his or her agency, including approval for IT procurements and oversight of IT staff; agencies are also charged with leveraging commercial best practices. FITARA requires CIOs to lead reviews of IT portfolios that enhance transparency and improve risk management, with additional provisions to improve IT management that include expanded training for IT staff, data center consolidation, enterprise software buys, and strategic sourcing.

OMB issued 2015 guidance[46] on FITARA implementation that further promoted institutionalization of sound digital management, largely by addressing the governance challenge cited above. The guidance set out a baseline for sound IT management and strong cybersecurity, and delineated specific roles and responsibilities for CIOs and their mission support brethren in integrating IT to improve performance across the enterprise: chief financial officers, chief acquisition officers, and chief human capital officers, among others. FITARA implementation is continuing to mature, with the Government Accountability Office (GAO) assessing agency progress through a set of metrics that ensure continued oversight for this important IT management statute. On the cyber side, FITARA has been complemented by the FISMA reauthorization noted above, as well as two other 2014 statutes that strengthen DHS authorities to collaborate with industry and help agencies address risk, increase skills, and build resilience: the Cybersecurity Enhancement Act of 2014[47] and the Cybersecurity Workforce Assessment Act.[48]

Two IBM Center reports capture activities led by CIOs to drive improvements in digital government. First, consistent with the longstanding focus from GAO and multiple administrations on the importance of IT metrics, CIOs increased their focus on measuring outcomes for their work. Kevin DeSouza's 2015 report, *Creating a Balanced Portfolio of Information Technology Metrics*, noted that CIOs over time had not done enough "to invest in the creation of metrics that capture the performance of IT assets and their contribution to organizational performance."[49] DeSouza found improvements being made by CIOs who recognize the value of metrics to guide IT strategic planning, contract oversight, cost management, and benchmarking against commercial best practice.

Second, as CIOs sought to integrate innovation into their operations, working alongside new digital services and innovation offices have represented a challenge. Because many of these offices do not fall under the purview of the CIO, and are often staffed by outside IT experts without much prior experience in federal operations, their path to innovation often differs from the experience of government CIOs. A 2015 report by Greg Dawson and James Denford, *A Playbook for CIO-Enabled Innovation in Government*, provides a roadmap for CIOs to move forward in driving innovation that adapts evolving digital transformation to government. The authors found that "few agencies have a defined and repeatable process for enacting innovation. Rather, often the person who generates the idea is unaware of a process to enact the innovation, and either tries to create a process or simply gives up trying to implement it."[50] In understanding how to overcome this constraint, Dawson and Denford interviewed successful CIOs and concluded that "committed leadership and an enterprise-wide ecosystem can foster a culture of innovation, institutionalized through repeatable processes that garner buy-in from all stakeholders—from digital service teams to program offices."

New Approaches to Funding Innovation: The Modernizing Government Technology (MGT) Act of 2017

Another major challenge to institutionalization identified above revolves around funding for digital transformation. In order to provide agencies with flexibility to invest in change and benefit from returns on that investment, agencies need funding flexibility. The MGT Act[51] now gives OMB and agencies the authority to establish working capital funds that support IT modernization by authorizing multi-year, commercial-style budgeting; this provides agencies with more tools to move to the cloud, implement shared services, and improve cybersecurity. MGT implementation has just begun, with federal CIO

Suzette Kent leading a cross-agency board that selects and oversees investments in a central Technology Management Fund.

The President's Management Agenda Redux: The Cross-Agency Priority Goal for IT Modernization

MGT Act implementation is one part of a broader strategic imperative for IT modernization that will fuel progress in digital government. Just as a three-part E-Gov Strategy brought IT into focus as a major administration priority in the President's Management Agenda of 2001, the current administration's Management Agenda designates IT Modernization as its first Cross-Agency Priority (CAP) Goal (see the discussion of CAP goals in Chapter Four). The new 2018 IT Modernization goal, which builds on the previous administration's Cross-Agency Priority Goal of "Smarter IT Delivery,"[52] captures recommendations made by government and industry leaders over the past year, and reflects on lessons learned over the past twenty years. The goal's central tenet calls on agencies to "build and maintain more modern, secure, and resilient information technology (IT) to enhance mission delivery and productivity—driving value by increasing efficiencies of Government IT spending while potentially reducing costs, increasing efficiencies, and enhancing citizen engagement and satisfaction."[53]

Another element of the CAP Goal drives forward toward greater use of cloud computing, furthering the efforts discussed earlier in this chapter. Eight years after the federal government adopted the 2010 Cloud First policy, agencies still faced hurdles in deploying cloud solutions. An interagency working group led by GSA has started to make headway on smoothing the path to the cloud for agencies. The group, called the Cloud Center of Excellence, kicked off in January 2017 and aims to provide agencies with advice on best practices for cloud adoption. The Center of Excellence, one of five such Centers at GSA helping to drive IT modernization forward, includes more than 140 participants representing 48 different agencies, and serves as a knowledge-sharing network and a clearinghouse for cloud adoption tips. The group is working on documents to help agencies address cloud funding challenges, acquire cloud solutions more rapidly, and provide for enhanced cloud security.

Importantly, the IT Modernization agenda is overseen by a strong governance coalition that includes OMB, GSA, the new White House Office of American Innovation, and lead agencies (starting with the U.S. Department of Agriculture). The agenda focuses on accelerating agency movement to the cloud, carries forward agile principles, and strengthens collaboration among CIOs, digital service offices, and other stakeholders—with strong support from the OMB Deputy Director for Management. Another key element of this agenda draws from a digital evolution in the commercial sector reflecting new technologies that rely more on data and less on the computing platforms that produce that data, as well as a workforce with 21st century skills to implement these emerging innovations; the pairing of the IT Modernization initiative with related CAP goals that focus on data and workforce modernization will help expand institutionalization of digital government.

A 2018 report by Greg Dawson, *A Roadmap for IT Modernization in Government*,[54] recommends a series of key actions and steps that agencies can take to plan, assess, execute, and measure modernization activities, based on research into recent successes in public and private sector IT modernization. Dawson presents several findings that CIOs and other IT leaders can adapt to help drive digital transformation:

- Modernization must be an ongoing process rather than a single stand-alone event, to allow for continuous improvement.
- Technology must support mission goals.
- IT implementation must include a strong technical approach and acquisition strategy.
- Collaborative governance, measurement identification and communication, and stakeholder feedback must occur throughout the process to capture lessons learned.

LESSONS LEARNED

Much of the government's digital experience over the past 20 years demonstrates the need to balance disruptive innovation with sound IT management, cost-effective outcome measurement, and strong cybersecurity. A leading government-industry IT partnership, the American Council for Technology and Industry Advisory Council, issued a framework entitled *7S for Success*[55] that captures 7 key findings to assist in delivering positive results and reducing risk for digital government. These lessons demonstrate how agencies can move from traditional command-and-control implementation, and toward an emphasis on business outcomes delivered in short increments with continuous improvement in the face of inevitable change.

This framework, the subject of congressional testimony and an influence on government policy and practice, recommends seven actions for effective digital transformation based on lessons learned—many of which echo key findings described throughout this chapter.

- **Stakeholder commitment and collaborative governance:** Most complex programs involve numerous stakeholders at political, policy, and management levels, and often multiple agencies, contractors, and other non-government constituencies. These players should have clear roles and responsibilities, and engage key stakeholders. Finally, there should be a shared commitment to the program's outcomes.
- **Skilled program manager and team:** An accountable, qualified, and properly positioned senior leader of the team should be highly proficient at technical, business (both government and commercial business process), organizational, programmatic, and interpersonal levels.

- **Systematic program reviews:** Governance leaders and the program manager should review progress in achieving key results on a regular basis. As part of these reviews, success should be celebrated and actual or potential problems promptly and openly identified for correction. This will promote timely consideration of whether the program is making rapid progress and minimizing risk.
- **Shared technology and business architecture:** Major IT programs involve complex interfaces with internal and external users, back-end applications, operational processes, policies, and supporting infrastructure. A business and technology architecture should guide activities across the team.
- **Strategic, modular, and outcomes-focused acquisition strategy:** The program manager must collaborate with the acquisition organization and other stakeholders, and then work with the private sector early on, to define a set of strategic requirements, a program management model that relies on incremental improvements, and an acquisition strategy that supports the program's outcome-based goals.
- **Software development that is agile:** Applications should be developed in an iterative fashion whenever possible, with small-scale rollouts, frequent feedback from end users, and communication with program management and governance leaders on changes. This approach reduces risk and increases the chances for program success.
- **Security and performance testing throughout:** Software modules should be tested and released in phases throughout design, development, and operations—both for individual components and collective system performance.

LOOKING FORWARD

For digital technology to transform operations, governments will also need to change both culture and policy. To take full advantage of the transformational changes made possible through the speed and scale of digital technologies, citizens must help drive how agencies work with them. Digital government in the future must adapt to the needs and expectations of citizens, businesses, non-profits, and other partners, creating user experiences that are personalized, interactive, and easy to access and use. Digital technologies can enable "cognitive systems" that help agencies understand, reason, and learn, allowing government to interact in real time with the public to deliver mission and mission support services with strong security and privacy protections.

Ultimately, new technologies will continue to help government drive performance improvements based on leveraging data and analytics over the cloud, in a secure manner, and in real time—emerging technologies that include artificial intelligence, blockchain, the internet of things, and initial steps toward quantum computing. Early innovators have shown a path for agencies to move forward in engaging with and serving the public. For example, two 2018 reports on artificial intelligence—*The Future Has Begun: Using Artificial Intelligence to Transform Government*[56] (published with the Partnership for Public Service) and *Delivering Artificial Intelligence in Government: Challenges and Opportunities*[57] by Kevin DeSouza—highlight visible progress in the adaptation of that revolutionary technology to government at all levels—federal, state, local, and international.

The evolution of digital government over the past two decades shows that when implemented effectively, securely, and with cost-effective approaches, agencies can drive significant and positive change while managing risk to the government and the taxpayer. As discussed in Part II, government in the next twenty years can act responsibly to accelerate this progress.

Daniel J. Chenok *is Executive Director of the IBM Center for The Business of Government, where he oversees all of the Center's activities in connecting research to benefit government. He serves in numerous industry leadership positions, with organizations that include the Partnership for Public Service, the National Academy of Public Administration, and the Senior Executives Association. His previous positions included Chair of the Industry Advisory Council (IAC) for the government-led American Council for Technology (ACT). As a career government executive, Mr. Chenok served as Branch Chief for Information Policy and Technology with the Office of Management and Budget.*

Endnotes

1   Kevin Desouza, *Delivering Artificial Intelligence in Government: Challenges and Opportunities,* IBM Center for The Business of Government, 2018.

2   Jane Fountain, *Building the Virtual State* (Washington, DC: Brookings Institution Press, 2001).

3   U.S. Federal CIO Council, *State of Federal Information Technology Report*, January 2017, https:www.cio.gov/sofit.

4   *The Privacy Act of 1974*, Public Law 93-479, 5 U.S.C. 552(a), Dec 31, 1974.

5   *The Paperwork Reduction Act of 1995*, Public Law 104-13, May 22, 1995.

6   *The Computer Security Act of 1987*, Public Law 100-235, June 11, 1987.

7   *The Clinger Cohen Act of 1996*, Public Law 104-106, Feb 10, 1996.

8   Diana Gant and Jon Gant, *State Web Portals: Delivering and Financing E-Service*, IBM Center for The Business of Government, 2002, 3.

9   Genie Stowers, *The State of Federal Websites: The Pursuit of Excellence*, IBM Center for The Business of Government, 2001, 8.

10   France Belanger and Janine Hiller, *Privacy Strategies for Electronic Government*, IBM Center for The Business of Government, 2001, 6.

11   Stephen Holden, *Understanding Electronic Signatures: The Key to E-Government*, IBM Center for The Business of Government, 2004.

12   *Electronic and Information Technology*, Section 508 of the Rehabilitation Act of 1973, as amended, 29 U.S. Code §794d, 1998.

13   *The E-Government Act of 2002*, Public Law 107-347, Dec 17, 2002.

14 Cynthia Farina, *Rulemaking 2.0: Understanding and Getting Better Public Participation*, IBM Center for The Business of Government, 2013.

15 Stephen Holden, *A Model for Increasing Innovation Adoption: Lessons Learned from the IRS e-file Program*, IBM Center for The Business of Government, 2006.

16 Marc Holzer, James Melitski, Seung-Yong Rho and Richard Schwester, *Restoring Trust in Government: The Potential of Digital Citizen Participation,* IBM Center for The Business of Government, 2004, 3.

17 M. Jae Moon, *State Government E-Procurement in the Information Age: Issues, Practices, and Trends*, IBM Center for The Business of Government, 2002; and Mita Marra, *Innovation in E-Procurement: The Italian Experience*, IBM Center for The Business of Government, 2004.

18 *Federal Information Security Modernization Act of 2014*, Public Law 113-283, Dec 18, 2014.

19 George W. Bush, HSPD-12, *Policy for a Common Identification Standard for Federal Employees and Contractors,* August 27, 2004.

20 The White House, *National Strategy for Trusted Identities in Cyberspace*, April 2011.

21 U.S. Office of Management and Budget, *M-18-XX (Draft, as of April 6, 2018) Strengthening the Cybersecurity of Federal Agencies through Improved Identity, Credential, and Access Management.*

22 Beth Noveck and Stefaan Verlhust, *Encouraging and Sustaining Innovation in Government,* IBM Center for The Business of Government, 2016.

23 The White House, *Transparency and Open Government*, January 21, 2009.

24 Phillipe Kruchten and Paul Gorans, *A Guide to Critical Success Factors in Agile Delivery,* IBM Center for The Business of Government, 2013.

25 Jacob Parcell, "Making Mobile Gov Project," *DigitalGov*, published June 21, 2011. https://www.digitalgov.gov/2011/06/21/making-mobile-gov-project.

26 Bob Brown, "Mobile Apps Still Have a Long Way to Go in State Governments: But Arkansas Stands Out with Gov2Go Mobile App" *Networked World*, September 21, 2016.

27 Sukumar Ganapati, *Using Mobile Apps in Government*, IBM Center for The Business of Government, 2016.

28 David Wyld, *Moving to the Cloud: An Introduction to Cloud Computing in Government*, IBM Center for The Business of Government, 2009.

29 The White House, *Federal Cloud Computing Strategy*, February 8, 2011.

30 The White House, *Federal Cloud Computing Strategy*.

31 FedRAMP, accessed May 25, 2018, https://www.fedramp.gov.

32 Sujatha Perepa, "Why the US Government is Moving to Cloud Computing," *Wired.com*, (September 2013).

33 Shannon Tufts and Meredith Weiss, *Cloudy with a Chance of Success*, IBM Center for The Business of Government, 2013.

34 Paul Wormeli, *Mitigating Risks in the Application of Cloud Computing in Law Enforcement*, IBM Center for The Business of Government, 2012.

35 Digital Gov, "2012 Digital Government Strategy." Accessed June 20, 2018, https://digital.gov/resources/2012-digital-government-strategy.

36 The White House, *25 Point Implementation Plan to Reform Federal Information Technology Management*, December 9, 2010.

37 Presidential Innovation Fellows, accessed May 25, 2018, https://presidentialinnovationfellows.gov.

38 Noveck and Verhulst, *Encouraging and Sustaining Innovation in Government,* 20.

39 General Services Administration, 18F, accessed May 25, 2018, https://18f.gsa.gov.

40 Adam Mazmanian, "GSA Launches Digital Incubator," *Federal Computer Week* (March 19, 2014).

41 Alyssa Black and Rachel Burstein, *A Guide to Making Innovation Offices Work*, IBM Center for The Business of Government, 2014, 4.

42 The U.S. Digital Service, accessed May 25, 2018, https://www.usds.gov.

43 Ines Mergel, *Digital Service Teams: Challenges and Recommendations for Government*, IBM Center for The Business of Government, 2017, 6.

44 "Digital Services Playbook," The U.S. Digital Service, accessed May 25, 2018. https://playbook.cio.gov.

45 *Federal Information Technology and Acquisition Reform Act*, Public Law 113-291, December 19, 2014.

46 U.S. Office of Management and Budget, *M-15-14: Management and Oversight of Information Technology*, June 10, 2015.

47 *Cybersecurity Enhancement Act of 2014*, Public Law 113-274, December 18, 2014.

48 *Cybersecurity Workforce Assessment Act*, Public Law 113-246, December 18, 2014.

49 Kevin DeSouza, *Creating A Balanced Portfolio of IT Metrics*, IBM Center for The Business of Government, 2014, 8.

50 Greg Dawson and James Denford, *A Playbook for CIO-Enabled Innovation in the Federal Government*, IBM Center for The Business of Government, 2015.

51 *National Defense Authorization Act for Fiscal Year 2018*, Title X, Subtitle G, Public Law 115-91, January 3, 2017.

52 "Cross-Agency Performance Goals," Performance.gov, accessed May 25, 2018, https://obamaadministration.archives.performance.gov/cap-goals-list.html.

53 "Modernize IT to Increase Productivity and Security," Performance.gov, accessed May 25, 2018, https://www.performance.gov/CAP/CAP_goal_1.html.

54 Greg Dawson, *A Roadmap for IT Modernization in Government*, IBM Center for The Business of Government, 2018.

55 ACT-IAC, *Key Success Factors for Major Programs that Leverage IT: The '7-S for Success' Framework*, May 2014.

56 IBM Center for The Business of Government and Partnership for Public Service, *Using Artificial Intelligence to Transform Government*, 2018.

57 Kevin Desouza, *Delivering Artificial Intelligence in Government: Challenges and Opportunities*, IBM Center for The Business of Government, 2018.

CHAPTER THREE

Using Data

Mark A. Abramson

Highlights

- The use of data has risen exponentially. However, government agencies face challenges in transforming data into actionable insights.

- With the increased use of data, the challenges of handling data have also increased. As government makes open data more accessible, challenges include finding data experts and managing data accessibility, data quality, and data sharing.

- Data sharing by the private sector, data sharing among government agencies, and the government's capacity to manage and analyze its increasing volumes of data will be critical factors in the years ahead.

USING DATA

By Mark A. Abramson

In 2016, the Department of Justice (DOJ) and the Department of Health and Human Services (HHS) worked together to uncover a money laundering and health care fraud case involving a $1 billion scheme being perpetrated by a ring of Miami-based health care providers. Caryl Brzymiakliewicz, chief data officer in the Office of the Inspector General (OIG) at HHS, said, "Three co-conspirators had figured out how to try to hide in the data. But it was really about using data analytics and partnering with DOJ and the FBI to uncover the money laundering, to understand in the data what was happening, really understand between the provider and all of the networks really what was going on."[1]

This effort involved working closely with Centers for Medicare & Medicaid Services (CMS), which gave their claims to the HHS OIG who then used the claims in their investigation with the Department of Justice. Jessica Kahn, director of the Data and System Group at CMS, said that it is not always easy to share data across agencies. "We put it (our data) in the cloud because I want people to use it," said Kahn.[2] She said she gives her data to Brzymi-akliewicz because she wants the Inspector General "to catch the bad guys."

INTRODUCTION

Data as a Strategic Asset

The chapters in this book are closely interrelated. As seen in the previous chapter, the rapid movement to "going digital" over the last twenty years served as a key enabler to the increased capability of government to collect and analyze data. New technologies, also discussed in Chapter Two, dramatically reduced the cost of collecting and reporting data. The ability of government to collect and analyze data has similarly been a valuable tool enabling the performance management movement to shift the emphasis from complying with reporting requirements to generating more useful data that informs performance improvement efforts. Performance management is examined in Chapter Four.

This chapter focuses on data collected and used by government managers and decision makers in managing their organizations. In 2018, the President's Management Agenda designated "Leveraging Data as a Strategic Asset" as a Cross-Agency Priority (CAP) Goal. In its description of the CAP

Goal, the Administration set out three key opportunities to more effectively use data in coming years:[3]

- Develop a long-term enterprise Federal Data Strategy to better govern and leverage the federal government's data.
- Enable government data to be accessible and useful for the American public, businesses, and researchers.
- Improve the use of data for decision making and accountability for the Federal Government, including policy making, innovation, oversight, and learning.

While all three are interrelated, and the development of a Federal Data Strategy will have an influence on the use of data by decision-makers, this chapter focuses on what the CAP Goal describes as "providing high quality and timely information to inform evidence-based decision-making and learning." This chapter will not address the host of policy and legal questions, such as citizen privacy and the security of data, collected by statistical agencies, and administrative data collected by other agencies (privacy and security are addressed in Chapter Two and Chapter Seven).

In order to understand the evolution of data and data policy, it is important to note that the root of federal data policy goes back to the Paperwork Reduction Act of 1980 and Office of Management and Budget (OMB) Circular A-130, *Management of Federal Information Resources*. Both the Paperwork Reduction Act and the OMB Circular established the following key principles:

- sound information management policies are crucial
- government will provide free and open access to data
- data will be treated as a strategic asset by government

The key challenge now is transforming data into actionable insights for government executives. In short, how can government make sense of its vast and growing amounts of data to develop new understandings that inform decisions? While new technologies now allow for the collection, analysis, and sharing of real time data, agencies face the challenge of making data relevant and meaningful to decision makers.

The last two decades have been characterized by a more robust supply of useful data and performance information that can serve as a foundation for more evidence-based insights and decisions in the future. Government policy in recent years has encouraged the greater availability of open data, which has contributed to the growing supply of useful information. The increased emphasis on open data occurred via administrative and legal channels, including policies surrounding Open Data commitments, the adoption of the Digital Accountability and Transparency Act (DATA Act), and additional commitments to make routine administrative data more widely available via channels such as Data.gov.

Organization of Chapter

This chapter addresses major developments in how government has evolved its use of data between 1998 to 2018. As seen in the chart, "Evolution of Data: 1998–2018," the evolution of data can be divided into three phases:

- **Early action:** This phase was characterized by an important shift from simply collecting and reporting data to using and analyzing data. Government organizations at the federal, state, and local levels all demonstrated an increased interest in timelier, more useful data. This emphasis was seen in the creation of PerformanceStat initiatives in localities across the nation. During this phase, the federal government also continued its interest in the use of data generated by state and local governments.
- **Expansion:** Based on the increased production of data, government organizations began to focus on new ways to more effectively use the datasets that were being produced. New, more effective uses of data included increased used of analytics, data visualization tools, and big data.
- **Institutionalization:** Based on government's increased experience with the creation and use of data, government policies needed to change. These changes resulted in a series of new policies, increased use of open datasets, and the creation of chief data officer positions.

Evolution of Data: 1998—2018

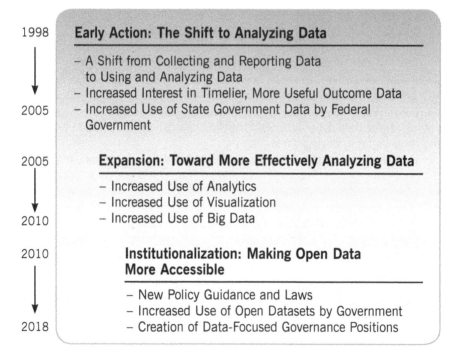

1998

Early Action: The Shift to Analyzing Data

- A Shift from Collecting and Reporting Data to Using and Analyzing Data
- Increased Interest in Timelier, More Useful Outcome Data
2005
- Increased Use of State Government Data by Federal Government

2005

Expansion: Toward More Effectively Analyzing Data

- Increased Use of Analytics
- Increased Use of Visualization
2010
- Increased Use of Big Data

2010

Institutionalization: Making Open Data More Accessible

- New Policy Guidance and Laws
- Increased Use of Open Datasets by Government
2018
- Creation of Data-Focused Governance Positions

EARLY ACTION:
THE SHIFT TO ANALYZING DATA

While interest in performance management has a long history (as described in Chapter Four), great strides were made in the early 1990s to mandate and stimulate the collection of data which could be used in performance management systems. A notable impetus to organized data collection (for use in performance management) was the passage of the Government Performance and Results Act of 1993 (GPRA). GPRA mandated the development of agency strategic plans, annual operating plans, performance measures, and reporting systems.

A Shift from Collecting and Reporting Data to Using and Analyzing Data

The late 1990s and early 2000s witnessed the shift in emphasis from the collecting and reporting of data to the analysis and use of data. These uses included identifying and understanding problems in need of attention in specific government activities and setting goals to measure progress. Traditionally, government organizations have collected administrative data on operations, but the use of such data was often limited. This began to change in the 1990s.

A prime example of the movement to using and analyzing data is the implementation of PerformanceStat initiatives that were created at the local level and spread throughout the nation in the 1990s. Robert Behn characterizes PerformanceStat as action-oriented, data-informed problem solving meetings in government agencies, which focus on using data to find problems in need of attention.[4] Behn notes that one of the key components of these Stat systems is the use of data to analyze specific aspects of an organization's performance.

The first well-known and most widely publicized "Stat" initiative was CompStat, which was created by the New York City Police Department in the mid-1990s. Creation of "Stat" initiatives followed in other localities throughout the next decade. Numerous IBM Center reports chronicled the development of these Stat systems, also discussed in Chapter Four, including a 2001 examination of CompStat by Paul O'Connell, *Using Performance Data for Accountability: The New York City Police Department's CompStat Model of Police Management.*[5]

O'Connell noted that a fundamental, essential principle of CompStat was the collection of accurate and timely information (data), and the meaningful analysis and dissemination of the data. It is hard today to recall the state of technology in the mid-1990s and early 2000s. One of the consistent recommendations from the early years of the Stat movement was the need to have an updated information technology infrastructure in place for a Stat system to operate effectively. Equally important, according to O'Connell, was the need to compile timely and accurate data to share in advance of the Stat meeting (meetings held among senior staff and front-line managers to discuss the data presented and take appropriate action). The PerformanceStat movement also represented the start of increased attention to the need to make data transparent and publicly available.

The second well-known PerformanceStat program was CitiStat, which originated in Baltimore and was spearheaded by former Mayor Martin O'Malley. In his 2003 report, *The Baltimore Citi-State Program: Performance and Accountability*, Lenneal Henderson also focused on the importance of data collection to the Stat process.[6] Henderson wrote that a key to the success of the Stat model is the identification, collection, and analysis of agency performance and personnel data. While it is easy to underestimate the challenges facing the early Stat programs, one of CitiStat's accomplishments was the creation of a computerized information network to collect biweekly data from agencies. This biweekly data generated analyses of performance trends used in early Geographical Information System (GIS) formats to examine the distribution of city services, needs, and challenges. Henderson recommended that CitiStat data needed to be better compiled and simplified for both internal use and broader public use. He also observed that the next challenge for CitStat data would be to develop indicators to mark progress on citywide mayoral initiatives such as crime reduction, public safety and security, housing, and health care. The first wave of Stat programs tended to focus on the progress and accomplishments of single departments.

The Stat movement has also been also used in school systems. In their 2007 report, *The Philadelphia SchoolStat Model,* Christopher Patusky, Leigh Botwinik, and Mary Shelley examined the Philadelphia School Stat program.[7] This Stat program identified key performance indicators that quantified school and student performance in multiple areas. The report's authors found that the collection of data did impact the culture of the organization. The authors wrote that, based on their interviews with school district staff, "the District's culture has begun to operationalize the regular use of data as part of its management routines, and this represents an important step toward establishing a data-driven organizational culture."[8] Data began to be reviewed by both staff and students. SchoolStat and other Stat programs were challenged by the faulty assumption that staff would make effective use of data generated by the initiative.

Increased Interest in Timelier, More Useful Outcome Data by Federal Government Agencies

During this same time period, the early and mid-2000s, federal agencies also increased their emphasis on outcome-focused management, in response to GPRA as well as changes in authorizing legislation. In a 2004 report, *How Federal Programs Use Outcome Information: Opportunities for Federal*

Managers, Harry Hatry, Elaine Morley, Shelli Rossman, and Joseph Wholey examined how federal programs used outcome information.[9] The authors found that the quality of data continued to be a major problem in successfully assessing program outcomes. Specifically, Hatry and his colleagues found:

* datasets were often "old" by the time they reached program managers
* even if the datasets were not "old," the timing as to when the data became available for use by program managers was an issue
* some of the datasets were not actionable to be useful to many program managers

These findings led Hatry and his colleagues to recommend that timelier data be sought, and that the data be presented in a user-friendly form. The federal government would spend the remainder of the decade addressing the accuracy and timely collection of data.

Increased Use of State Government Data by Federal Government

Prior to cities implementing Stat initiatives, the federal government had begun developing strategies for better using information from state governments. In a 2003 report, *Strategies for Using State Information: Measuring and Improving Program Performance,* Shelley Metzenbaum examined the use of state information by the federal government.[10] Metzenbaum found that state performance information was helpful to federal and state government when used to identify successes and problems, as well as to trigger focused follow-up inquiries that enabled everyone in the delivery systems—from the front-line to the federal program office—to better understand the causes of problems and contributors to success.

EXPANSION: TOWARD MORE EFFECTIVELY ANALYZING DATA

During this time period, substantial progress was made on three fronts. First, great strides were made in better analyzing the data collected. Second, improvements emerged in the use of visualization tools to better communicate the data which had been collected and analyzed. And third, the use of big data expanded the capability of government to access and analyze large datasets with increased speed.

Increased Use of Analytics

The mid-2000s saw significant breakthroughs in data-capturing technologies, data standards, and data storage, accompanied by improvements in modeling and optimization science. With the increase in available data, the challenge became placing the data in context to understand its implications for decision-making. As a result, noted Tom Davenport and Sirkka Jarvenpaa, new opportunities arose for the use of analytics. In their 2008 report, *Strategic Use of Analytics in Government*, Davenport and Jarvenpaa defined analytics as "the extensive use of data, statistical and quantitative analysis, explanatory and predictive models, and fact-based management to drive decisions and actions."[11]

The increased interest in the use of analytics during this time period reflected the realization that many government agencies had considerable administrative data at their disposal. *Administrative data* refers to information collected primarily for administrative (not research or statistical) purposes collected by government organizations as part of their transactional activities and record keeping. Examples of administrative data include information gathered from tax filings, registrations, and in connection to applications for government benefits and other administrative activities. However, most agencies did not analyze administrative data in detail, which would have enabled them to identify opportunities to improve services or increase revenue.

A major problem identified during this time period, which continues to this day, is the limited availability of skilled resources in government agencies to analyze data. A key recommendation from Davenport and Jarvenpaa, echoed by other reports discussed in this chapter, was that "...government organizations need to develop a cadre of analysts—both professional and amateur."[12]

During this same time period, the IBM Center and the Partnership for Public Service undertook a multi-year project examining the use of data and analytics by government agencies. A key lesson that emerged from these studies was the insufficiency of merely collecting and reporting data. Government had indeed improved its ability to collect and store data. In their 2011 report, *From Data to Decision: Power of Analytics*, the Partnership wrote, "... we learned that data is only the starting point. The data need to be analyzed, turned into information and made accessible to staff and executives, and the data also is needed to meet varying needs and to be understandable to different audiences."[13]

The Partnership conducted a series of interviews with federal executives for this 2011 report. The interviews identified several significant challenges regarding data for use in analytics:
- ownership of data
- availability of data
- maintaining data integrity

The 2012 study, *From Data to Decisions II: Building an Analytics Culture,* from the Partnership and the IBM Center echoed the recommendation from Davenport and Jarvenpaa—skilled staff were a critical piece in the effective use of analytics in government.[14] This report found that the government was increasing its use of analytics to document what it does, assess effectiveness, and determine measurement processes. Based on the use of analytics, agencies were identifying changes which needed to be made to improve program performance and achieve better results.

The need to "embed" an analytics culture into government was a key focus of the 2013 study *From Data to Decisions III.*[15] This report emphasized encouraging the use of data by employees. The report recommended that employees be able to easily see, combine, analyze, and use data. The report found that, "Leaders and managers should demand and use data and provide employees with targeted on-the-job training."[16]

A good example of the use of analytics in the public sector was the increased interest in predictive policing. Predictive policing can be viewed as a descendent of CompStat in which crime data was used as one input into the deployment of police officers in the field. In her 2013 report, *Predictive Policing: Preventing Crime with Data and Analytics,* Jennifer Bachner wrote that the fundamental notion of predictive policing "is that we can make probabilistic inferences about future criminal activity based on existing data."[17] Bachner found that predictive policing faced several major challenges which focused on the quality of data and the training of analysts to use the data. Bachner found that collecting and managing large volumes of accurate data pointed to one major challenge facing the use of predictive policing. A second major challenge was ensuring that analysts possessed sufficient domain knowledge about law enforcement to analyze the available data. An additional challenge emerged as maintaining adequate analytical resources to use the data, a reoccurring theme in studies on the effective use of data. In her recommendations, Bachner emphasized the need to collect accurate and timely data, and to designate leaders who were committed to the use of analytics.

Increased Use of Visualization

A major factor in increasing the use of data by government in this time period was making it more accessible for users, enabled by the significant advance in the visualization of data. While data visualization has a long history, advances in both hardware and software made it substantially easier to use.

One type of visualization is enabled by the increased use of GIS and, more specifically, geo-coding of data. In a 2010 report, *Using Geographic Information Systems to Increase Citizen Engagement,* Sukumar Ganapati examined the use of GIS.[18] The ability of citizens to visually see transit routes, obtain transit information, and to provide citizen-volunteered information was made possible by government agencies providing data in standardized formats. This access to public domain data enabled government agencies and third parties to develop GIS apps aimed at citizens. The importance of open data and standardized formats is discussed further, later in this chapter.

Another type of data visualization is the use of dashboards by government managers to track performance. In a 2011 report, *Use of Dashboards in Government,* Sukumar Ganapati assessed the impact of dashboards.[19] Ganapati writes, "Organizational dashboards are often likened to dashboards in plane cockpits and cars, which allow the pilot or the driver to see instant information about various metrics...and make travel adjustments or spot vehicular issues on the fly." [20] He found that the quality of data was key to the credibility of dashboard performance measures. Like other research on the use of data, he noted that dashboards were only tools and their effectiveness depended on the use by managers.

In her 2013 report, *The Use of Data Visualization in Government,* Genie Stowers noted that effective data visualization, or graphic display, has been used to understand data patterns since 1854 when a doctor in London mapped cases of cholera.[21] Her report tracked the movement toward increased use of visualization in government. She wrote, "The movement is the result of numerous converging trends—the open data and transparency movements, growing citizen engagement with data, new tools for data mining and analysis that use ever larger datasets, advances in web graphic technology and interactive online mapping and graphing, and new awareness of the need for more proactive citizen engagement."[22]

Increased Use of Big Data

The mid-2010s saw an increase in the use of big data. As noted earlier, technological advances made it dramatically easier to collect and store data, with the cost of storing data falling sharply over the years. In his 2014 report, *Realizing the Promise of Big Data: Implementing Big Data Projects,* Kevin Desouza reported that not only were storage devices cheaper, significant advancements in the science of databases and information retrieval emerged as well.[23]

In his report, Desouza defined big data as an evolving concept that refers to the growth, value, and speed of data, and how data can be analyzed to optimize business processes, create customer value, and mitigate risks. Desouza quotes authors Viktor Mayer-Schonberger and Kenneth Cukier that "big data refers to things one can do at a large scale that cannot be done at a smaller one, to extract new insights or create new forms of values, in ways that change markets, organizations, the relationships between citizens and governments, and more."[24]

In their 2016 report, *Ten Actions to Implement Big Data Initiatives: A Study of 65 Cities,* Alfred Ho and Bo McCall referred to big data as "using massive amount of data to conduct analyses so that the data patterns and relationships can be used for classification, clustering, anomaly detection, prediction, and other analytic needs in decision making."[25] Ho and McCall also reported that, with the advancement of computing technologies and the emergence of many data analytic tools, user-friendly platforms can be used to conduct more sophisticated program and customer analysis.

Ho and McCall surveyed 65 cities to understand their use of big data and analytics. They found that 75 percent of the cities surveyed reported having undertaken big data initiatives, including increased used of analytics, better integration of data with budgeting, and using a team approach or multi-departmental governance structures for their data initiatives. Their survey also found that many cities were creating chief data officer positions to lead these data initiatives. Cities were also increasingly providing citizen-friendly ways to visualize city and access data, as well as empowering citizens to conduct their own data inquiries and analysis of city-generated data.

While Ho and McCall found that big data was being used in the cities they surveyed, and had much potential, a variety of issues involving data began to surface. The increase in the availability of data created new ethical and legal challenges in both the public and private sectors. These issues included potential privacy and individual rights infringement, hidden inequity and discrimination in algorithm-driven decision making, and potential conflicts between efficiency, customization, and equal access to government services by all. Specific privacy issues include how data should be collected, stored, and analyzed, as well as how data should be shared with non-government entities.

Case Study in Collecting and Using Data: The American Recovery and Reinvestment Act of 2009

A key event in advancing government's ability to collect and use federal financial and performance data was the implementation of the American Recovery and Reinvestment Act of 2009 (Recovery Act). An implementation goal set by the Office of Management and Budget was that the use of all Recovery Act funds be transparent to the public and that public benefits of the Act be reported clearly, accurately, and in a timely manner. Oversight of the implementation of the Act was assigned to the newly created independent Recovery Accountability and Transparency Board (Recovery Board), comprised of agency Inspectors General. The Recovery Board had the responsibility to establish and maintain a user-friendly, public-facing website, Recovery.gov, to foster accountability and transparency in the use of Recovery Act funds over the course over the six-year initiative. The Recovery Board also created a Recovery Operations Center which was responsible for cross-referencing data from recipient reports and other government databases to detect fraud and misuse of funds.[26]

The experience of implementing the Recovery Act was a significant "learning experience" for the federal government and helped lead to the DATA Act of

2014 that codified many of the lessons learned by the Recovery Board. In addition, implementation of the Recovery Act demonstrated many of the capabilities and tools discussed in this chapter:

- **Standardization of data collected**
  The Recovery Board required the recipients of its funds to input 99 fields of numerical and narrative data related to six dimensions of spending. By generating detailed, multilayered recipient reports tracking Recovery Act financial data, the Act acted as "proof of concept" for future, more ambitious public transparency initiatives regarding federal spending.

- **Use of predictive analytics**
  The Recovery Operations Center used a variety of tools to mine more than 25 government and open-source databases, looking for anomalies and indicators of fraud or waste.

- **Use of new technologies**
  According to Earl Devaney, former chair of the Recovery Board, the success of the Recovery Operations Center was based on the Board's ability to find the right set of tools to collect, manage, and analyze numerous datasets.

- **Mapping**
  The Recovery.gov website provided comprehensive geospatial capability for citizens to find Recovery Act spending in their localities and for use by the Recovery Board to map incidents of fraud and waste.

- **Cloud computing**
  The Board had a clear need to seek new levels of efficiency and cost savings in the collection and analysis of data. Their efforts were an early demonstration of the value of cloud computing. The move to the cloud meant that the Board no longer had to manage the Recovery.gov's physical data center and related computer equipment.

- **Continuous monitoring**
  The concept of continuous monitoring helped reduce the reliance on human analysts to perform predictive analytics. By leveraging big data systems, the continuous monitoring process eliminated the need for additional interpretation of data before taking action.

Identification of Challenges in the Use of Data

A 2018 study by the Pew Charitable Trusts, *How States Use Data to Inform Decisions*, reported the challenges that government executives at the state level faced in using data, were similar to those faced at both the federal and local levels.[27] The report found the following major challenges:

- **Challenge One: Staffing.** Few state employees were experienced in both policy and data analytics. Many states reported that existing staff lacked skills in data analytics or the ability to interpret data findings to make policy recommendations.
- **Challenge Two: Data accessibility.** Many state agencies had archaic data systems, some developed in the 1980s, which made it very difficult to access and use data.
- **Challenge Three: Data quality.** Data quality issues impaired the analyses of data. Many state databases suffered from quality issues which made them difficult to use and interpret.
- **Challenge Four: Data sharing.** If a state agency wanted to make quality data accessible, a combination of problems including organizational culture, laws, or other factors often prohibited the data from being shared.

While the Pew report found that data were indeed being used in strategic ways in state decision making, the above four challenges all need to be addressed to enhance more effective use of data. The report contains a series of recommendations, including the need for a more organized and centralized approach to data in the future. Key actions for state leaders include the development of "governance structures to guide data use and access while also prioritizing privacy" and the need to "take stock of their data systems and perform an inventory of data sets."[28] A major part of the data governance process involves the need to ensure that quality data could be accessed and used by stakeholders. Key steps include improving data quality and accessibility, developing an enterprise view of data, and establishing data sharing agreements.

As has been seen throughout this chapter, concerns continue about the need to build government's capacity to effectively use data. The Pew report recommended hiring new staff skilled in data analytics. The report also recommended that funding be dedicated to support data-driven projects. The federal government now faces the same challenges of skilled staff and adequate funding for data-driven projects.

In addition to addressing governance, staff capacity, and the quality of data, the Pew report made a series of recommendations concerning the use of data. While this chapter focuses on the availability (or supply) of data, Chapter Four addresses issues surrounding the use (demand) of data. The Pew report recommended an increase in the use of visualization techniques in charts, dashboards, and reports to make the data easier for decision makers to analyze and understand. Findings from the analysis of data can inform, guide, or alter decisions. The Pew report concluded with recommendations that agencies should create an organizational culture that prioritizes data collection, and that new legislation and policies are needed to support data use.

INSTITUTIONALIZATION:
MAKING OPEN DATA MORE ACCESSIBLE

Institutionalization is reflected in several major developments in recent years: a series of directives and new policies at the federal level to open up government datasets, increased use of existing administrative datasets by government executives, and the creation of chief data officer positions.

New Policy Guidance and Laws

Starting in 2009, a series of federal policies and laws contributed to the opening of data sources to the public. In addition to becoming available for use by the public, these open datasets also proved highly useful to government agencies as they delivered their missions. In addition to improving accessibility to these datasets, emphasis was also placed on increasing the quality of data. Key policy directives included:

- **Open Government Directive:** This 2009 directive required agencies to publish more information online in open and accessible ways. It also required agencies to increase the amount of high-value datasets available to researchers and directed OMB officials to create an interagency process for sharing and coordinating data policies.[29]
- **Open Data Policy—Managing Information as an Asset:** This 2013 directive was to promote interoperability, accessibility, and openness in regard to data. Agencies were required to use data standards and extensible metadata for information creation and collection efforts, and to ensure information stewardship.[30]
- **Guidance for Providing and Using Administrative Data for Statistical Purposes:** This 2014 directive called for greater collaboration between program and statistical offices and encouraged agencies to promote the use of administrative data for statistical purposes.[31]
- **The Digital Accountability and Transparency Act of 2014 (DATA Act):** This law aims to make federal spending information more accessible and transparent. The law requires the Department of the Treasury to establish common standards for financial data provided by all government agencies and to expand the amount of data that agencies must provide to USASpending.gov, which is discussed below.[32]

Increased Use of Open Data Datasets by Government

The policy directives and new laws outlined above have had a significant impact on making government datasets more widely accessible to the public and more user-focused. These datasets also proved useful to some government agencies in achieving their missions. Two types of new web portals—

data repository websites operated by the federal government, and external data repository websites which used government data—saw increased use.

Key government-hosted data web portals include:

- **USASpending.gov**, initially launched in 2007 in response to the Federal Funding Accountability and Transparency Act of 2005 (FFATA) mandated that federal contract, grant, loan, and other financial assistance awards of more than $25,000 be displayed on a publicly accessible and searchable website to give the public access to information on how its tax dollars were spent. The Digital Accountability and Transparency Act of 2014 expanded FFATA by establishing government-wide data standards for financial data and providing consistent, reliable, searchable, and accurate data. The website was relaunched in April 2018 with expanded analytical tools and visualization capabilities.
- **Data.gov**, launched in 2009 by the Obama Administration to improve public access to high-value datasets generated by the federal government. In response to the 2013 Federal Open Data Policy discussed above, all future government data must be made available in open, machine-readable formats, while continuing to ensure privacy and security.
- **HealthData.gov**, created in 2012 as an outgrowth of the Health Data Initiative (HDI) established within the Department of Health of Human Services to make health data more available. At its launch, the website contained over 2,000 datasets. The website makes high-value health data more accessible to entrepreneurs, researchers, and policy makers in the hopes of better health outcomes for all.

In addition to the establishment of government data web portals, there has been an increase in the number of commercial web portals using government data. These new websites benefited greatly from the Open Data policies of the late 2000s and early 2010s, which made government datasets more available and accessible. Notable non-government data portals include:

- **DataUSA**, created in 2014 as a comprehensive website and visualization engine for publicly available U.S. government data. The site provides an easy-to-use platform that allows individuals to conduct their own analyses and turn data into knowledge.
- **USAFacts**, created in 2018 as a non-partisan, not-for-profit civic initiative which presents a data-driven portrait of the American population, government's finances, and government's impact.

Creation of Data-Focused Governance Positions

In her 2018 report, *Data-Driven Government: The Role of Chief Data Officers*, Jane Wiseman found that there are currently few individuals in the federal government with the official title of chief data officer (CDO) at the departmental level.[33] There is, however, a clear trend to designate individuals who will have data responsibilities, some with the CDO title. While few of these individuals will have the same set of responsibilities, most CDO-type positions will have a portfolio of activities that include data governance, data analytics, geographic information systems, data culture, smart technology, data infrastructure, and digital services. There has also been an increase in the number of data scientist positions throughout the federal government.

LESSONS LEARNED

Based on our review of research on this topic over the past twenty years, we identified two key lessons:

First, data made available for public use has also proved to be useful to government organizations themselves. A case study on the impact of the transparency requirements from the American Recovery and Reinvestment Act of 2009 found that government officials became the primary users of the Recovery Act data because it allowed them to manage and track federal spending in near-real time. In a 2012 report, *Recovery Act Transparency: Learning from States' Experience,* Francisca Rojas found that spending transparency became institutionalized in some states and at the federal level in response to reporting requirements and that the data was used effectively by government executives.[34]

Second, standardization of data provides a crucial step in the collection and sharing of data. Significant strides have been made since the implementation of the Recovery Act. In describing his experience as chair of the Recovery Accountability and Transparency Board to monitor Recovery Act spending, Earl Devaney noted the difficulty of harmonizing spending data across agencies with different data standards. He concluded that, in order to effectively track money and to use data to make better-informed decisions, government will have to reevaluate how its databases interact and leverage each other. Many of the lessons learned in implementing the Recovery Act influenced the DATA Act of 2014, which moved government to a more cohesive, centralized accountability framework to track and oversee spending with standardized data formats.

LOOKING FORWARD

A variety of important issues appear on the horizon regarding the future use of data by government agencies.

How can government use data collected by the private sector? To date, the emphasis has been on making data "open" from the government to the public, including the private sector. A future challenge will face the private sector to make its data "open" to the government and other users. This sharing would create the possibility of effectively combining data collected by the government and the private sector.

A series of issues relate to sharing of data between federal government agencies themselves, between the federal government and other levels of government, and between local governments. Presently, the sharing of data between federal agencies poses problems because of statutory limits on sharing data. Proposed legislation, the Foundations for Evidence-Based Policymaking Act of 2017, would ease barriers which currently make the sharing of data between agencies difficult.[35]

The capacity of the federal government to both manage and analyze its data continues to be a major issue, as discussed earlier in findings from the Pew Charitable Trusts report on the state use of data. Another report, the 2017 report of the Commission on Evidence-Based Policymaking, set forth two key capacity challenges for the federal government related to data:

- The capacity to support the full range of evidence-building functions is uneven, and where capacity for evidence building does exist, it is often poorly coordinated within departments.
- The federal evidence community has insufficient resources and limited flexibilities that restrict the ability to expand evidence-building activities.[36] A key recommendation of the Commission is that the President direct Federal departments to increase capacity for evidence building throughout government.

Mark A. Abramson *is the President, Leadership Inc. and the founding Executive Director of the IBM Center for The Business of Government. His recently published books include* Getting It Done: A Guide for Government Executives *(with Daniel J. Chenok and John M. Kamensky) and* Succeeding as a Political Executive: 50 Insights from Experience *(with Paul R. Lawrence). He is also the author of* What Government Does: How Political Executives Manage *(with Paul R. Lawrence).*

Endnotes
1   Meredith Somers, "Federal managers working on 'culture change' for cross-component data sharing," *Federal News Radio* (April 26, 2017).

2   Somers, "Federal managers working on culture change."

3   For additional information on the President's Management Agenda, see https://www.performance.gov/PMA/.

4   Robert D. Behn, *The PerformanceStat Potential: A Leadership Strategy for Producing Results* (Washington, DC: Brookings Institution Press, 2014).

5   Paul O'Connell, *Using Performance Data for Accountability: The New York City Police Department's CompStat Model of Police Management,* IBM Center for The Business of Government, 2001.

6   Lenneal Henderson, *The Baltimore Citi-State Program: Performance and Accountability,* IBM Center for The Business of Government, 2003.

7   *Christopher Patusky, Leigh Botwinik, and Mary Shelley The Philadelphia SchoolStat Model,* IBM Center for The Business of Government, 2007.

8   Patusky, et al., *Philadelphia SchoolStat,* 32-33.

9   Harry P. Hatry, Elaine Morley, Shelli B. Rossman, and Joseph S. Wholey, *How Federal Programs Use Outcome Information: Opportunities for Federal Managers,* IBM Center for The Business of Government, 2004.

10 Shelley Metzenbaum, *Using State Information: Measuring and Improving Program Performance,* IBM Center for The Business of Government, 2003.

11 Tom Davenport and Sirkka Jarvenpaa, *Strategic Use of Analytics in Government,* IBM Center for The Business of Government, 2008, 6.

12 Davenport and Jarvenpaa, *Strategic Use of Analytics,* 28.

13 Partnership for Public Service, *From Data to Decisions,* 2011, 3.

14 Partnership for Public Service, *From Data to Decisions II: Building an Analytics Culture,* 2012.

15 Partnership for Public Service, *From Data to Decisions III,* 2013.

16 Partnership for Public Service, *From Data to Decisions III,* 4.

17 Jennifer Bachner, *Predictive Policing: Preventing Crime with Data and Analytics,* IBM Center for The Business of Government, 2013, 14.

18 Sukumar Ganapati, *Using Geographic Information Systems to Increase Citizen Engagement,* IBM Center for The Business of Government, 2010.

19 Sukumar Ganapati, *Use of Dashboards in Government,* IBM Center for The Business of Government, 2011.

20 Ganapati, *Use of Dashboards,* 15.

21 Genie Stowers, *The Use of Data Visualization in Government,* IBM Center for The Business of Government, 2013.

22 Stowers, *Data Visualization,* 8.

23 Kevin Desouza, *Realizing the Promise of Big Data: Implementing Big Data Projects,* IBM Center for The Business of Government, 2014.

24 Desouza, *Realizing the Promise,* 10.

25 Alfred Tat-Kei Ho with Bo McCall, *Ten Actions to Implement Big Data Initiatives: A Study of 65 Cities,* IBM Center for The Business of Government, 2016, 6.

26 For more detailed discussions of the Recovery Act, see Francisca M. Rojas, *Recovery Act Transparency: Learning from State's Experience,* IBM Center for the Business of Government, 2012; and Earl Devaney, "Using Predictive Analysis to Prevent Rather than React and Respond: A Case Study of the Recovery Accountability and Transparency Board," *Fast Government: Accelerating Service Quality While Reducing Cost and Time,* IBM Center for the Business of Government, 2013.

27 The Pew Charitable Trusts, *How States Use Data to Inform Decisions,* 2018.

28 Pew Charitable Trusts, *How States Use Data,* 23.

29 Office of Management and Budget, *M-10-06: Open Government Directive,* December 8, 2009.

30 Office of Management and Budget, *M-13-13: Open Data Policy – Managing Information as an Asset,* May 9, 2013.

31 Office of Management and Budget, *M-14-06: Guidance for Providing and Using Administrative Data for Statistical Purposes,* February 4, 2014.

32 *Digital Accountability and Transparency Act of 2014,* Public Law 113-101 (May 9, 2014).

33 Jane Wiseman, *Data-Driven Government: The Role of Chief Data Officers,* IBM Center for The Business of Government, 2018

34 Francisca M. Rojas, *Recovery Act Transparency: Learning from States' Experience,* IBM Center for The Business of Government, 2012.

35 The Foundations for Evidence-based Policymaking Act, H.R. 4174, was introduced in October, 2017, 115th Congress (2017-2018).

36 Commission on Evidence-based Policymaking, *The Promise of Evidence-Based Policymaking,* 2017.

CHAPTER FOUR

Managing Performance

John M. Kamensky

Highlights

- Performance management initiatives over the past two decades helped shift the conversation within and across U.S. government agencies—from a focus on measuring program activities and outputs to a focus on achieving mission outcomes.

- These performance management initiatives started with developing a supply of information via new routines, then moved to the use of more sophisticated techniques. Together, these information-gathering efforts have gradually contributed to a greater demand for performance information by decision makers.

- Trial and error led to the development and institutionalization of a performance management framework for the federal government, and this performance management framework has successfully navigated the transition to successive administrations.

MANAGING PERFORMANCE

By John M Kamensky

In the early 1990s, the U.S. Coast Guard had based its marine safety efforts on inspections and certifications of vessels such as tug boats. The Coast Guard measured its marine safety performance by counting the number of inspections and outstanding inspection results that it conducted. A new law encouraged it to shift its performance focus to counting the number of accidents, injuries and deaths. The Coast Guard then investigated the causes of accidents and found they were largely caused by human error, not equipment failures. As a result, the Coast Guard shifted its enforcement strategy from inspections of vessels to a joint effort with industry to train crew members how to avoid accidents. For the towing industry, the fatality rate dropped 70 percent between 1990 and 1995.[1]

INTRODUCTION

The U.S. federal performance management movement is rooted in the passage of the Government Performance and Results Act of 1993. But this was only one milestone in a much broader trend toward the development and use of performance information that includes international, state, local, and nonprofit participants.

The scope and depth of different approaches to performance management makes this topic difficult to characterize, but academics offer several conceptual models to describe the many variations. For example, Geert Bouckaert and John Halligan offer four models of performance management systems that constitute a continuum of four different levels of maturity:

- **The performance administration model**: Formal, procedural mechanisms create a linear input/output measurement system that focuses on program productivity and efficiency.
- **The siloed performance model**: Specialized performance systems for different functions and programs are disconnected and lack integration among components, even within the same organization.
- **The performance management model**: Performance measurement used not just for accountability but for learning and improvement of operations within an agency. Performance information is systematically generated, integrated, and used.
- **The performance governance model**: Collaborative approaches replace hierarchical performance management, and are cross-agency and cross-sector in approach. Multiple independent actors contribute to the delivery of public services and inform policy making in conjunction with non-governmental actors.[2]

These four notional performance management models do not exist in a pure form anywhere, but they provide a useful construct for understanding how different approaches to performance management have evolved over the past 20 years, and where it might go in coming years.

Enduring Challenges of Performance Management Drive Reform Efforts

Performance information has long been collected and used to varying degrees at the federal, state, and local levels in the U.S. since the early 1900s, as part of the reforms brought about by the Progressive Movement. Localities and several state governments began developing performance measurement systems more methodically in the 1970s. The federal government undertook some performance-related initiatives, such the Defense Department's Planning, Programming, and Budgeting System (PPBS) of the 1960s, but other agencies did not begin in earnest until the passage of the Government Performance and Results Act of 1993 (GPRA). That law required federal departments and agencies to develop strategic plans, annual performance plans, performance measures, and annual performance reports.

By 2010, a number of lessons had been learned in how to effectively develop, use, and govern a performance management system. Many of these lessons came from the Government Accountability Office's (GAO's) observations in various reports on GPRA's implementation, but also from agencies' practical experiences with the effectiveness and impact of various performance management routines. Changes based on these lessons were incorporated into the GPRA Modernization Act of 2010.

The overarching implementation challenges highlighted by GAO and others pointed to two enduring realities faced by agency implementers, which continue today:

- **Too much focus on measuring outputs vs. outcomes**: The traditional hierarchical governance model, especially at the federal level, tends to be more suited to focusing on accountability for producing "outputs," such as the student-teacher ratio in classrooms, or the number of hours of instruction in given subjects. It is less suited to producing "outcomes," such as the percentage of high school students who graduate and either get a job or pursue higher education. Achieving outcomes requires dynamic cross-agency measures and the use of collaborative governance approaches (see Chapter Six). Again, some progress has been made in this dimension, but largely around the edges of the performance management framework.
- **Lack of a demand for performance information:** The law effectively mandated a supply of performance plans, measures, and reports, but did not influence decision makers' behaviors sufficiently to create a demand for performance information. Numerous efforts, ranging from creating incentives through the use of scorecards to creating new organizational models, have yet to "crack the code" to embed the use of performance

information more systematically in budgeting. In contrast, agencies have made progress in using performance information more regularly to administer programs. One area of focus in recent years has been on the supply of information—making it more readily interpretable via visualization and other interpretive tools, as well as more timely so decision makers will see it as more relevant. However, absent a stronger integration between performance and budget systems, the use of performance information by decision makers may continue to be episodic.

In addition to federal performance-related efforts, a number of state governments adopted similar laws to GPRA. Similarly, professional communities (such as those involved with the implementation of foster care programs) and municipal professional associations developed standard measures for common functions, such as waste collection and emergency response. In addition, by the 2010s, a number of nonprofits, foundations, and advocacy groups supported initiatives related to improved performance, evidence, and analysis.

Organization of Chapter

As seen in the chart titled, "Evolution of Performance Management: 1998-2018," the evolution of the performance movement in the U.S. federal government during this time period can be divided into three phases:
- **Early action**: In response to the adoption of the Government Performance and Results Act of 1993, federal agencies began developing performance management routines to create a supply of performance information. This started with the development of agency strategic plans, annual operating plans, performance measures, data collection systems, and data reporting systems. These efforts reflect the first two of the four performance management models described by Bouckaert and Halligan. In addition, there was a new focus by agency leaders on achieving program "outcomes" instead of "outputs." While agencies made a limited use of performance information to manage at the federal level, there were pioneering efforts to do so at the local level.
- **Expansion**: This phase reflects the beginning in the shift from creating a supply of performance information, to creating a demand for its use by managers and policy decision makers. This included uses such as for accountability, operational management, and to inform budget and pay decisions. This phase can also be characterized as the beginning of the development of more sophisticated approaches to collecting and using information, such as measures of "unobserved events" (e.g., illegal drug smuggling) and predictive measures, such as where and when crimes are more likely to occur.
- **Institutionalization:** Lessons learned from more than a decade of experimentation and observation were incorporated into an update of the

GPRA law in 2010. This included newly defined governance structures, a more stable operating framework, and new authority for agencies to work collaboratively on shared outcomes. In parallel, technological advances made data collection and reporting less burdensome and more available for analysts and decision makers. This contributed to new demands for evidence-based decisions and new performance-based program models, such as tiered evidence grants and Pay-for-Success programs.

Even with expanded institutional capacity, enduring challenges continue for the performance management movement's efforts to mature to the point of achieving the "performance governance" model described above by Bouckaert and Halligan. This will require better integration with other management

Evolution of Performance Management: 1998—2018

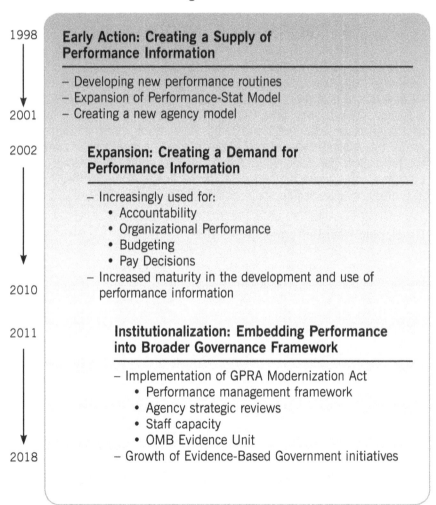

1998

Early Action: Creating a Supply of Performance Information

- Developing new performance routines
- Expansion of Performance-Stat Model
2001
- Creating a new agency model

2002

Expansion: Creating a Demand for Performance Information

- Increasingly used for:
  • Accountability
  • Organizational Performance
  • Budgeting
  • Pay Decisions
- Increased maturity in the development and use of
2010
performance information

2011

Institutionalization: Embedding Performance into Broader Governance Framework

- Implementation of GPRA Modernization Act
  • Performance management framework
  • Agency strategic reviews
  • Staff capacity
  • OMB Evidence Unit
2018
- Growth of Evidence-Based Government initiatives

systems in use within government—personnel, technology, regulatory, budget, etc.—and a greater availability of granular, real-time, and contextually-relevant performance information. However, the most significant challenge facing government leaders will involve adopting performance management approaches as their day-to-day leadership strategy, and not just another set of government compliance processes.

The remainder of this chapter details these three phases and concludes with lessons learned and observations as to what policy makers may face in the next few years as the performance movement continues to evolve.

The reader will note that this chapter discusses issues that are also raised in Chapter Three, "Using Data," and Chapter Six, "Becoming Collaborative."

EARLY ACTION: CREATING A SUPPLY OF PERFORMANCE INFORMATION

By 1998, GPRA had been in place for five years, but its requirements were only beginning to be applied governmentwide. The 1993 law called for at least ten pilot projects for performance goal-setting in agencies before a governmentwide launch in 1997, but OMB actually approved about 70 pilot projects between 1994 and 1996. As a result, many efforts emerged across the federal government to develop a set of routines—or administrative processes—for planning, measuring, and reporting. Multiple agencies or programs also significantly rethought approaches to achieving their missions as a result of implementing the new law.

Developing New Performance Routines

Even with the passage of the Government Performance and Results Act of 1993, it took a long time before agencies developed the necessary administrative routines to meet the law's requirements. The law required a series of pilot projects for developing approaches to:
- strategic plans and goal setting
- annual performance plans, measures, and targets
- performance reports and program evaluation

GAO was directed by Congress to assess agencies' compliance with the implementation of the law's requirements. The first agency strategic plans were to be in place by September 30, 1997, the first annual performance plans by September 30, 1998, and the first annual performance reports by early 2000. These requirements trickled down to the bureau and program levels in departments and agencies at different rates, with different experiences in how the new performance routines were adopted. Some were compliance-oriented, while others used the new routines to rethink how they met their mission objectives.

Strategic Planning and Goal Setting

GPRA required agencies to develop strategic plans covering at least a three- to five-year period. This included the development of mission statements and setting long-term goals. For example, the U.S. Air Force in 1997 completed a corporate strategic plan with stretch goals that reached out to 2025. Colin Campbell, in a 2000 report, *Corporate Strategic Planning in Government: Lessons from the United States Air Force,* described how the then-chief of staff of the Air Force, General Ronald Fogelman, assembled all of the Air Force's four-star generals in 1996 to develop a long-term vision via a collaborative process.[3] He then staffed the development of the plan via a Board of Directors comprised of the Air Force's three-star generals. This led to the identification of 16 key potential issues, of which four were then further fleshed out.

However, General Fogelman retired before the plan was implemented. The transition to a new Air Force chief of staff with different priorities led to a delay and then the development of a new plan, completed in 2000. Unlike the 1997 plan, the process leading to this new plan engaged the Secretary of the Air Force—not just uniformed military officers—and resulted in a shorter timeframe. Instead of 30 years, it focused 20 years out.

Campbell observed, "Corporate strategic planning does not come naturally to organizations within the U.S. federal government."[4] He found insufficient staff capacity and too much turnover of top leaders to gain commitment to longer-term objectives, but that efforts to be collaborative and engage stakeholders helped ensure ultimate success. He concludes that the development of a strategic planning routine would likely involve a good deal of trial and error to develop a sustainable process. This observation was borne out in many other agencies, according to GAO's assessment of the implementation of agency strategic plans.[5]

Annual Plans, Measures, and Targets

Effective strategic plans should tie to an agency's day-to-day operations in order to be meaningful. This requires the development of annual operating plans linked to resources, meaningful measures of progress, and target-setting.

A particularly challenging example of the development of action plans and measures is when this kind of effort is undertaken across multiple agencies that are working toward a common result. The Office of National Drug Control Policy (ONDCP) pioneered the creation of a Performance Measurement and Evaluation System in 1997. ONDCP orchestrates the joint efforts and strategies of more than 50 federal agencies, with combined resources of $19 billion, toward anti-drug efforts.

In a 2001 report, *The Challenge of Developing Cross-Agency Measures: A Case Study of the Office of National Drug Control Policy*, Patrick Murphy and John Carnevale described the evolution of ONDCP's performance system that spans organizational boundaries. They concluded that even with the statutory limitations of ONDCP to focus primarily on coordination—without any authority to direct agency compliance—"it managed to produce an impressive set of goals, objectives, and performance measures intended to improve the management of federal drug control efforts.[6]

However, measurement systems sometimes have unintended consequences. In response to GPRA, the Department of Labor pioneered the development of a performance management system in the late 1990s for the then-new Workforce Investment Act. In a 2005 study, Carolyn Heinrich examined the implementation of the new system and found the target-setting problematic for unforeseen reasons.[7] The system had three elements:

- performance measures to evaluate progress toward goals
- a method for setting standards and performance targets, and for measuring progress against those targets
- rewards and sanctions for achieving goals

The performance targets to be achieved were negotiated with each state using prior year baseline data. But economic conditions changed with the 2000 recession, so states began to miss their targets for reasons outside their control. Heinrich noted: "...states were not prepared or in a position to adjust for dramatic economic changes that led to significant risks of failure to meet performance targets during an economic downturn."[8]

Performance Reporting and Program Evaluation

A key rationale for performance management systems lies in their value in creating accountability and learning opportunities, so as to improve performance in the future. This is typically manifested in performance reporting and program evaluation routines. Program evaluation routines were pioneered in agencies—beginning in the 1970s, in social services agencies such as the Department of Health, Education and Welfare (HEW)—but experienced a lack of support until the early 2000s.

In a 2009 report, *Performance Reporting: Insights from International Practice,* Richard Boyle examined the performance information in a sample of performance reports from four countries (Australia, Canada, Ireland, and the U.S.) in order to identify commonalities, differences, and key attributes of effective reporting of output and outcome information.[9] He found: "On the whole, indicators in the U.S. reports are more likely to report on outcomes, be quantitative in nature, meet data quality criteria, and have associated targets and multiyear baseline data." Interestingly, the U.S. went a step further with the adoption of the GPRA Modernization Act of 2010 stipulating that agency performance reporting should be *at least* annual, with more frequent updates of actual performance.

Performance information helps program managers and stakeholders understand "what" happens, but typically does not explain "why" a certain level of performance occurs. Understanding "why" requires deeper knowledge about a program. This is often found by conducting program evaluations. In a 2001 report, *Using Evaluation to Support Performance Management: A Guide for Federal Executives,* Kathy Newcomer and Mary Ann Schierer examined the capacities of 13 large federal departments and 10 large agencies.[10] They found federal agencies generally had a low capacity for conducting program evaluations, but a high demand for valid and reliable evidence to meet the requirements of GPRA.[11] They also found that program evaluation could improve agencies' strategic planning, program delivery, accountability to Congress, and link performance results to specific programs.[12] They concluded that strengthening program evaluation capacity with additional personnel and dedicated financial resources "will enhance the likelihood that the performance measurement and management framework...will result in both improved program management and desired results."[13] Newcomer and Schierer recommended bringing together agency-level program evaluation and program management staffs to "transfer knowledge" between the two professional communities.

Examples of the Early Uses of Performance Information

The use of performance information by managers and political leaders happened more rapidly in the 1990s at the local level than at the federal level. But, as federal agencies began to define outcome-focused goals for their programs, the dialogue between the federal government and states and localities changed with regard to how federal grants should focus more on societal outcomes.

Expansion of the PerformanceStat Model

A new data-driven model for managing performance and accountability—ultimately dubbed "PerformanceStat"—was created in the early 1990s in New York City, rapidly spread to other cities, and was adopted by various state governments and federal agencies over the next decade.

As noted earlier in Chapter Three, "Using Data," the New York City police pioneered the use of what was initially called "CompStat," beginning in 1994, by redesigning the city's police department accountability approach to institutionalize a data-driven approach to policing. Paul O'Connell, in a 2002 report, *Using Performance Data for Accountability: The New York City Police Department's CompStat Model of Police Management,* described how New York City Police Commissioner William Bratton "shocked his subordinates by establishing new, exacting standards of operational performance." CompStat data was gathered and analyzed on a near-real-time basis at the precinct level. Crime reduction strategies were derived from these data via twice-weekly meetings between the commissioner and precinct commanders.[14] O'Connell wrote: "CompStat has transformed the department into a learning organization that can 'analyze, reflect, learn, and change based on experience.'"[15] By 2001, the CompStat approach was attributed to having reduced major crimes in New York City by 63 percent.[16] Because of the success of the CompStat approach in New York City, its use was rapidly expanded over the following decade, covering all city services in Baltimore's CitiStat program under Mayor Martin O'Malley, as described in Lenneal Henderson's 2003 report, *The Baltimore CitiStat Program: Performance and Accountability*,[17] and Robert Behn's 2007 report, *What All Mayors Would Like to Know About Baltimore's CitiStat Performance Strategy*.[18] It also spread to school systems, such as the case detailed in *Philadelphia's SchoolStat Model*, a 2007 report by Christopher Patusky, Leigh Botwink, and Mary Shelley.[19] It then spread to entire states, such as Maryland's StateStat and Washington State's Government Management, Accountability, and Performance (GMAP) system.

Collectively, professor Robert Behn called these related performance management systems "PerformanceStat" in his 2014 book on this management phenomena.[20] However, this approach did not always carry over intact from one elected official to another. Many of these systems disappeared when the top political leaders left; others were sustained, but often evolved in new directions (e.g., Washington State's GMAP became "Results Washington," with a new focus). This probably could have been anticipated, notes Behn, who says "PerformanceStat is not a system, or a model. It is a leadership strategy. For to achieve the strategy's potential to produce real results requires active leadership. Moreover, the leadership team must adapt the strategy to fit its specific public purposes."[21] Thus, it should not be expected that the management styles of one political leader can readily transition to the next political leader.

In a 2003 report, *Strategies for Using State Information: Measuring and Improving Program Performance,* Shelley Metzenbaum found that federal GPRA requirements reinforced existing performance-related conversations between states, localities, and the federal government. Would federal agencies use state- and local-generated data about their performance? Would federal agencies define desired national outcome goals and require states and localities to report on progress towards those goals? How would federal agencies treat goals that states set for themselves?[22] None of these issues were addressed in GPRA. Metzenbaum examined how federal agencies resolved these kinds of issues in a series of case studies involving environmental protection, highway construction, highway safety, and public education.

Metzenbaum found that, "Common measures across states and across time are useful for identifying problems to be addressed and successes to be replicated."[23] She observed that comparative data was a powerful motivator for states to act. She also found that federally mandated goals and measures can work, but that if federal agencies "make it a priority to build measurement systems that serve the needs of those they measure" it would lessen the chances that states would organize to dismantle the measurement system via appeals to Congress.

Creating a New Agency Model

The National Performance Review in 1996 (later renamed the National Partnership for Reinventing Government) attempted to embed performance management into federal government culture by creating a new agency model that would, "Give agencies that deliver measurable services a greater degree of autonomy from governmentwide rules in exchange for greater accountability for achieving results."[24] This model was inspired by the British "Next Steps" executive agencies initiative which began converting away from traditional agencies in the 1980s. By 1997, about three-quarters of the British government had converted to this new agency model, which remains its dominant organizational approach even today. Independent assessments of the model—which had been adopted by other countries as well—found it an effective way to shift agency cultures to focus more on performance than on administrative processes.

The U.S. version was termed a "performance-based organization" (PBO), defined as "a government program, office, or other discrete management unit with strong incentives to manage for results. The organization commits to specific measurable goals with targets for improved performance. In exchange, the PBO is allowed more flexibility to manage its personnel, procurement, and other services." In a PBO, the agency head would not be a civil servant nor a political appointee, but rather someone with strong managerial experience hired via a term contract, with a portion of his or her salary contingent on meeting agreed-upon performance targets. The PBO would receive statutory flexibilities to operate outside traditional governmentwide personnel, pay, and procurement systems.[25]

By the end of the Clinton Administration, three agencies had been designated as PBOs: Air Traffic Operations, within the Federal Aviation Administration; the Office of Federal Student Aid, within the Department of Education; and the Patent and Trademark Office, within the Department of Commerce. The Bush Administration considered adding additional agencies, but never pursued the effort. These three agencies continue in their PBO status.

A New Focus on Outcomes Over Outputs

In addition to developing measurement systems and capacity, GPRA changed the conversation within many agencies. Harry Hatry, Elaine Morley, Shelli Rossman, and Joseph Wholey, in a 2003 report, *How Federal Programs Use Outcome Information: Opportunities for Federal Managers,* profiled 16 federal programs that made use of regularly collected outcome information.[26] A number of these initiatives were initiated in response to GPRA. For example, the Department of Housing and Urban Development (HUD) created in 1998 its Real Estate Assessment Center to collect and assess information on public housing. These data were provided to local HUD program offices to help them "identify risks and direct resources to improve the quality of public housing."[27] The Assessment Center used its data to create scores for housing projects, which in turn informed improvement plans for "standard" performance and helped teams for troubled performers. The resulting outcome data identified high performers, poor performers, common problems, and solutions.

The focus on outcomes had become part of a worldwide performance management trend. In a 2006 report, *Moving from Outputs to Outcomes: Practical Advice from Governments Around the World*, Burt Perrin provided substantial evidence from a World Bank roundtable of government officials from around the world that a wide range of countries—both developing and developed—were moving toward a results-oriented approach. He wrote: "Implementing an outcome focus represents a fundamental shift in the nature of thinking, acting, and managing within the public sector, away from a focus on *process* and on what one needs to do, to a focus on *benefits*."[28] He described how the motivating force behind this trend was expressed by participants as: "We are supposed to be in the business of improving services to citizens, and outcomes are what are important to them."[29] Like in the U.S., other countries used both a top-down and bottom-up approach to linking outcomes to strategy. Perrin concluded with the observation that a focus on outcomes is not so much an administrative initiative as a "fundamental change in the approach to thinking and managing within government."[30]

EXPANSION: CREATING A DEMAND FOR PERFORMANCE INFORMATION

Performance management routines that created a supply of performance information in the 1990s and early 2000s did not necessarily lead to an expected demand for the information by managers and decision makers. Starting in 1997, GAO conducted periodic surveys of mid-level federal managers on their use of performance information to support operational decisions. Every GAO survey found that only about one-third of managers responded that they used available performance information.[31]

While GAO could not identify why there was so little use, Behn wrote in a 2003 article that: "The leaders of public agencies can use performance measures to achieve a number of very different purposes, and they need to carefully and explicitly choose their purposes. Only then can they identify or create specific measures that are appropriate for each individual purpose."[32] He also described a series of purposes for which agency leaders and managers could use performance information, such as to evaluate performance, to control subordinates, and to learn and improve performance. Understanding these potential uses helps target strategies to better engage leaders and managers about using performance information in the course of their decision making.

An Increase in Ways Performance Information is Used in Decision Making

Following are four ways that expanded the use of performance information in government agencies:
- greater accountability
- improving organizational performance
- making budget decisions
- informing employee pay decisions

Using Performance Information for Greater Accountability

Metzenbaum, in a 2006 report, *Performance Accountability: The Five Building Blocks and Six Essential Practices,* explored what it means to "hold someone accountable" without creating a culture that would worry primarily about avoiding punishment.[31] Typically, if a measurement system focuses on accountability, managers are incentivized to set lower performance targets for their organizations and themselves. But, she found, if a measurement system focuses on performance improvement, then managers tend to be more comfortable with higher performance targets. Ideally leaders want both, but there are trade-offs. Managing this tension is possible, by creating five building blocks:
- **Goals:** clear, measurable goals that drive the performance of an organization
- **Framework:** a measurement framework that connects individual efforts to the progress and overall outcomes related to the organization's goals
- **Individual Feedback:** one-on-one verbal feedback that stimulates ideas and specific plans for meeting goals
- **Group Feedback:** group feedback that encourages "interactive inquiry," such as the approach used in Baltimore's CitiStat sessions
- **Incentives:** a cautious use of incentives, with a focus on group rather than individual performance

Along with these building blocks, Metzenbaum described managerial practices to ensure the building blocks work. These include actions such as "measurement mastery," where managers study their data to look for patterns, anomalies, and relationships to find what works and what doesn't; and developing longer-term strategies, coupled with shorter-term action plans based on the best available evidence and ideas.

President George W. Bush launched the first President's Management Agenda in 2001. The Agenda included an initiative to "create an integrated plan/budget and to monitor and evaluate its implementation." But this approach was soon seen as too ambitious and vague. The focus of the Agenda became more targeted with the creation of an accountability system for individual federal programs in 2003 in order to make them more results-oriented. The Office of Management and Budget developed an assessment framework, which it named the Program Assessment Rating Tool (PART). The PART was based on a scoring system, ultimately used to assess about 1,000 individual programs. OMB intended to use these scores to hold program managers accountable and to make funding decisions.

In a 2006 report, *Implementing OMB's Program Assessment Rating Tool (PART): Meeting the Challenges of Integrating Budget and Performance,* John Gilmour assessed the progress of the PART initiative and found "little evidence that PART has caused significant changes in program management."[34] Later assessments by GAO confirmed this assessment, noting: "of the federal managers familiar with PART, a minority—26 percent—indicated that PART results are used in management decision making, and 14 percent viewed PART as improving performance."[35]

Using Performance Information to Improve Organizational Performance

Other approaches were employed in attempts to use performance information to improve organizational performance. These approaches met with varying degrees of success. For example, a private sector approach called Balanced Scorecard was adopted by several federal agencies. A 2006 report by Nicholas Mathys and Kenneth Thompson, *Using the Balanced Scorecard: Lessons Learned from the U.S. Postal Service and the Defense Finance and Accounting Service,* examined these two agencies' experiences.[36]

The Balanced Scorecard calls for forward-looking measures that balance different perspectives of an organization's performance in order to create a more strategic assessment of how well that organization meets its vision and strategy. As Mathys and Thompson describe it, "The balanced scorecard, or BSC, is primarily a tool for translating an organization's strategy into action."[37] The typical Scorecard includes financial, customer, learning and growth, and internal business process measures. In their assessment, they concluded, "we have seen some dramatic improvements in their performance resulting from the use of the balanced scorecard and the organizational culture and fact-based improvement that are part of the process," but that it takes a focused effort from top management to sustain.[38] When agency leaders who championed these approaches left, the systems fell into disuse.

A second approach was the expanded use of the PerformanceStat model at the federal level. In a 2010 report, *A Guide to Data-Driven Performance Reviews*, Elizabeth Davies and Harry Hatry described the use of data-driven performance reviews pioneered by several federal agencies.[39] The federal "data driven" reviews were patterned after the PerformanceStat reviews initially developed by states and localities. They consisted of regular, data-driven review meetings led by senior agency officials. For example, the Department of Housing and Urban Development's HUDStat launched in 2010 and focused on four priority goals. Meetings focused on the progress of one of the four goals and were attended by the secretary and up to 30 invited participants from across the department engaged in that particular performance goal.

Based on their observations, Davies and Hatry developed a "how-to" guide for implementing data-driven reviews in other agencies. This approach was ultimately endorsed by OMB and used by agencies to conduct effective, data-driven decision forums. The most notable of these, which successfully navigated the transition from the Obama to the Trump administration, are the annual agency reviews of progress against strategic objectives, and the statutorily required quarterly reviews of progress of agency priority goals.

Using Performance Information to Inform Budget Decisions

A third use of performance information that expanded in recent years has been to inform budget decisions. Anecdotal experience suggests that, at the federal level, Congress only intermittently uses performance information to inform budget decisions—but that executive branch agencies do so on a more consistent basis.

In a 2003 report, *Linking Performance and Budgeting: Opportunities in the Federal Budget Process*, Phil Joyce identifies challenges to tying budget to performance information within executive branch agencies, mainly in the context of the PART tool. At the time, the Bush Administration was also preparing a performance budget based on demonstrated effectiveness of programs. However, Joyce noted, "the relationship between funding and performance is not well understood, even where good performance data exist."[40] He further observed that *saying* budgeting and performance should be integrated "is not the same thing as *doing* it."

A more optimistic assessment was provided by Lloyd Blanchard in a 2006 report, *Performance Budgeting: How NASA and SBA Link Costs and Performance*.[41] Blanchard had been an appointed executive in two large federal agencies (NASA and the Small Business Administration) where he introduced two different methodologies—Full Cost and Activity-Based Costing—in an attempt to connect cost information with performance information. He described each approach, along with their strengths and weaknesses, and offered advice on ways to improve cost allocations in order to better link budget and performance decisions. However, this approach never gained traction with other agencies, and fell into disuse in the two agencies after he left.

A third report, *Four Actions to Integrate Performance Information with Budget Formulation*, by John Whitley in 2014, offered four pragmatic actions agencies could undertake in order to better integrate performance and budget information at a more granular level. He observed that the budget and performance professional disciplines have different data needs and processes and that they need better alignment so performance measurement is seen "as a key component of an agency's internal analysis function, not just a collection and reporting function for external accountability."[42] Whitley's four suggested actions are:

- **Engage agency leadership:** Ensure interest and constructive involvement in using performance information to improve outcomes when making budgeting decisions.

- **Focus on the development and use of analytic talent:** Talent needs to bridge both performance and budget functions within the agency, and analyses that offer alternatives for decision makers.
- **Improve the budget formulation process:** Budget formulation should be "capable of isolating, analyzing, and constructively presenting issues for decisions to leadership."[43]
- **Reform agency budget account structures:** Account structures should align costs of an activity or program within a single budget account and define cost elements that occur in different years so that agency staffs can construct more accurate cost estimates.

While agency-wide use of performance information in budgeting has not been widely adopted, it has been woven into selected elements of budgeting. For example, beginning in 1999, OMB began requiring greater justifications for information technology investments by agencies, requiring agencies to include performance information via its "Exhibit 300B," used by agencies to justify information technology investments. OMB required agencies to "Identify performance targets for evaluating operations," and other performance-related metrics. In the late 2010s, this requirement was absorbed into a broader IT Dashboard that tracks the implementation of IT investments across all agencies.[44]

The topic of performance-informed budgeting will likely remain of interest to government reformers, but past experience shows that acting on any such initiatives will require top-level sustained attention.[45]

Using Performance Information to Inform Pay Decisions

A fourth potential use of performance information has been to inform decisions about levels of pay for civil servants and career executives. Much like performance-informed budgeting, more has been written than done in this area. Nevertheless, it is a perennial topic of interest.

In 2002, legislation creating the Department of Homeland Security authorized the creation of a performance pay system for the department and for the career Senior Executive Service across the entire government. And, in 2003, the Defense Department was authorized to overhaul its personnel performance management system to be more performance-based as well. A 2004 report by Howard Risher, *Pay for Performance: A Guide for Federal Managers,* describes different pay-for-performance models and offers advice to managers in these agencies on lessons learned in designing successful performance-based pay systems in the private sector and in a dozen federal pilot programs. Risher "warns that the transition to a pay-for-performance environment is not going to be easy."[46]

GAO, in a 2009 report assessing the implementation of the new Defense pay system, observed: "As DOD and the components proceeded with implementation of the system, survey results showed a decrease in employees' optimism about the system's ability to fulfill its intent and reward employees for performance." In response to GAO's observations and other complaints about the fairness of the pay-for-performance systems, Congress abolished both the Defense and Homeland Security pay-for-performance systems in early 2010.[47] Nevertheless, in a 2017 testimony before Congress, GAO did not recommend abandoning this approach. It noted that "implementing a more market-based and more performance-oriented pay system is both doable and desirable. However, we also found that it is not easy."[48] In 2018, the President's budget proposed to move from a tenure-based pay system to a performance-based pay system.[49]

An alternative approach being used by some federal agencies is the use of performance-oriented pay-banding. A 2007 report by James Thompson, *Designing and Implementing Performance-Oriented Payband Systems,* examined initial efforts by nine federal agencies that adopted performance-oriented pay banding systems.[50] Pay banding takes the existing 15-step pay structure used by the federal government over the past six decades and allows agencies to restructure job positions into broader categories. For example, one agency reduced its existing 15-step structure into three broad pay bands.

According to Thompson, "With paybanding, there is no need to make fine distinctions between the duties or responsibilities of different jobs because many related titles can be accommodated within a single band."[51] Pay banding provides greater organizational agility by allowing greater lateral movement within an agency. For managers, it shifts the emphasis within the performance system from the "job" to the "person." Thompson "makes the case that successful designs are those that (1) achieve a balance between efficiency, equity, and employee acceptance; (2) acknowledge the importance of soft as well as hard design features; and (3) fit the organization's context."[52] However, to date, this approach has not expanded more widely in the federal government.

Increased Maturity in Development and Use of Performance Information

Another aspect that increased demand for performance information during the expansion years was the availability of new techniques to collect and use data, and more sophisticated treatment of data in analyses that increased the utility of performance information to decision makers.

Easier Data Collection and Visualization Tools

Over the past decade, government began to share administrative data more readily, both within and across agencies. For example, OMB's 2013 directive on open data directs agencies to treat data "as an asset" and to make administrative data interoperable and machine-readable.[53] This is described in more detail in Chapter Three. Related to making data more readily available was the drive to make data more consumable by decision makers.

This is exemplified by the rapid spread of geographical data and dashboards across government agencies. In 2013, a report by Genie Stowers, *The Use of Data Visualization in Government,* noted that, "The best visualizations help viewers understand not only the data, but also their implications."[54]

In a 2010 report, *Using Geographic Information Systems to Increase Citizen Engagement,* Sukumar Ganapati described the rapid spread of mapped data, such as the location of Recovery Act projects around the country, so that citizens could see where these funds were being spent, and by whom.[55] And in a 2011 report, *Use of Dashboards in Government,* Ganapati described the expanded use of dashboards for internal agency and public use, such as the Recovery.gov and Performance.gov websites.[56] Dashboards can put easily digestible information in one place for a busy reader. As Stowers notes, "Even with these more sophisticated means of analysis, government managers still have the challenge of explaining issues and results to decision-makers and the public; that is where data visualization comes in."[57]

More Sophisticated and Nuanced Uses of Performance Information

Probably one of the most interesting developments during the expansion phase was the evolution of more sophisticated and nuanced uses of performance information by program managers and decision makers.

In a 2013 report, *Incident Reporting Systems: Lessons from the Federal Aviation Administration's Air Traffic Organization,* Russell Mills described how the Federal Aviation Administration (FAA) developed a performance reporting system that tracks operational errors by air traffic controllers.[58] By analyzing patterns of these errors, FAA revised its operating procedures and training protocols to reduce or preclude future incidents, thereby reducing risks of accidents. Mills addressed FAA's strategies over the previous decade to systematically develop measures, targets, and reporting methods to create an effective incident reporting system. The lessons from FAA's approach to developing its incident reporting system apply in other policy domains, such as food safety violations, reporting sexual assaults in the military, or privacy breaches.

Another challenge to performance analysts is how to measure "unobserved events." For example, how can we know if law enforcement strategies actually work to prevent or deter crime? To assess this requires an ability to measure events that cannot be observed, such as tax cheating, drug smuggling, or illegal immigration. In a 2012 report, *Five Methods for Measuring Unobserved Events: A Case Study of Federal Law Enforcement,* John Whitley described five data estimation methods being pioneered in different federal law enforcement agencies. He concluded that when decision makers systematically analyze their existing data, "it is possible to bring about radical reforms" and achieve impressive improvements in performance.[59]

A third example of using performance information in a more sophisticated manner was reflected in a 2013 report by Jennifer Bachner, *Predictive Polic-*

ing: Preventing Crime with Data and Analytics, on the use of data and analytics to predict crimes in city neighborhoods and prevent them from occurring.[60] Bachner describes how new policing approaches in selected communities are using "big data" techniques common among commercial retail stores such as Walmart, to predict criminal behavior. These same tools apply in other policy areas such as predicting and preventing homelessness, reducing tax fraud, and mitigating communities vulnerable to natural disasters.

A fourth example of the increase in sophistication in the use of performance information has been the growing interest in the use of evidence-based decision making and program evaluation. A 2018 paper by Nick Hart and Kathy Newcomer describes a wide range of initiatives undertaken in both the Bush and Obama Administrations to use evidence and performance information to improve organizational performance. In the Bush Administration, assessments of the efficacy of individual programs was integral to its Program Assessment Rating Tool and created a new demand for program evaluations. And in the Obama Administration, Hart and Newcomer wrote, "The administration emphasized using evaluation to assess causal impacts for determining whether to fund or not fund programs."[61] They concluded that the value of evaluation holds bipartisan interest.

These evidence and evaluation initiatives have operated separate from, but in parallel to, the performance management movement. But a 2018 article by Alexander Kroll and Donald Moynihan observes that "evaluations facilitate performance information use by reducing the causal uncertainty that managers face as they try to make sense of what performance data mean."[62] They recommend greater integration between these two professional disciplines, much like Newcomer and Schrier did in their 2002 report, discussed earlier.

Identifying Challenges to Institutionalization

During the expansion years, the development and use of performance information revealed a number of implementation challenges. The following five challenges were subsequently addressed during the institutionalization phase that followed, as discussed in the next section.

Challenge One: Developing a Governance Framework

A federal performance management framework did not exist in law until GPRA in 1993. An earlier law, the Chief Financial Officers Act of 1990, placed a statutory duty on CFOs to provide for "the systematic measurement of performance," but most CFOs focused their energies on other priorities. Consequently, OMB and agencies varied widely in their approaches to define roles and responsibilities, during the early steps and expansion phases.

Challenge Two: Defining the Unit of Analysis

The organizing construct for measuring performance changed between the Clinton, Bush, and Obama administrations, from a focus on agency performance, to program-level performance, to a focus on strategic outcomes. As the focus for the organizing construct changed, significant shifts occurred in what agencies and program managers focused on to comply with the expectations of their respective administrations. In many cases this drained energy from agencies' ability to use the performance management system to improve performance.

Challenge Three: Linking Performance Information to Decision Making

As noted earlier, multiple potential uses of performance information exist, as well as multiple potential users. The goal of "using data, evidence, and analytics to create insight that influences decision making, actions, and results" became the focal point of most agency performance management systems, but only after much trial and error in terms of agencies producing various reports and data feeds in response to the requirement of GPRA.

Challenge Four: Distinguishing Between Executive Versus Legislative Uses

The GPRA statute and many policy makers presumed that Congress would be a key user of performance information. When congressional appropriation committees explicitly rejected using performance information being reported by agencies, some observers felt that the law was a failure. However, agencies have made greater use of performance information in the budget development and execution processes than previously thought.

Challenge Five: Using Performance Information for Accountability Versus Learning Purposes

Because performance information has multiple uses and users, there is a constant tension between its use for accountability versus its use as a learning device. The emphasis on accountability versus learning varied significantly during the early stages and expansion phases, often depending on the philosophy of political leaders at the time.

INSTITUTIONALIZATION: EMBEDDING PERFORMANCE INTO A BROADER GOVERNANCE FRAMEWORK

The institutionalization phase, which began roughly around 2010, addressed many of the issues identified above. The GPRA Modernization Act of 2010 incorporated many of the lessons learned during the expansion phase. It put into place a statutory governance structure by:

- designating agency chief operating officers (typically deputy secretaries or equivalents)
- designating agency performance improvement officers, who report to the chief operating officers
- creating a cross-agency Performance Improvement Council, comprised of agency performance improvement officers, to coordinate performance-related initiatives

The new law also clarified the authority of agencies to work across agency boundaries on common goals, authorized the designation of cross-agency goal leaders, and mandated quarterly progress assessments towards cross-agency goals, released publicly for accountability purposes.

In a 2013 report, *The New Federal Performance System: Implementing the GPRA Modernization Act,* Donald Moynihan described key challenges facing the new law's implementers: the need to ensure that the law's many procedural requirements do not overwhelm federal agencies through a focus on compliance rather than on improving performance. He optimistically noted that, if implemented thoughtfully, the new law could catalyze a culture that thrives on outstanding performance.[63]

Implementing the GPRA Modernization Act by Embedding New Routines into Existing Administrative Processes

In a 2016 article, Moynihan and Kroll assessed early efforts to implement the GPRA Modernization Act's goal of establishing a series of new routines to encourage the use of performance information. They wrote that these "routines centered on the pursuit of cross-agency priority goals, the prioritization of a small number of agency goals, and data-driven reviews." They concluded that agency managers were using data from these routines at a higher rate than before these routines were put in place.[64] They saw this as an encouraging sign of progress.

In addition to these new statutory routines, several other actions further institutionalized the use of performance information. These include:

- the creation of an overarching federal performance management framework and performance management cycle that successfully made the transition from the Obama to the Trump administration.[65]

- the creation of agency annual reviews of strategic objectives outlined in their strategic plans. These reviews inform long-term strategy and budget formulation, and identify areas for improvement.[66]
- the creation of an Evidence and Innovation Unit within OMB in 2013 to serve as the catalyst, convener, and champion for the development and use of evidence in agency program decision making. The unit works with the OMB office responsible for performance management issues, in order to integrate with budget, performance, and risk management routines.

Growth of Evidence-Based Government Initiatives

Efforts began in the late 2000s to take a longer, more strategic look at how to manage austerity by finding what works and targeting dollars accordingly instead of funding programs that cannot demonstrate effectiveness. This trend is the heart of what is being called "evidence-based government," and there are initiatives both inside and outside the federal government to use evidence and program evaluations to reframe budget debates in ways that reflect value created, not just dollars spent.

In addition to OMB's Evidence and Innovation Unit's efforts, bipartisan congressional support for a wide range of initiatives at the federal, state, local, and non-profit levels includes:

- the creation of tiered-evidence grants, where new, untested programs receive small amounts of funds and funding increases over time as programs can demonstrate their effectiveness
- performance contracting, where service contractors deliver results based on pre-defined targets to government purchasers
- pay-for-success programs, where investors fund social services up front and, based on demonstrated success, government pays for results achieved

Following are examples of how these initiatives result in new service delivery models:

- **Tiered Evidence Grants**: GAO examined this relatively new grant-making approach in 2016. According to GAO: "Under this approach, agencies establish tiers of grant funding based on the level of evidence of effectiveness provided for a grantee's service model. Agencies award smaller amounts to promising service models with a smaller evidence base, while providing larger amounts to those with more supporting evidence."[67]

    GAO further noted: "Proponents of tiered-evidence grants contend that they create incentives for grantees to use approaches backed by strong evidence of effectiveness, encourage learning and feedback loops to inform future investment decisions, and provide some funding to test innovative approaches." Patrick Lester, in a 2017 report, *Tiered Evidence Grants—An Assessment of the Education Innovation and Research Program,* examined the U.S. Department of Education's Education and Innovation Research program and found promising success in distinguishing effective from ineffective projects.[68]

- **Performance Contracting:** Patrick Lester, in a 2016 report, *Building Performance Systems for Social Service Programs: Case Studies in Tennessee,* writes that performance-based contracts create financial incentives or penalties for providers to meet pre-defined performance benchmark targets in social services. This approach differs from traditional fee-for-service contracts that use fixed payment rates for services provided. In the case studies in Lester's report, the performance incentives are to place children in permanent homes with foster families instead of housing them in group homes. He says that performance-based contracts can take a policy initiative to scale because they are straightforward and easy to understand, and they allow flexibility in changing service delivery approaches over the course of the contract because "Most performance-based contracts...specify only the outcomes to be achieved, leaving providers freedom to decide how to meet them."[69]

- **Pay-for-Success Programs:** Like performance-based contracts, pay-for-success programs (also called "social impact bonds") tie payments to a provider's performance in delivering outcomes. However, social impact bonds link funding to meeting pre-determined performance goals. Payments are not made until results are achieved. This creates substantial risks for providers, but has attracted bipartisan political attention and the support of various non-profits, universities, and foundations.

Beginning in 2009, OMB and agencies undertook a series of initiatives to build or expand the skills and capabilities of federal agency staff to be more evidence- and evaluation-based in their decision making. In some cases, this required new money. But, in many other cases, this changed how existing work was done. Initiatives developed in subsequent years included: building greater agency-level analytic capacity, increasing the amount and variety of data available for analysis, increased use of existing administrative data, and the creation of "what works" repositories in agencies.[70]

LESSONS LEARNED

Government has made substantial progress over the past twenty years in developing a results-oriented performance management framework. Most of the progress has been iterative, with many setbacks but steady progress.

As many of the examples cited above demonstrate, successes have not often taken root with long-term sustainability over time. In fact, one long-time observer, Beryl Radin, has expressed some skepticism as to the ability of the performance movement to institutionalize an overarching approach into the federal system, given its complexity. She notes there are at least seven different perspectives or users, such as program managers, planners, policy staffs, budgeteers, and political leaders. She suggests that, absent a single agreed-upon theory or model across these varied perspectives, modesty and a rejection of one-size-fits-all approaches will be important attributes for the future success of the performance movement.[71]

Nevertheless, because of the statutory framework and a bipartisan commitment by top government executives, the performance movement seems assured of a place at the table. Yet, still more that needs to be done before performance becomes embedded as part of the government's culture. Following are several lessons gleaned from observations over the past two decades.

- **First, it takes time, effort, and commitment.** The seemingly simple goal of "creating performance information that is useful and used" sounds easy, but in reality there are substantial challenges, both technical and personal, to meeting that goal. There are challenges related to definitions, measurement, analysis and methodology. And there are organizational, political, and human behavioral challenges. Developing a multi-dimensional strategy and long-term commitment is essential. Robert Behn probably puts it best when he says that performance management isn't a system, but rather a leadership strategy.

- **Second, successfully linking performance information to decisions is less a technical issue than a human behavioral issue.** Both managers and employees must trust data before they will use it for actions that may have significant consequences. Analyses of performance information have to be readily interpretable by busy leaders or they will revert to intuition instead of using data to make decisions. Ideally, causal links between the data and results will allow leaders to have confidence in making decisions on data that will result in the change desired. In addition, agency leaders will need to create and embed both individual and organizational incentives to be more results-oriented and performance-based. And in the end, the insights derived from data need to be tied to concrete steps that can be taken to influence desired results.

- **Third, performance information is increasingly used by a broader set of government and public users**. While congressional use lags, performance information is increasingly used by government executives and program managers to inform operational decisions and budget choices. In addition, more performance information is being shared with the public to inform a wide range of individuals' decisions—on healthcare choices, travel routes, education opportunities, and housing locations, to name but a few. As the use of artificial intelligence expands and creates the ability to tailor information needs to specific individuals or situations in real time, the potential for greater use in day-to-day decisions becomes more likely.

LOOKING FORWARD

While performance management may now be formally institutionalized via the GPRA Modernization of 2010, it still is not ingrained as part of the organizational culture in government. Moynihan and Kroll write that, as performance routines become embedded into government, they will drive a new culture. However, Behn says that leaders need to explicitly adopt performance management as their leadership strategy, and that this will foster culture change. Most likely, both approaches will be needed.

Going forward, three key steps could help further ingrain the use of performance management approaches to create a culture where decisions are based on data and evidence, including:

- **Embedding performance management as a part of the front-line culture:** Line managers need to view performance management not as a compliance cost but a way of doing business. But studies show little progress on this front over the past two decades. Interestingly, some potential for addressing this comes via the relatively new field of "behavioral sciences," which may provide new strategies to incentivize behaviors and attitudes regarding the integration of performance information into frontline work.[72]

- **Creating stronger, more explicit "line-of-sight" links:** Creating links between broader strategies, program budgets, and individuals will improve decision making and demonstrate relevance. For example, one approach might involve "portfolio budgeting" to frame broader strategic tradeoffs in the allocation of resources. This could be a long-term outgrowth of the agency annual strategic review process.[73]

- **Making performance information more granular, real-time, contextual, predictive, and intuitive:** Managers are more likely to use information that is relevant and reliable for their specific needs, and tied to how they normally "do business," whether through administrative systems or their agency's budget process. If performance information is easy to use, and seen as integrated into their existing administrative routines, then the likelihood it will be used will increase.

Taking steps such as these could help move the U.S. federal government closer to the "ideal" performance governance model described by Bouckaert and Halligan in their 2009 book, as well as a long-term vision for modernizing the federal government.

John M. Kamensky is a Senior Fellow with the IBM Center for The Business of Government. He previously served as deputy director of Vice President Gore's National Performance Review (later renamed the National Partnership for Reinventing Government) and a special assistant to the Deputy Director for Management at the U.S. Office of Management and Budget. Before that, he worked at the U.S. Government Accountability Office. He is a Fellow of the National Academy of Public Administration.

Endnotes

1   Harry Hatry, Elaine Morley, Shelli Rossman, and Joseph Wholey, *How Federal Programs Use Outcome Information: Opportunities for Federal Managers*, IBM Center for The Business of Government, 2003, 57.

2   Geert Bouckaert and John Halligan, *Managing Performance: International Comparisons* (New York: Routledge Press, 2009).

3   Colin Campbell, *Corporate Strategic Planning in Government: Lessons from the United States Air Force*, IBM Center for The Business of Government, 2000.

4   Campbell, *Corporate Strategic Planning*, 40.

5   U.S. Government Accountability Office, *Results-Oriented Government: GPRA Has Established a Solid Foundation for Achieving Greater Results*, GAO-04-38 (Washington, DC, 2004), 46.

6   Patrick Murphy and John Carnevale, *The Challenge of Developing Cross-Agency Measures: A Case Study of the Office of National Drug Control Policy*, IBM Center for The Business of Government, 2001, 56.

7   Carolyn Heinrich, "Chapter Seven: Setting Performance Targets: Lessons from the Workforce Investment Act System," *Managing for Results: 2005* (Lanham, MD: Rowman & Littlefield Publishers, Inc., 2005), 351-378.

8   Heinrich, *Managing for Results: 2005*, 369.

9   Richard Boyle, *Performance Reporting: Insights from International Practice*, IBM Center for The Business of Government, 2009.

10   Kathy Newcomer and Mary Ann Scheirer, *Using Evaluation to Support Performance Management: A Guide for Federal Executives*, IBM Center for The Business of Government, 2001.

11   Newcomer and Scheirer, *Using Evaluation*, 8.

12   Newcomer and Scheirer, *Using Evaluation*, 32.

13   Newcomer and Scheirer, *Using Evaluation*, 33.

14   Paul E. O'Connell, *Using Performance Data for Accountability: The New York City Police Department's CompStat Model of Police Management*, IBM Center for The Business of Government, 2001, 8.

15   O'Connell, *Using Performance Data*, 10.

16   O'Connell, *Using Performance Data*, 13.

17   Lenneal Henderson, *The Baltimore CitiStat Program: Performance and Accountability*, IBM Center for The Business of Government, 2003.

18   Robert D. Behn, *What All Mayors Would Like to Know About Baltimore's CitiStat Performance Strategy*, IBM Center for The Business of Government, 2007.

19   Christopher Patusky, Leigh Botwinik, and Mary Shelley, *The Philadelphia SchooStat Model*, IBM Center for The Business of Government, 2007.

20   Robert Behn, *PerformanceStat: A Leadership Strategy for Producing Results*, (Washington, DC: Brookings Institution Press, 2014).

21   Robert Behn, "PeformanceStat Leadership Strategy," *Bob Behn's Performance Leadership Report* 8, No. 3 (2009), https://thebehnreport.hks.harvard.edu/files/thebehnreport/files/november2009.pdf. Accessed June 22, 2018.

22 Shelley Metzenbaum, *Strategies for Using State Information: Measuring and Improving Program Performance,* IBM Center for The Business of Government, 2003, 11.

23 Metzenbaum, *Strategies,* 43.

24 ibid.

25 National Partnership for Reinventing Government, *Performance-Based Organizations,* 1997, https://govinfo.library.unt.edu/npr/initiati/21cent/. Accessed June 22, 2018.

26 Hatry, et al., *How Federal Programs Use Outcome Information.*

27 Hatry, et al., *How Federal Programs Use Outcome Information,* 37.

28 Burt Perrin, *Moving from Outputs to Outcomes: Practical Advice from Governments Around the World,* IBM Center for The Business of Government, 2006.

29 Perrin, *Moving from Outputs to Outcomes,* 21.

30 Perrin, *Moving from Outputs to Outcomes,* 51.

31 U.S. Government Accountability Office, *Results-Oriented Government: GPRA Has Established a Solid Foundation for Achieving Greater Results,* GAO-04-38 (Washington, DC, 2004); *Government Performance: Lessons Learned for the Next Administration on Using Performance Information to Improve Results,* GAO-08-1026T (Washington, DC, 2008); and *Managing for Results: Further Progress Made in Implementing the GPRA Modernization Act, but Additional Actions Needed to Address Pressing Governance Challenges,* GAO-17-775 (Washington, DC, 2017).

32 Robert Behn, "Why Measure Performance? Different Purposes Require Different Measures." *Public Administration Review* 63, No. 5 (2003): 586-606.

33 Shelley H. Metzenbaum, *Performance Accountability: The Five Building Blocks and Six Essential Practices,* IBM Center for The Business of Government, 2006.

34 John B. Gilmour, *Implementing OMB's Program Assessment Rating Tool (PART): Meeting the Challenges of Integrating Budget and Performance,* IBM Center for The Business of Government, 2006.

35 U.S. Government Accountability Office, *Government Performance: Lessons Learned for the Next Administration on Using Performance Information to Improve Results,* GAO-08-1026T (Washington, DC, 2008), 9.

36 Nicholas J. Mathys and Kenneth Thompson, *Using the Balanced Scorecard: Lessons Learned from the U.S. Postal Service and the Defense Finance and Accounting Service,* IBM Center for The Business of Government, 2006.

37 Mathys and Thompson, *Using the Balanced Scorecard,* 56.

38 ibid.

39 Elizabeth Davies and Harry Hatry, *A Guide to Data-Driven Performance Reviews,* IBM Center for The Business of Government, 2011.

40 Philip G. Joyce, *Linking Performance and Budgeting: Opportunities in the Federal Budget Process,* IBM Center for The Business of Government, 2003, 13.

41 Lloyd A. Blanchard, *Performance Budgeting: How NASA and SBA Link Costs and Performance,* IBM Center for The Business of Government, 2006.

42 John Whitley, *Four Actions to Integrate Performance Information with Budget Formulation,* IBM Center for The Business of Government, 2014, 4.

43 Whitley, *Four Actions,* 26.

44 Office of Management and Budget, "Guidance on Exhibit 300—Planning, Budgeting, Acquisition, and Management of Information Technology Capital Assets," 2011, 17.

45 While the link between performance information and budgeting is not a consistent practice at the federal level, there are examples of its use in local government. A new book by Andrew Kleine, *City on the Line: How Baltimore Transformed its Budget to Beat the Great Recession and Deliver Outcomes* (Lanham, MD: Rowman & Littlefield Publishers, Inc., 2018) describes the evolution of the City of Baltimore's Outcome Budgeting system that pioneers a number of novel elements of performance budgeting that may serve as a future model for other governments.

46 Howard Risher, *Pay for Performance: A Guide for Federal Managers,* IBM Center for The Business of Government, 2004.

47 U.S. Government Accountability Office, *Human Capital: Continued Monitoring of Internal Safeguards and an Action Plan to Address Employee Concerns Could Improve Implementation of the National Security Personnel System,* GAO-09-840 (Washington, DC, 2009), 8.

48 U.S. Government Accountability Office, *Federal Workforce: Sustained Attention to Human Capital Leading Practices Can Help Improve Agency Performance,* GAO-17-627T (Washington, DC, 2017), 8.

49 Charles Clark, "Trump's Budget Will Push Performance-Based Pay for Feds," *Government Executive,* February 9, 2018.

50 James Thompson, *Designing and Implementing Performance-Oriented Payband Systems,* IBM Center for The Business of Government, 2007.

51 Thompson, *Designing and Implementing,* 12.

52 Thompson, *Designing and Implementing,* 4.

53 Office of Management and Budget, "Open Data Policy—Managing Information as an Asset," *M-13-13, Memorandum for the Heads of Executive Departments and Agencies,* 2013.

54 Genie Stowers, *The Use of Data Visualization in Government,* IBM Center for The Business of Government, 2013.

55 Sukumar Ganapati, *Using Geographic Information Systems to Increase Citizen Engagement,* IBM Center for The Business of Government, 2010.

56 Sukumar Ganapati, *Use of Dashboards in Government,* IBM Center for The Business of Government, 2011.

57 Stowers, *The Use of Data Visualization,* 8.

58 Russell W. Mills, *Incident Reporting Systems: Lessons from the Federal Aviation Administration's Air Traffic Organization,* IBM Center for The Business of Government, 2013.

59 John Whitley, *Five Methods for Measuring Unobserved Events: A Case Study of Federal Law Enforcement,* IBM Center for The Business of Government, 2012.

60 Jennifer Bachner, *Predictive Policing: Preventing Crime with Data and Analytics,* IBM Center for The Business of Government, 2013.

61 Nick Hart and Kathy Newcomer, *Presidential Evidence Initiatives: Lessons from the Bush and Obama Administrations' Efforts to Improve Government Performance,* Bipartisan Policy Center, 2018, 13.

62 Alexander Kroll and Donald Moynihan, "The Design and Practice of Integrating Evidence: Connecting Performance Management with Program Evaluation," *Public Administration Review* 78, No. 2 (2018): 183-194.

63 Donald Moynihan, *The New Federal Performance System: Implementing the GPRA Modernization Act,* IBM Center for The Business of Government, 2013.

64 Donald Moynihan and Alexander Kroll, "Performance Management Routines That Work? An Early Assessment of the GPRA Modernization Act," *Public Administration Review,* 76, 2 (2016): 314-323.

65 Office of Management and Budget, "Part 6, Section 200: Overview of the Federal Performance Framework," *Circular A-11 Preparation, Submission, and Execution of the Budget,* 2017.

66 OMB, Part 6, Section 200.

67 U.S. Government Accountability Office. *Tiered Evidence Grants: Opportunities Exist to Share Lessons from Early Implementation and Inform Future Federal Efforts,* GAO-16-818 (Washington, DC, 2016).

68 Patrick Lester, *Tiered Evidence Grants—An Assessment of the Education Innovation and Research Program,* IBM Center for The Business of Government, 2017.

69 Patrick Lester, *Building Performance Systems for Social Service Programs: Case Studies in Tennessee,* IBM Center for The Business of Government, 2016.

70 Office of Management and Budget, *M-12-14 Use of Evidence and Evaluation in the 2014 Budget*, May 18, 2012.

71 Beryl Radin. *Challenging the Performance Movement: Accountability, Complexity, and Democratic Values* (Washington, DC: Georgetown University Press, 2006).

72 S. Grimmelikhuijsen, S. Jilke, A. L. Olsen, and L. Tummers, "Behavioral public administration: Combining insights from public administration and psychology," *Public Administration Review* 77, No. 1 (2017): 45-56.

73 F. Stevens Redburn and Paul Posner, "Portfolio Budgeting: How a New Approach to the Budget Could Yield Better Decisions," *Economic Studies at Brookings* 1 (September 2015).

CHAPTER FIVE

"Liking" Social Media

Mark A. Abramson

Highlights

- The rise of social media has provided a highly useful set of tools for government at all levels in its quest to both inform and engage citizens. New technology-based tools can engage citizens through crowdsourcing and a variety of social media platforms.

- Government now uses social media to more effectively communicate with its own employees via tools such as ideation platforms, social intranets, and wikis.

- The federal government institutionalized the use of social media by creating new policies and guidance, as well as enhancing its organizational and staff capabilities.

- In the future, government will need to devote increased attention to managing the risks associated with social media. The future is also likely to see a greater emphasis on improving the user experience and engaging citizens.

"LIKING" SOCIAL MEDIA

By Mark A. Abramson

Bob Burns began his career as a Transportation Security Administration (TSA) screener at the Cincinnati-Northern Kentucky International Airport in 2002. Brand new to TSA, Burns says he volunteered for "anything and every-thing." In 2008, he started a blog for TSA. Today, the award-winning Burns is a TSA public affairs specialist and the agency's social media lead in charge of its popular Instagram account which now has 870,000 followers. In 2016, it was ranked as the fourth best Instagram account by Rolling Stone on a list of the top 100 accounts.

Photos on the TSA Instagram account include items and weapons confiscated by TSA, including a giant lobster and a life-size prop from the Texas Chainsaw Massacre. Burns says the lighthearted posts complement the serious busi-ness of keeping Americans safe. "It's a very important balance," Burns said. "There's a cheekiness to it, but I also try to educate and provide travel tips. A lot of officers says that they appreciate that, that it makes their job easier."[1]

INTRODUCTION

The Evolution of Social Media

To appreciate the growth of social media, one only has to look back to 1998. At that point, the internet (then more commonly called the World Wide Web) was just five years old, the creation of Facebook was still six years away (2004), and the creation of Twitter eight years away (2006). Today, the impact of social media is clearly seen at all levels of government.

Social media is commonly defined as computer-assisted technologies that facilitate the creation and sharing of information via virtual communities and networks. At the federal level, nearly all agencies now invite citizens to "con-nect with us" on a vast array of social media platforms, including Facebook, Twitter, Instagram, YouTube, Flickr, Pinterest, LinkedIn, Digg, and Google+. In addition, nearly all agencies have internal social media platforms that encour-age greater communication and engagement with employees.

Social media offers the government a new set of tools and platforms in which to both inform and engage the public. The quest for meaningful citizen engagement has been long been a public sector goal. In the past, this quest largely focused on face-to-face engagement. For example, town hall meetings have been a staple of American government dating back to colonial times. In addition to attending meetings, citizens have had the option of visiting a government office. If an individual could not physically attend a face-to-face meeting to either gain information or comment on government activity, citizen engagement was limited to either writing a letter to a government official or agency, or simply reading about a government action in a newspaper or an official notice from government (usually delivered through the mail).

A good example of engagement "before" and "after" is clearly seen in the evolution of the public review and comment process of government regulations. Before the rise of social media in the 2000s, government began to explore new ways to engage citizens.[2] Up until 2002, citizens faced a cumbersome process to comment on a pending government regulation. An individual commenter would have to know the following: which agency issued the regulation, when the regulation would be published, and the deadline for public comment—they then had to review the proposed regulation either in a government reading room, or find a copy of the *Federal Register* at a local library. This changed as government entered the 21st century, as discussed below, and directly contributed to the ability of agencies to further engage the public through social media tools.

Organization of Chapter

This chapter addresses major developments in how government has evolved its use of social media between 1998 and 2018. As seen in the chart titled "Evolution of Social Media: 1998–2018," the evolution of government's use can be divided into three phases:

- **Early action:** This phase was characterized by government's experimentation with the internet and the development of websites which were static and non-interactive. This early period saw new ways to engage citizens undertaken and assessed.
- **Expansion:** The decade of the 2000s was characterized by the rapid expansion of the number of websites across government, as well as the emergence of new tools, such as blogs—and new platforms, including Facebook, Twitter, and Instagram. During the expansion period, new strategies for engaging citizens and civil servants were deployed. This period was also characterized by the identification of barriers which hindered further expansion of the use of social media by government agencies.
- **Institutionalization:** The decade of the 2010s can be characterized by the institutionalization of social media, in which barriers were overcome by the development of new policies and guidance, enhancing organizational and staff capacity, and developing assessment capability.

Evolution of Social Media: 1998—2018

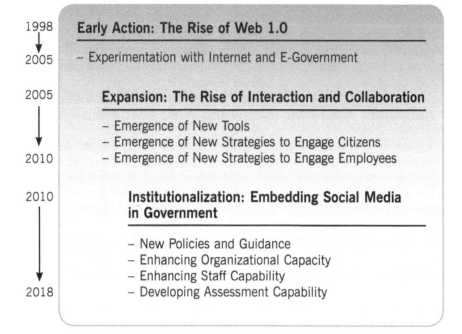

1998
↓
2005

2005
↓
2010

2010
↓
2018

Early Action: The Rise of Web 1.0

– Experimentation with Internet and E-Government

Expansion: The Rise of Interaction and Collaboration

– Emergence of New Tools
– Emergence of New Strategies to Engage Citizens
– Emergence of New Strategies to Engage Employees

Institutionalization: Embedding Social Media in Government

– New Policies and Guidance
– Enhancing Organizational Capacity
– Enhancing Staff Capability
– Developing Assessment Capability

EARLY ACTION: THE RISE OF WEB 1.0

Experimentation with the Internet and E-Government

In the 1990s, the use of the internet began to spread. The early years of the internet, often termed "Web 1.0," were characterized by static non-interactive web pages and one-way communication. Personal, commercial, and a limited number of government web sites began to appear, and some interactivity (such as guestbook pages) appeared.

During the early years (which lasted until the mid 2000s), government began to explore the use of the internet as a vehicle for citizen engagement. These early initiatives reflected a first step toward today's world of ubiquitous social media. The term most commonly used in this time period was "e-Government," defined as the use of electronic information to improve performance, create value, and enable new relationships between governments, businesses, and citizens. E-Government was a precursor to government's use of social media (see further detail in Chapter Two, "Going Digital").

A good example of e-Government's efforts to change the way in which citizens engaged government was the creation of Regulations.gov. In 2002, the federal government unveiled its new eRulemaking program, which enabled easier access to participate in a high-quality, efficient, and open rulemaking process. The goals of the eRulemaking program were to:

- increase public access to federal regulatory materials
- increase public participation and understanding of the federal rulemaking process
- improve federal agency efficiency and effectiveness

Instead of physically visiting a government reading room or finding a copy of the *Federal Register*, citizens could now go online and visit Regulations.gov, where they could search all publicly available regulatory materials, submit a comment on a regulation, submit an application or adjudication document, download agency regulatory materials, sign up for email alerts, and access regulations.

In addition to Regulations.gov, other interesting early efforts emerged to improve engagement with citizens. In a 2004 report, *Restoring Trust in Government: The Potential of Digital Citizen Participation*, Marc Holzer and his colleagues described these early efforts: "Information and communication technologies (ICTs) have the potential to help make citizen participation a more dynamic element of the policy-making process. Citizen participation advocates are optimistic that ICTs will facilitate direct interactions between citizens and government through the integration of digital democratic applications."[3] Holzer and colleagues focused on two types of digital citizen participation: information dissemination and citizen deliberation. Their report presented two examples of citizen participation:

- **The Environmental Protection Agency's National Dialogue of Public Involvement in EPA Decisions:** EPA conducted an experimental 10-day online discussion in 2001 on public participation. The dialogue took the form of messages posted to a website, linked together in an ongoing conversation among participants. Participants could either initiate a new discussion thread or comment on an ongoing thread. More than 1,000 individuals registered to participate.
- **CitizenSpace, United Kingdom:** This initiative sought public comments on a variety of public policy issues then facing the U.K. government. Background documents were available for citizens to review prior to commenting on specific issues. The initiative, according to U.K. officials, promoted a more meaningful discourse between elected officials and their constituents, one in which citizen feedback could be incorporated into policymaking.

EXPANSION: THE RISE OF INTERACTION
AND COLLABORATION

Emergence of New Tools

Use of Web 2.0 Websites

In the mid-2000s, a new term became popularized—Web 2.0. The number of total websites passed 100 million in 2006 (in April 2018, the count was over 1.8 billion). With advances in both hardware and software, the stage was set for a dramatic increase in the interaction between users and the development of user generated content. In a 2008 report, *Leveraging Web 2.0 in Government*, Ai-Mei Chang and P. K. Kannan defined Web 2.0 as a "networked world supporting individual users creating content individually and collectively, sharing and updating information and knowledge using...diverse sharing devices and tools, and remixing and improving on content created by each other."[4] These new and enhanced websites allowed users to interact and collaborate in a social media "dialogue" as creators of user-generated content in a virtual community, in contrast to the Web 1.0 era where people passivley viewed content.

Chang and Kannan reported that around 2008, government began to move away from relying solely on citizens to visit government-hosted portals and websites: "Reaching citizens where they are—in their communities—will... enable government to harness the collective intelligence of citizens, such as feedback on services, ways to improve the design of content and services, and ways to distribute content and services efficiently to various citizens groups."[5]

The expansion phase was characterized by the increased use of a variety of new technologies for citizen collaboration with government, including blogs, wikis, Facebook, Twitter, and Instagram. During this phase, the use of social media was characterized by a "let a thousand flowers bloom" approach. As government gained more experience with new tools, the need for a consistent approach was clear.

Use of Blogs

One of the first big "success stories" in government during the expansion phase of social media was the use of blogging by government agencies. Blogging was also one of the first social media tools to be quickly adopted by government at all levels as an interactive communication device for citizens. A blog was defined as an online journal that can be updated regularly, with entries typically displayed in chronological order.

In a 2007 report, *The Blogging Revolution: Government in the Age of Web 2.0*, David Wyld examined blogs being published by members of Congress, congressional committees and caucuses, federal government leaders, governors, state legislators, city managers and mayors, police and fire departments, and college and university presidents.[6] In an early demonstration of the future of social media communications, Wyld found that government officials used blogs as a new vehicle for communicating with citizens on their activities, expressing their views on issues, describing their contacts and travels, and providing information on their personal lives and interests.

The use of blogs has dramatically increased as an important vehicle for government to communicate at greater length than through other forms of social media, such as Twitter or Facebook. Nearly all federal websites now feature a blog on their home page. Several agencies have created separate websites devoted solely to the publication of blogs. Most notable among these websites are two by the Department of Defense (DoD)–DoD Live and Armed with Science—and the Department of Veterans Affairs website VAntage Point. In an interview with the IBM Center, Tiffany Miller, Director of Social Media and Strategy, Department of Defense, said: "Blogs allow us to give more information than we can on social media. We will 'tease' to these blogs on social media with engaging photos and text. People aren't always looking for information, so it's our job to bring it to them via social media. We are really moving away from the traditional website. Obviously, we have Defense.gov, but people aren't necessarily going there to find out what the Department of Defense is doing."

Use of New Platforms

Facebook

Nearly every federal agency has a strong Facebook presence and uses it as a major communication platform. Table 1 lists the top federal Facebook accounts.

A major initial challenge for federal agencies was the need to verify that Facebook pages were legitimate and operated by federal departments and agencies. For example, numerous Facebook pages had names containing the acronym "CIA". It was difficult to tell these "fake" pages from those of the real agency. In 2014, Facebook became the first social media platform to verify all federal government Facebook pages with their signature "blue checkmark" using the Federal Social Media Registry. Other social media platforms quickly followed Facebook's verification model.

Today, Facebook is used effectively by federal departments and agencies to convey key information to citizens and make them aware of government activities and announcements. In many cases, agency Facebook pages drive citizens to agency websites for more information and details about specific announcements. In an interview with the IBM Center, Dana Allen-Greil, Web and Social Media Branch Chief at the National Archives and Record Administration, said that Facebook and other social media sites have served to "humanize" government agencies. Reflecting on her experience, Ms. Allen-Greil said that social media offers agencies an opportunity "to touch people in unexpected ways and to show how we are here to serve the public."[7]

Table 1—Top Federal Facebook Accounts

Agency	Followers (February 2018)
NASA	20.0 million
The White House	8.3 million
U.S. Army	4.6 million
U.S. Marine Corps	3.3 million
U.S. Navy	3.0 million
U.S. Air Force	2.6 million
Federal Bureau of Investigation	2.1 million
State Department	1.8 million
The National Guard	1.7 million
Department of Veterans' Affairs	1.1 million

Twitter

Twitter was created in 2006 and has now become a leading vehicle for government agencies to communicate to the public. Many agencies now have multiple Twitter accounts. The leading government Twitter accounts are listed in Table 2.

Table 2—Top Federal Twitter Accounts

Agency	Account	Number of Followers (February 2018)
National Aeronautics and Space Administration	@NASA	28.4 million
White House	@whitehouse	16.6 million
Department of Defense	@DeptofDefense	5.5 million
Department of State	@StateDept	4.9 million
Smithsonian Institution	@smithsonian	2.7 million
Central Intelligence Agency	@CIA	2.3 million
Federal Bureau of Investigation	@FBI	2.1 million
Centers for Disease Control	@CDCEMERGENCY	1.9 million
Peace Corps	@PeaceCorps	1.7 million
Department of Justice	@The JusticeDept.	1.5 million
Department of Agriculture	@USDAFoodSafety	1.4 million
U.S. Army	@USArmy	1.2 million
National Science Foundation	@NSF	1.1 million

Twitter is a microblogging tool in which users write brief text updates (initially limited to 140 characters, changed in 2017 to allow up to 280 characters). Many users combine their Twitter updates with content generated in other social media accounts, such as Facebook, YouTube, or blogs. In her examination of the use of Twitter by government in a 2012 report, *Working the Network: A Managers Guide for Using Twitter in Government*, Ines Mergel wrote, "Twitter can be used effectively to involve a large number of citizens and create conversations with an engaged, networked public. The outcomes of these conversations can be new insights and even innovations in the public sector including suggestions on how to make government more effective, or rapidly accelerating emergency responses that help to improve public safety."[8] Twitter has become a useful tool for government to communicate to citizens during an emergency, such a hurricane and other natural disasters.

Instagram

In 2013, many federal agencies started using Instagram. Agencies quick to see the potential of Facebook and Twitter also saw the potential of Instagram and quickly built a presence. In announcing its availability to federal agencies, Justin Herman, the General Services Administration's social media program manager, said: "Instagram can be used by federal agencies as part of an overall social and mobile strategy to ensure citizens can access valuable government content anywhere, anytime, on any device."[9]

Agency success on Instagram relies on the ability to regularly post compelling photographs. Many of these photographs look into the "day in the life" of an agency, and provide an opportunity to better understand agency missions. For example, the Transportation Security Administration (TSA) has become a highly popular Instagram site, identifying what travelers can and cannot bring onto planes. In addition, photos of strange items confiscated by TSA have proven entertaining and received much attention. Jennifer Plozai, TSA social media manager, comments, "Our goal was...to be able to help passengers. And I think this program (Instagram) has really helped us soften the public perception of TSA."[10]

High-quality photographs have led to a large number of followers for other federal agencies, such as the Smithsonian National Zoo. The Department of the Interior now has 1.6 million followers and has become one of the more active federal Instagram accounts, featuring nature and animal photos. Within the department, other popular Instagram accounts include the National Park Service, the Bureau of Reclamation, and the U.S. Fish and Wildlife Service. The National Aeronautics and Space Administration (NASA) has been widely praised for advancing its mission through photography. Instagram gives NASA a powerful tool for publishing photographs.

In describing the Department of the Interior's Instagram account, Melody Kramer, senior digital media strategist for the department, says, "A lot of work goes into finding great photos for Interior's Instagram account. We try to share pictures of what it currently looks like on the ground at national parks and other public sites. At the same time, we try to balance the different types of photos (sunrise, night sky, wildlife, etc.), geographic location, and type of public lands."[11]

Emergence of New Strategies to Engage Citizens

Crowdsourcing

The late 2000s saw the rise of crowdsourcing as a new tool in the portfolio of government initiatives to engage citizens. While the concept of crowdsourcing dates to 2004 with the publication of the *Wisdom of Crowds* by James Surowiecki, the term crowdsourcing was not defined until two years later. The accepted definition of crowdsourcing is "a type of participative online activity in which an individual, an institution, a non-profit organization, or company proposes to a group of individuals...the voluntary undertaking of a task."[12]

In his 2013 report, *Use of Crowdsourcing in Government*, Daren Brabham set forth four approaches to how an organization tasks a crowd:[13]

- **Knowledge discovery and management:** Finding and collecting information into a common location and format, ideal for information gathering, organizing and reporting problems.
- **Distributed human intelligence tasking:** Analyzing large amounts of information, ideal for large-scale data analysis where human intelligence is more efficient or effective than computer analysis.
- **Broadcast search:** Solving empirical problems, ideal for problems with empirically provable solutions, such as scientific problems.
- **Peer-vetted production:** Creating and selecting creative ideas, ideal for problems where solutions are matters of taste or market support.

The federal government now has increasing experience in the use of the broadcast search approach for soliciting solutions to specific problems, such as the use of prizes and challenges. Prizes have a long history, dating back to 1714 with the British government-sponsored prize offered to invent an instrument for accurately measuring longitude at sea. In his 2011 report, *Managing Innovation Prizes in Government*, Luciano Kay cites prizes as being used to accelerate the initial development of the aviation industry in the early 20th century, which included the Orteig Prize for the first aviator to fly nonstop from New York to Paris.[14] Examples of the use of broadcast searches by government include the Defense Advanced Research Projects Agency (DARPA) Challenges, the government wide Challenge.gov platform, and the Center of Excellence for Collaborative Innovation at NASA.

- **DARPA:** DARPA pioneered the development of challenges. Between 2004 and 2007, DARPA held three challenges for the development of an autonomous ground robotic vehicle (now known as driverless cars) which would perform specified maneuvers in both off-road and urban environments. The most recent DARPA Challenge was announced in April 2018. In 2019, qualified teams will compete for the top prize of $10 million to launch payloads to orbit with an extremely short notice and no prior knowledge of the content, destination orbit, or launch site.
- **Challenge.gov:** The federal government dramatically increased its use of crowdsourcing in 2010 with the creation of Challenge.gov. The Challenge.gov website presents information on competitions (usually with financial rewards) conducted in various federal departments and agencies. Since 2010, more than 800 challenges have been held. Prizes have ranged from $3,000 to $20 million. In assessing the initial impact of Challenge.gov in a 2012 report, *Challenge.gov: Using Competitions and Awards to Spur Innovation*, Kevin Desouza wrote: "By addressing key issues and seizing improvement opportunities, Challenge.gov can advance the missions of federal agencies and enhance their relevancy, legitimacy, and impact by empowering citizens to help solve problems and enable the realization of goals that matter to the nation."[15]

- **Center for Excellence for Collaborative Innovation (CoECI):** CoECI was created in 2011, after the success of a pilot program to determine if a crowdsourcing initiative could help NASA accelerate and augment research and development. NASA challenges are managed by CoECI, through the NASA Tournament Lab. The Lab now offers a variety of open innovation platforms that engage the crowdsourcing community in challenges to create innovative, efficient, and optimal solutions for specific, real-world challenges faced by NASA.

Co-production

The use of competitions in which citizens send their best solutions for specific problems is just one new type of citizen engagement in which citizens actively contribute to the accomplishment of a government mission. Increasing attention in the 2010s has been given to the concept of co-production. In a 2013 report, *Beyond Citizen Engagement: Involving the Public in Co-Delivering Government Services*, P. K. Kannan and Ai-Mei Chang define this new approach to engagement as "an active, creative, and social process, based on collaboration between governments and citizens and/or between citizens and citizens, that is facilitated by government to generate value for citizens through innovative services."[16]

The use of social media is a key vehicle for co-production in which individual citizens or groups of citizens participate in the delivery of a government service. A good example of the use of social media in co-production is the Library of Congress' Veterans History Project, in which citizen volunteers interview veterans to gather their first-person recollections for preservation.

Another prominent example of the use of social media in co-production is the Citizen Archivist program of the U.S. National Archives and Records Administration. With the support of virtual volunteers, the National Archives has increased online access to its historical records. Citizens assist the Archives in tagging, transcribing, or adding comments to the National Archives Catalog. The Archives website presents an updated list of new citizen archivist missions and newly added records. Citizen archivist missions now underway include tagging and transcribing captions from photographs of the U.S. Marine Corps activities during World War II and Korea, transcribing logbooks of the U.S. Coast guard vessels that served in the Vietnam War, and transcribing records of Watergate-related cases.

Emergence of New Strategies to Engage Employees

Just as new strategies have emerged and been used by government to engage citizens in recent years, these tools have also been used to engage federal employees. These strategies include ideation platforms, social intranets, and wikis.

Ideation Platforms

During the late 2000s and early 2010s, federal departments began to develop platforms to engage their own employees. According to Gwanhoo Lee in a 2013 report, *Federal Ideation Programs: Challenges and Best Practices,* ideation platforms include online brainstorming or social voting platforms for employees to submit new ideas, search previously submitted ideas, post questions and challenges, discuss and expand on ideas, vote them up or down, and flag them.[17] Federal government ideation platforms include Idea Hub (Department of Transportation), Sounding Board (Department of State), IdeaFactory (Department of Homeland Security), and IdeaLab (Department of Health and Human Services).

Social Intranets

In addition to the ideation platforms discussed above, many federal departments created social intranets. Ideation tools can be viewed as an example of one tool on an agency's social intranet platform. In her 2016 report, *The Social Intranet: Insights on Managing and Sharing Knowledge Internally,* Ines Mergel defined social intranets as "in-house social networks that use technologies—such as automated newsfeeds, wikis, chats, or blogs—to create engagement opportunities among employees."[18] Federal government social intranets include Corridor (Department of State), Space-book (NASA), and i-Space (Intelligence Community). In addition, Canada also created a government-wide social intranet called GCconnex for use by Canadian civil servants.

The Intelligence Community has pioneered the use of social intranet platforms. In his 2016 report, *New Tools for Collaboration: The Experience of the U.S. Intelligence Community,* Gregory Treverton describes Intelink as the backbone for Intelligence Community-wide tools.[19] Intelink provides platforms where the Community can use social media tools for collaboration and information sharing, such as Intelink Search, Inteldocs, IntelShare, Intellipedia (discussed below), Intelink Blogs, e-Chirp, and Jabber. Treverton presents a series of recommendations for the increased use of such sites, including making access to these type tools easier and providing more training on the use of such tools.

As part of the CoECI, NASA sponsors the NASA@work intranet site as an agency-wide virtual platform that seeks innovation by fostering collaboration within the NASA community, through the contribution of interactive discussions and submissions of solutions to posted challenges.

Wikis

The early 2000s saw the rise of wikis. While wikis can be used for citizen engagement, their greatest impact to date has been as a vehicle for government employees to share information among themselves and encourage deliberation. Wikis are websites which can be created, edited, discussed, and changed by users working in collaboration. The most well-known wiki, Wikipedia, was founded in 2001. In government, two wikis have received a high degree of public attention:

- **Diplopedia:** Launched in 2006 by the Department of State, Diplopedia provides a central information space for foreign service specialists to contribute their knowledge. It has proven an effective way for diplomats to prepare for new assignments by reading the posts of diplomats who previously served in those assignments. Diplopedia now has more than 25,000 entries. In an interview with the IBM Center, Andre Goodfriend, Director of the Department of State's Office of eDiplomacy, said "Each individual has the ability to share their expertise directly without having to go through someone else. We are creating a group culture of sharing information and internal transparency rather than the old model of siloed information. Diplopedia has helped encourage a culture of people sharing their expertise."[20]
- **Intellipedia:** Launched in 2005 as a pilot project and officially launched in 2006, Intellipedia has been one of the most successful and acclaimed wikis in government. It has become a valuable tool for those in the Intelligence Community and is part of the Intelink platform discussed above. In her 2011 report, *Using Wikis in Government: A Guide to Public Managers*, Ines Mergel wrote, "The goal of Intellipedia is described by one user as providing new ways of capturing knowledge of 'what we know, what the intelligence community knows about various topics."[21]

While Diplopedia and Intellipedia were primarily for intra- and inter-organizational use within the federal government, wikis have also been used to engage citizens by state and local governments and other nations. For example, the City of San Jose, California, used a wiki as a "virtual charrette" to improve civic engagement in urban planning initiatives for San Jose.

Identification of Challenges to Institutionalization

During the expansion years, it became obvious to the government executives charged with implementing social media throughout government that the federal government's policy apparatus had not kept pace with the rapid expansion of the use of social media by government agencies. The "let a thousand flowers bloom" approach resulted in a host of issues for managing privacy, security, and records—and Freedom of Information Act regulations quickly began to surface as agencies implemented a variety of social media tools.

In 2004, an interagency group of federal web managers came together to formally create the Federal Web Managers Council as a community of practice. The new Council built upon earlier initiatives which supported "webmaster" networks. In addition, the new Web Managers Council also served an advisory function for government policy-makers trying to resolve government-wide issues regarding the web and social media.

In December 2008, the Federal Web Managers Council developed a paper on "Social Media and the Federal Government: Perceived and Real Barriers and Potential Solutions" for use by the incoming Obama Administration in updating government regulatory policies to reflect the increased use of social media by government agencies. The Council found that the use of social media raised a myriad of legal, contractual, and policy questions for the new administration. The varying interpretations of government policy regarding social media impeded the use of these tools in many agencies. Among the challenges to be resolved were the need for:

- A government-wide digital strategy
- Government-wide terms of service agreement with social media sites
- Procurement policy on the use of free web products and services
- A policy on whether the Paperwork Reduction Act and the Administrative Procedure Act applied to social media sites

The Federal Web Managers Council's paper served as a valuable guide for the first social media policies in the Obama White House, which began to focus on analyzing barriers to the increased use of social media in government.

INSTITUTIONALIZATION: EMBEDDING SOCIAL MEDIA IN GOVERNMENT

The late 2000s saw the "institutionalization" of social media as a permanent part of the federal government landscape. In addition, other nations also began to institutionalize social media. Institutionalization has four characteristics:

- new policies and guidance
- enhancing organizational capacity
- enhancing staff capability
- developing assessment capability

New Policies and Guidance

In response to the barriers identified by the Federal Web Managers Council, the Obama Administration began to develop a government-wide strategy and new policies throughout the first of year of the administration in 2009. These efforts resulted in a series of new government-wide policies.

- In 2010, Cass Sunstein, Administrator of the Office of Information and Regulatory Affairs, Office of Management and Budget, issued a Memorandum on "Social Media, Web-Based Interactive Technologies, and the Paperwork Reduction Act."[22] The memo said that the Paperwork Reduction Act (PRA) does not apply to the use of social media by agencies. The Memo explained that the use of social media and web-based interactive technologies will be treated as activities *excluded* from the PRA.
- In 2011, the President issued an Executive Order on "Streamlining Service Delivery and Improving Customer Service."[23] The order required departments and agencies to "identify ways to use innovative technologies to streamline their delivery of services to lower costs, decrease service delivery times, and improve the customer experience." The order was followed by a charge to the federal chief information officer to develop a government-wide strategy to deliver better digital services to the American public.
- In 2012, the President issued a Memorandum for the Heads on Executive Departments and Agencies, "Building a 21st Century Digital Government."[24] The memo mandated that each federal department implement a 12-month strategy to enhance their digital service delivery.

These new policies are further addressed in Chapter Two on "Going Digital."

Enhancing Organizational Capacity

Digital service offices were formed to respond to and repair urgent technology failures, or as an alternative structural approach to rethinking processes and implementation strategies in government digital transformation efforts.[25] In the United States, three types of digital service teams were created, as discussed further in Chapter Two:

- **The U.S. Digital Service** was created in 2014 to focus on specific technology projects determined to be national priorities.
- **18F** was created as a team of software engineers and product managers located at the General Services Administration to assist departments and agencies with their technology initiatives.
- **Agency-level in-house digital service teams** focus on high-priority policy areas within their own department and agency.

Enhancing Staff Capability

The third aspect of institutionalization is enhancing staff capability. This takes the form of creating resource websites, communities of practice, and providing training. The newness of social media to government pointed to a clear need for enhancing staff capability and knowledge regarding the effective use of social media to reach out to the public.

- **DigitalGov:** DigitalGov, created by the General Services Administration, provides government employees with the tools, methods, practices, and policy guidance they need to deliver effective and accessible digital services. The website was created based on the need that government staff had for:
    - Guidance on implementing digital policies and initiatives
    - Open access to modern methods, practices, policies, and tools
    - Focused training and events that help teams learn and adopt new concepts
    - Easy access to collaborate with others across government who are working on the same problems

- **Communities of Practice:** DigitalGov also serves as a resource for communities of practice which have developed over time. As of 2018, 19 communities of practice existed in which more than 10,000 federal employees participated. The federal SocialGov Community included over 1,200 digital managers and specialists at more than 160 agencies and offices, in a collaborative program aimed at improving the creation, adoption and evaluation of social media and other digital engagement programs.

- **DigitalGov University (DGU):** Sponsored by the GSA, DGU serves as the events platform for the DigitalGov community. According to GSA, DGU "provides programming to build and accelerate digital capacity by providing webinars and in-person events highlighting innovations, case studies, tools, and resources."

Developing Assessment Capability

The fourth characteristic of institutionalization is the assessment of government's social media efforts. In her 2014 report, *A Managers Guide to Assessing the Impact of Government's Social Media Interactions*, Ines Mergel describes how public managers now assess whether social media is making a difference to citizens, improving their trust in government, increasing accountability, and making government communication more effective and efficient.[26] There are common performance measures, collection methodologies, and web analytics tools used in the assessment of government's social media. In her report, Mergel describes how government managers can now measure the degree of engagement between citizens and agencies on social media. The use of metrics is also an important component for agencies making the business case for the continued and increased use of social media.

LESSONS LEARNED

Based on our review of research on this topic over the past twenty years, we identified four key lessons:

First, as with any innovation, government agencies can be divided between innovators, early adopters, and laggards. Innovators and early adopters have a special role to play in implementing future social initiatives. Innovative agencies need to be recognized, rewarded, and encouraged to share their knowledge and experience with agencies moving more slowly along the adoption curve.

Second, agencies can become more effective and improve their performance by engaging the public through social media. By engaging citizens through social media, agencies can obtain crucial feedback on current performance and how their performance could be improved. Such engagement can also assist government organizations in developing clearer and more effective policies.

Third, the role of interagency communities of practice helps with the successful implementation of social media initiatives. Central management agencies can take responsibility for catalyzing and encouraging communities of practice on new management initiatives. Creation of interagency communities of practice serve two primary purposes:

- Providing a vehicle for agencies to share their experiences of what has worked well and what has not
- By sharing information and participating in a government-wide initiative, agencies begin to take ownership of a given initiative

Fourth, interagency communities of practice can play a key role in identifying government-wide policy changes needed in response to a new initiative. In the case of social media, a host of government-wide policies required change or updates to reflect the use of new social media tools.

LOOKING FORWARD

As agencies continue to develop their social media capabilities and strategies while expanding internal and public use, they will need to focus on several areas:

- **Managing the evolving risks associated with social media:** The government needs to develop policies, practices, and approaches for creating and maintaining trust when citizens interact with agencies on social media platforms. This will include attention to privacy and security issues related to users' identities, as well as tracking individual users across platforms to create integrated profiles of their interactions.

- **Managing the increasing convergence of the uses of social media:** Social media tools and platforms will increasingly provide the foundation for new forms of collaboration and engagement among agencies and between government and citizens. These new models of interaction could serve as powerful accelerators for how government works in the future.
- **Improving the user experience with social media:** The user experience is defined as the overall experience of an individual with using a product, such as a website or platform. The federal government will need to focus in the future on improving user experiences for:
  - **Citizens:** Government agencies now involve citizens in testing new platforms to make them easier to use, to increase customer satisfaction.
  - **Government employees:** The user experience by government employees is also crucial in that employees now seek a more consistent experience in working across multiple platforms to better serve citizens. An emphasis on the employee user experience will increase the adoption rate of social media as "the way of doing business" in government.

Addressing these opportunities will set the stage for longer-term innovations and increased adoption of social media strategies in government.

Mark A. Abramson is the President of Leadership Inc. and the founding Executive Director of the IBM Center for The Business of Government. His recently published books include Getting It Done: A Guide for Government Executives *(with Daniel J. Chenok and John M. Kamensky) and* Succeeding as a Political Executive: 50 Insights from Experience *(with Paul R. Lawrence). He is also the author of* What Government Does: How Political Executives Manage *(with Paul R. Lawrence).*

Endnotes

1 Elizabeth Chuck, "Why the TSA's award-winning Instagram account is hilarious and unexpected," *NBC News*, April 29, 2018.

2 For further discussions of the early days of e-government and e-commerce, see Mark A. Abramson and Grady E. Means, *E-Government 2001* (Lanham: Rowman & Littlefield Publishers, 2001), *and* Mark A. Abramson and Therese L. Morin, *E-Government 2003* (Lanham: Rowman & Littlefield Publishers, 2003).

3 Marc Holzer, James Melitski, Seung-Yong Rho, and Richard Schwester, *Restoring Trust in Government: The Potential of Digital Citizen Participation*, IBM Center for The Business of Government, 2004.

4 Ai-Mei Chang and P.K. Kannan, *Leveraging Web 2.0 in Government*, IBM Center for The Business of Government, 2008, 10.

5 Chang and Kannan, *Leveraging Web 2.0*, 18.

6 David C. Wyld, *The Blogging Revolution: Government in the Age of Web 2.0*, IBM Center for The Business of Government, 2007.

7 Dana Allen-Greil, telephone interview with IBM Center for The Business of Government, February 23, 2018.

8   Ines Mergel, *Working the Network: A Managers Guide for Using Twitter in Government,* IBM Center for The Business of Government, 2012, 6.

9   Colby Hochmuth, "Federal agencies get green light for Instagram," *FedScoop,* January 9, 2015.

10   "TSA gains popular following on Instagram," *CBS News,* July 27, 2017.

11   Melody Kramer, "What we can learn from the Interior's social feeds," *18F,* January 21, 2016.

12   Daren C. Brabham, *Use of Crowdsourcing in Government,* IBM Center for The Business of Government, 2013, 7.

13   Brabham, *Use of Crowdsourcing.*

14   Lucian Kay, *Managing Innovation Prizes in Government,* IBM Center for The Business of Government, 2011.

15   Kevin C. Desouza, *Challenge.gov: Using Competitions and Awards to Spur Innovation,* IBM Center for The Business of Government, 6.

16   P.K. Kannan and Ai-Mei Chang, *Beyond Citizen Engagement: Involving the Public in Co-Delivering Government Services,* IBM Center for The Business of Government, 2013, *11.*

17   Gwanhoo Lee, *Federal Ideation Programs: Challenges and Best Practices,* IBM Center for The Business of Government, 2013.

18   Ines Mergel, *The Social Intranet: Insights on Managing and Sharing Knowledge Internally,* IBM Center for The Business of Government, 2016, 7

19   Gregory F. Treverton, *New Tools for Collaboration: The Experience of the U.S. Intelligence Community,* Center for Strategic and International Studies, 2016

20   Andre Goodfriend, telephone interview with IBM Center for the Business of Government, February 1, 2018.

21   Ines Mergel, *Using Wikis in Government: A Guide to Public Managers,* IBM Center for The Business of Government, 2011, 16.

22   Office of Management and Budget, *Social Media, Web-Based Interactive Technologies, and the Paperwork Reduction Act,* April 7, 2010.

23   The White House, *Executive Order 13571—Streamlining Service Delivery and Improving Customer Service,* April 27, 2011.

24   The White House, *Presidential Memorandum—Building a 21st Century Digital Government,* May 23, 2012.

25   For a further discussion of digital service offices, see Chapter Two and Ines Mergel, *Digital Service Teams: Challenges and Recommendations for Action,* IBM Center for The Business of Government, 2014.

26   Ines Mergel, *A Managers Guide to Assessing the Impact of Government's Social Media Interactions,* IBM Center for The Business of Government, 2014.

CHAPTER SIX

Becoming Collaborative

John M. Kamensky

Highlights

- Collaborative governance—that is, working jointly across the traditional boundaries of governmental agencies, and between the public and private sectors—has proven to be an effective strategy for implementing policy initiatives over the past two decades in an increasingly interdependent environment.

- The increased demand for collaborative governance stems from a changing policy environment which has become more dynamic and demanding. A wide range of tools, techniques, and legal authorities have evolved in recent years in response to the increased demand.

- As the use of networked collaborative governance models goes to scale, we will likely see a shift to a greater use of "platform-based networks"—a business model inspired by the digital world.

BECOMING COLLABORATIVE

By John M. Kamensky

In October 2002, an outbreak of a highly contagious disease among chickens was detected in Compton, California. If allowed to spread, it would devastate the $40 billion poultry industry in the U.S. The response involved dozens of public and private sector organizations over the course of a year and the outbreak was successfully quelled, but this emergency and the governmental response to it barely reached public attention.

Government operations such as this oftentimes run in the background out of public view, hiding how government works in ways that increasingly depends on multiple players for success in areas in which no single agency has the span of resources or legal authority to act.

Containing the outbreak required a highly coordinated effort among federal, state, and local actors. Dr. Annette Whitford, with the U.S. Department of Agriculture, was designated as the joint area commander of a task force formed to stem the outbreak. Her task force was modeled on a collaborative emergency response governance approach developed in the 1970s by the Forest Service to combat forest fires. Based on pre-defined protocols, she orchestrated the containment effort across 10 major state and federal agencies, in 19 counties, involving more than 7,000 workers over an 11-month period. The work involved diagnosing the disease, euthanizing and disposing more than 4.5 million birds, monitoring to ensure the disease was eradicated in commercial and private locations, and conducting appraisals to reimburse owners for birds destroyed.[1]

Organizing quickly, mobilizing people, exercising authority, and paying for the entire operation required significant collaboration among public and private actors. This approach to infrequent emergencies is just the tip of the iceberg of cross-agency collaboration occurring across the government.

INTRODUCTION

A decade ago, public management scholar Donald Kettl declared that government was failing to meet public expectations because "many of the most important problems we face simply do not match the institutions we have created to govern them."[2] He observed that many challenges—such as responding to disasters, organizing the delivery of services to disabled individuals, and orchestrating a response to climate change—have no single organization in charge. As a result, the traditional bureaucratic institutions defined by hierarchical agencies and programs that were so successful in the mid-twentieth century are not adequate for challenges that span across organizational boundaries.

The traditional hierarchical model of governing is increasingly being supplemented with a collaborative network model. Some stable and focused governmental functions remain under the hierarchical model, while other more fluid and dynamic functions are adopting a more network-based, collaborative approach. This networked collaborative model is still evolving and growing in importance—within agencies, between agencies, between levels of government, and between the public, private, and non-profit sectors.

What is "Collaborative Governance?"

The concept of "collaborative governance"—that is, working jointly across the traditional boundaries of governmental agencies, and between the public and private sectors—has proven an effective strategy for implementing policy initiatives over the past two decades in an increasingly interdependent environment. The descriptive terms for these phenomena vary: networks, collaborations, partnerships, horizontal government, boundary spanning, joined up government, and more.

This evolution has resulted from the need for new business models to address societal challenges where the traditional hierarchical organizational model no longer works. The evolution is also driven by the availability of new technologies that lower cross-functional collaboration barriers which existed in the past.

Academics say this collaborative networking phenomenon is one of the defining characteristics of "New Public Governance" where "multiple different actors contribute to the delivery of public services and the policymaking system" and the line between the public, private, and nonprofit sectors has become increasingly blurred.[3]

These new operating models have evolved largely through trial and error, beginning with the private sector and diffusing to cross-sectoral partnerships.[4] Public and private sector leaders have found the traditional hierarchical bureaucratic model increasingly inadequate for addressing increasingly complex challenges. They also found the market-based models of privatizing functions or creating contractual arrangements did not help. They tried different approaches to working horizontally across traditional hierarchical structures and stakeholders—typically by organizing around a common goal, customer, or geographic area.

What drives the use of collaborative governance? Rosemary O'Leary describes how government has steadily increased its use of collaborative approaches in lieu of the traditional hierarchical and bureaucratic approach. She says there are several explanations for this shift:

- First, "most public challenges are larger than one organization, requiring new approaches to addressing public issues" such as housing, pollution, transportation, and healthcare.
- Second, collaboration helps to improve the effectiveness and performance of programs "by encouraging new ways of providing services."
- Third, technology advances in recent years have helped "organizations and their employees to share information in a way that is integrative and interoperable."
- And finally, "citizens are seeking additional avenues for engaging in governance, resulting in new and different forms of collaborative problem solving and decision making."[5]

Early in his administration, President Obama's Open Government initiative placed a premium on the use of collaborative approaches. This led to the institutionalization of several specific initiatives, such as the creation of cross-agency priority goals described later in this chapter.[6]

The development and use of collaborative networks and partnerships happened faster than academics could keep up. There was a scramble to understand and classify them in the 1990s and early 2000s. The IBM Center sponsored a number of reports that undertook such efforts, addressing definitional issues such as:

- What do we mean by networks, partnerships, collaboration, and platforms?
- What can networks be used to accomplish?
- What are the different kinds of networks?
- How do collaborative networks differ from traditional hierarchical systems?
- What are the preconditions for success?
- What competencies and skills are needed to manage collaborative networks?

Responses to these types of questions were summarized in two publications: a 2004 book, *Collaboration Using Networks and Partnerships,* edited by John Kamensky and Tom Burlin,[7] and a 2014 literature review, *Inter-Organizational Networks: A Review of the Literature to Inform Practice,* by Janice Popp, Brint Milward, Gail MacKean, Ann Casebeer, and Ron Lindstrom.[8] These works provide useful conceptual frameworks to understand the evolution of collaborative networks and answers to questions like those above. However, the more inspiring stories have been case studies of practitioners in the "real world" over the past 20 years.

Organization of Chapter

As seen in the chart titled, "Evolution of Collaborative Networks: 1998–2018," the evolution can be divided into three phases:

- **Early action:** Informal networks of people, programs, and organizations—and the use of partnerships (a more formalized approach)—grew organically, largely from the bottom-up, as pragmatic responses to specific situations. These included community-led efforts to improve the water quality of rivers, and the Federal Emergency Management Agency's efforts to prevent future damage to communities facing natural disasters (versus only responding to a community after a disaster has occurred).
- **Expansion:** Policy makers began to proactively use network-based, collaborative governance models to address broader issues, such as improving food safety, addressing changes brought about by climate change, cross-agency law enforcement efforts, and creating veteran-centric approaches to myriad resources available to veterans.

Evolution of Collaborative Networks: 1998—2018

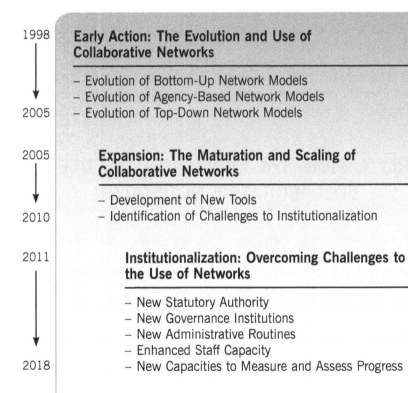

1998

Early Action: The Evolution and Use of Collaborative Networks

– Evolution of Bottom-Up Network Models
– Evolution of Agency-Based Network Models
2005 – Evolution of Top-Down Network Models

2005

Expansion: The Maturation and Scaling of Collaborative Networks

– Development of New Tools
2010 – Identification of Challenges to Institutionalization

2011

Institutionalization: Overcoming Challenges to the Use of Networks

– New Statutory Authority
– New Governance Institutions
– New Administrative Routines
– Enhanced Staff Capacity
2018 – New Capacities to Measure and Assess Progress

- **Institutionalization:** Statutory authority, strategic plans, and capacity-building efforts helped legitimize and provide the foundation for policy makers to use collaborative networks in a wide array of policy arenas. This has been reflected in statutory provisions creating cross-agency priority goals, Office of Management and Budget directives, and presidential directives to use collaborative approaches and to develop a cadre of career executives with experience working across organizational boundaries. Some congressionally appropriated funding has also specifically targeted these efforts.

In addition to the development of this new institutional capacity, there is a shift underway to create and use "platforms" to organize and deliver internal services. Platforms are electronic business models that have become a foundation for virtually frictionless transactions and interactions between "many-to-many"—like eBay, Facebook, Airbnb and Uber. Digital platforms may presage the future of how collaborative governance evolves. The lessons offered stem from the experiences of the many pioneers in the field of collaboration.

This shift to the use of platforms is reflected in the expansion of shared services for functions such as personnel and finance at the federal level. It is also seen in the delivery of citizen-facing services, such as the use of integrated networks of social services organized around the needs of families and individuals in cities like Los Angeles and San Diego and in countries like Canada, Australia, and Belgium.

The remainder of this chapter provides more detail about these three phases. The chapter concludes with lessons learned and observations on what's on the horizon—the evolution of digital "platforms" as the backbone for collaborative networks.

EARLY ACTION: THE EVOLUTION AND USE OF COLLABORATIVE NETWORKS

While state and local networks have tended to emerge bottom-up, networks at the federal level seemed to be largely an outgrowth of top-down initiatives to improve cross-agency or federal-state "coordination" efforts—in areas such as grants management, avoiding duplicative capital investments in hospital equipment in a common geographic area, or working across agency boundaries that shared a common geographic boundary. The dynamics within networks differ from those that are bottom-up versus top-down, and informal versus formal. Networks also start at the agency level, with agency leadership serving as "networking entrepreneurs." Observers judge the bottom-up and the mid-level manager approaches as more likely to be successful, generally due to better buy-in by those doing the actual work.

Evolution of Bottom-Up Network Models

The use of collaborative networks that cross organizational boundaries has a long history. Many of the early networks evolved in response to specific needs at the state and local levels, dealing with practical problems—such as sharing fire-fighting equipment and staff in emergencies via mutual aid agreements, joint economic development initiatives, or addressing natural resource issues in a common watershed.

In a 2003 report, *Leveraging Networks: A Guide for Public Managers Working Across Organizations,* Robert Agranoff described a dozen such locally-driven networks in the Midwest, observing: "Social capital, or the built-up reservoir of good will that flows from different organizations working together for mutual productive gain, no doubt is the 'glue' that holds people together or the 'motivator' that moves the process along."[9]

Mark Imperial, in a 2004 report, *Collaboration and Performance Management in Network Settings: Lessons from Three Watershed Governance Efforts,* provides a vivid case study of a bottom-up, local-level collaborative network.[10] He describes the collaborative efforts of three watershed governance efforts with activities dating back several decades in places as diverse as Lake Tahoe, NV; Tillamook Bay, OR; and Tampa Bay, FL. He observed that each watershed governance effort developed its own unique performance management system, to hold each of its participating members jointly accountable for the group's actions. He concluded that "collaboration is a strategy for getting things done" by improving both service delivery as well as environmental conditions. Common collaborative activities included "habitat restoration,...streamlining permitting processes, improving enforcement, and coordination land acquisition to improve service delivery." [11]

Evolution of Agency-Activated Network Models

Some networks evolved based on entrepreneurial efforts of leaders at the agency level within larger organizations. Following are two examples of federal-level collaborative initiatives that reached beyond their own agency boundaries. They include the Federal Emergency Management Agency's Safe Construction Networks launched in the late 1990s, and a Department of Health and Human Services initiative to improve community-level health care.

- **Federal Emergency Management Agency (FEMA):** A notable example of how one federal agency activated a collaborative network is a 2002 case study by William Waugh, Jr., *Leveraging Networks to Meet National Goals: FEMA and the Safe Construction Networks,* which describes the development of Safe Construction Networks by FEMA in the 1990s.[12] After a series of disastrous hurricanes, wildfires, and earthquakes, FEMA undertook in 1995 a National Mitigation Strategy to reduce property losses and protect lives. Pursuant to this strategy, FEMA created in

1997 an initiative called "Project Impact." A key focus of this initiative was to encourage safe construction. This included, for example, land-use regulations in flood plains that promoted elevated construction and flood-proofing buildings. It also required the collaboration of not only local jurisdictions, but also state coastal zone management programs, private insurance companies, building code standard-setting organizations, construction companies, and non-profits promoting disaster-resistant model home designs.

Initial distrust among the voluntary participants are because "Project Impact community participants [perceived] that FEMA officials were trying to foist certain kinds of projects on them rather than accept local priorities and proposals." FEMA quickly learned that working within a network "does require a less aggressive, more collaborative style of leadership." Ultimately, this pioneering network did not survive the transition from the Clinton to the Bush administration, but it offered clear lessons to other federal agencies on the importance of "strong interpersonal skills… and considerable political acumen in order to interact effectively."[13]

- **Department of Health and Human Services' Bureau of Primary Health Care (BPHC):** Another pioneering example of the use of an agency-activated collaborative approach to tackle an ambitious goal is the BPHC's "100% Access/0 Health Disparities" campaign from 1998–2002. John Scanlon, in his 2003 report, *Extraordinary Results on National Goals: Networks and Partnerships in the Bureau of Primary Health Care's 100%/0 Campaign,* describes how the BPHC, provided $1 billion in grants to community health centers and staffing support via the National Health Services Corps.[14] A leadership cadre within the BPHC collectively decided to set a national goal of providing 3,000 communities across the country with access to health care by all residents, focused on eliminating health-status disparities among the vulnerable and uninsured. Scanlon found that the strategy was to "launch a self-organizing, self-sustaining movement" with multiple levels of leadership at the national, state, and local levels sharing a common vision and measurable goals.

  The initial goal was to enroll 500 communities in the first three years of the initiative by gaining commitments from local doctors and other health care providers within these communities. As the initiative enrolled communities, it identified selected local benchmark models. BPHC then began to partner with existing national networks of physicians, hospitals, pharmacists, unions, local elected leaders, and faith communities. BPHC established performance partnerships with groups such as the United Way of America and the American Academy of Pediatrics to work with communities to restructure existing community assets and reinvestments to ensure access to care. By 2002, the campaign transitioned its leadership from BPHC to a non-profit, the Community Health Leadership Network, that continued the initiative as a "national movement."[15] By the late 2000s, the national network had disintegrated, but scattered local movements continue.

What triggered agencies like FEMA and BPHC to undertake efforts like this on their own initiative at an agency level within the federal government? In both cases, leaders of these initiatives said their efforts responded to the adoption of the Government Performance and Results Act of 1993, which requires agencies to develop plans and measures of performance. This Act signaled a shift in managerial attention from processes, programs, and activities to achieving mission-focused results. This new focus highlighted the need to collaborate more actively with stakeholders beyond their programs and agencies.

Evolution of Top-Down Network Models

The FEMA and BPHC examples were agency-activated and occurred within the context of larger organizations. Efforts to formalize the use of collaborative governance at the national cross-agency (and cross-sector) level first appeared in the mid-1990s and were dubbed "national strategies." These included the statutorily-mandated 1997 *National Military Strategy of the United States of America* and the *International Crime Control Strategy* in 1998.

These strategies, not signed by the President, largely dealt with issues within the bounds of a specific agency. For example, the national military strategy signed by the chairman of the Joint Chiefs of Staff focused on the armed forces—force structure, acquisition, doctrine, etc. Other agencies had developed cross-cutting national strategies. The Office of National Drug Control Policy's national strategy and the attorney general's interagency counterterrorism and technology crime plan pre-existed the Bush Administration's use of national strategies.

After the 9/11 terrorist attacks, President George W. Bush understood the criticality of developing a national—not just a federal—approach to fighting terrorism. He expanded the use of a relatively new policy vehicle—which the White House called a "national strategy" document—as a way of creating an overarching strategic plan around a specific need or outcome, signed by the President. One of the first signed by the President was the 90-page *National Strategy for Homeland Security,* issued in July 2002. It addressed the threat of terrorism in the U.S. and focused on the domestic efforts of the federal, state, local and private sectors.[16]

President Bush's Administration issued about a dozen other national strategies that addressed a pressing national—not just federal—issue, such as homeland security, cybersecurity, and pandemic preparation.[17] These strategies were typically orchestrated by the White House. The approach ebbed in the transition between the Bush and Obama Administrations, even though it was still being promoted by the Government Accountability Office (GAO) as late as 2017.[18]

GAO found that national strategies differed from other federal government planning documents in their national scope, and oftentimes had international components. The federal government did not control many of the sectors, entities, or resources involved in implementing these strategies. GAO also found a rough hierarchy among the various terror-related strategies with cross-references among them. For example, the *National Security* strategy provided an overarching strategy while the *Homeland Security* strategy provided more specific approaches to combating terrorism domestically.

Several of these early federal top-down collaborative networks were discontinued, largely because of changes in leadership between presidential administrations.

In the 1990s and early 2000s all levels of government experimented with different forms of inter-organizational collaborative networks. Some were emergent and bottom-up, some mandated and top-down. Some were

The Special Case of The Incident Command System

The Incident Command System (ICS) is an organizational model developed at the local level in California in the 1970s by firefighters struggling to overcome an organizational paradox that most crises create. Crises require a mix of skills and capacities beyond a single organizational hierarchy, or a single political jurisdiction, and therefore need a network of responders. Forest fires do not respect boundaries between counties or cities. At the same time, crises require coordination, rapid decision-making and decisive, coordinated action — characteristics associated with hiearchies.

In a pair of studies of the ICS approach, *Leveraging Collaborative Networks in Infrequent Emergency Situations (2005)* and *From Forest Fires to Hurricane Katrina: Case Studies of Incident Command Systems (2007)*, Donald Moynihan concludes that the ICS approach solves this paradox by leveraging the strengths of both networks and hierarchies.[19] This approach has since been applied successfully in a range of other crises, such as responding to contagious poultry diseases, the pandemic scare of 2004, and natural disasters. This organizational model involves a latent network among a wide range of participants that occasionally gather to share information and train together, but it does not come into action absent a specific triggering event. When that occurs, pre-defined roles and responsibilities and the latent network quickly becomes a hierarchical organization. After the event, it returns to being a latent network.

Dr. Moynihan's case studies found that ICS works best when the network size and the scale of the disaster are geographically limited, the responders are experienced with the ICS approach, and the responders have a strong positive working relationship with one another. While these limitations may bound the effectiveness of this approach in a wider range of situations, it was seen as compelling enough that, in 2004, the Department of Homeland Security extended the approach as national policy used in response to all national emergencies, called the National Incident Management System.

event-specific (e.g., local responses to a flood), some geographic-specific (e.g., watershed improvements), and some population-specific (e.g., reducing health disparities). But this approach gained traction in public management and moved beyond the experimentation phase, expanded into other policy domains, and scaled to larger and more complex public challenges.

EXPANSION: THE MATURATION AND SCALING OF COLLABORATIVE NETWORKS

In the 2000s, the use of collaborative networks expanded. This approach was used at all levels of government and in increasingly complex policy environments involving multi-sector partners. As collaborative networks matured, they often changed their composition of participants, strategic focus, and how they worked together. The growing pains of various networks helped identify common challenges that networks face as they strive for longer-term sustainability. Addressing these barriers systematically helped pave the path toward institutionalization of collaborative governance as a useful approach for public managers.

Expanded Use of Complex Collaborative Networks

The early 2000s saw the use of collaborative networks expand in complexity by involving multi-sector actors in different policy domains. The following four examples of such networks, demonstrate the breadth of issues in the network model:

- **Minnesota Traffic Congestion Program:** The U.S. Department of Transportation sponsored in 2007 a pilot program—Urban Partnerships—to reduce urban traffic congestion. One of the pilots focused on a cross-sector collaborative effort in the Twin Cities metropolitan area of Minnesota, the subject of a 2009 report, *Designing and Managing Cross-Sector Collaboration: A Case Study in Reducing Traffic Congestion,* by John Bryson, Barbara Crosby, Melissa Stone, and Emily Saunoi-Sandgren.[20] The Twin Cities traffic congestion management initiative led to the development of relationships among state and local government agencies and between the public and private sectors. This, in turn, led to changes in existing organizational structures, processes, and norms of interaction. The report examined the use of a system for charging road users during peak traffic times in order to reduce traffic congestion. But, because of the diverse mix of stakeholders involved, the report looked at other potential congestion-reduction strategies such as increasing public transit and telecommuting. Interestingly, as the project matured over time, the mix of stakeholders changed and the dynamics of the group of participants also changed. Critical factors in the success of the initiative involved having a project manager who could connect diverse stakeholders, as well as having respected, neutral organizations and conveners who could work with stakeholders.

- **Homeless Networks:** When President Obama took office in 2009, his Open Government initiative advocated the use of collaboration and set a new tone at the federal level. This supportive attitude contributed to the expanded use and scaling of collaborative networks at the federal level. For example, continuum of care homeless networks had been promoted via a 2009 federal law. They are comprised of multiple community-based or self-organized networks representing the public, private, and nonprofit sectors that work together to address homelessness within their communities. A number of these networks pre-existed the federal program, but they were able to expand as a result of the program. In 2014, about $1.8 billion in funding was provided to nearly 400 networks involved in planning, providing, and tracking the effectiveness of a range of services to eliminate homelessness. A 2016 report, *Effective Leadership in Network Collaboration: Lessons Learned from Continuum of Care Homeless Programs,* by Hee Soun Jang, Jesus Valero, and Kyujin Jung, found that the most successful of these networks had leaders who exhibited inclusive leadership styles, were agile and adaptive, and used performance information effectively in making decisions.[21]

- **Multi-National Networks:** Collaborative ventures sometimes result in multi-national and bi-national boundary efforts. A 2011 report, *Environmental Collaboration: Lessons Learned About Cross-Boundary Collaborations,* by Kathryn Bryk Friedman and Kathryn Foster, examined U.S.-Canadian-Mexican environmental efforts that resulted in collaboration around cleaner air and water.[22] While most collaborative efforts begin informally, multi-national and bi-national international efforts are seen as needing a formal written agreement to provide needed legitimacy to act jointly: "While they find that many of the elements necessary for effective collaborative ventures are critical—such as a clear purpose, dedicated staff, and the willingness to be flexible—they conclude that a bilateral collaborative venture is often more effective when it has formal legal structures in place that enhance its legitimacy in the eyes of various stakeholders. Informal collaborations are often useful precursors to more formal efforts. These informal efforts are often not seen as having the necessary legitimacy and resources in order to be as effective as their more formal counterparts."[23] For example, formalized bi-national technical groups were created between the U.S. and Canada with a commitment to "maintain and restore the chemical, physical, and biological integrity of the Great Lakes Basin ecosystem."[24]

- **Food Safety:** Not all efforts to create collaborative approaches succeed. For example, food safety responsibilities have historically been fragmented and decentralized among 16 federal agencies responsible for implementing 30 different laws and myriad state, local, and private sector entities. This policy area may be ripe for greater collaboration but, absent a willingness by key stakeholders, little progress has been made. Even presidential directions to increase cross-agency collaboration had largely failed to better integrate the food safety ecosystem. This resulted in GAO adding food safety to its list of high-risk programs. Nevertheless, efforts began in 2010 to integrate public and private sectors as partners in food safety to define an ecosystem approach, according to a report, *Food Safety—Emerging Public-Private Approaches: A Perspective for Local, State, and Federal Government Leaders,* by Noel Greis and Monica Nogueira.[25] However, absent congressional support and a consensus for action by key stakeholders, little progress has been made according to a 2017 report by GAO—in part because the U.S. food safety system never envisioned the regulation or coordination of global production and supply chains.[26] In June 2018, the Trump Administration's government reorganization plan included a proposal to create a single food safety agency.[27]

Development of New Tools to Support Collaborative Initiatives

As collaborative networks evolved in different policy domains, supporting technologies and network models evolved in parallel to support their growth. Technologies that support collaborative networks include:

- **Social Media Tools:** The evolution of a range of electronic tools, especially over the past decade, has dramatically lowered the "friction" of operating in collaborative networks. These tools include shared networks, shared data, video chat, and mobile devices. Together, they have helped lower the communication and coordination challenges endemic with the operation of interpersonal and highly dispersed collaborative networks. As noted in Chapter Five, the pervasive use of social media in individuals' private lives has led to the rapid adoption of these tools in the work place. A study by Greg Treverton, *New Tools for Collaboration: The Experience of the U.S. Intelligence Community*, describes how tools created for social media have been adapted for use in the Intelligence Community to foster greater collaboration in operational analyses and analytic processes.As examples, he writes: "An Intellipedia wiki is continuously updated with a timeline and links to various teams, portals and documents. *eChirp,* a variant of Twitter, is used to broadcast quick updates. GlobalScene is crowdsourcing, spontaneously relating, discovering and discussing across the hidden realms of the U.S. Intelligence Community."[28] He observes that these collaborative tools contribute to greater productivity, but still have "a long way to go" in terms of broader adoption across the community, in part because organizational cultures do not provide incentives for collaboration.

  Similarly, in a 2016 report, *The Social Intranet: Insights on Managing and Sharing Knowledge Internally*, Ines Mergel examines the use of "social intranets" in several agencies (also discussed in Chapter Five).[29] Social intranets are "in-house social networks that use technologies—such as automated newsfeeds, wikis, chats, or blogs—to create engagement opportunities among employees." Mergel found that social intranets can create broader communities within agencies. One manager she interviewed said "The real key was to increase the ability for people to find each other...And to have expertise emerge that wasn't explicit in the job description of that person."[30] For example, the State Department's Corridor initiative, launched in 2010, allowed a globally dispersed staff to quickly share information about events that might not be communicated as readily through the more traditional formal diplomatic cables. The platform "supports the creation of online communities to publish information and connect with employees across the department," she notes.[31]

- **Communities of Practice as a Tool:** Another tool for collaborative networks is "communities of practice," designed around common areas of interest rather than an event. In a 2003 report, *Communities of Practice: A New Tool for Government Managers,* William Snyder and Xavier Briggs wrote "Communities of practice provide a social context for building and sharing ideas and experiences together, and for getting help from colleagues to put them into practice."[32] In an example from the late 1990s, they describe how the Boost4Kids community of practice was formed as a pilot initiative to demonstrate the value of collaborative networks. This community focused on improving results for kids, such as school readiness, health insurance, and better nutrition. Network participants included not only a range of federal agencies, but also a number of foundations and nonprofits. Thirteen localities pioneered the community, and each brought state, local, and nonprofit partners to the table, as well. Each locality also developed a "performance partnership" with a federal agency champion to help measure results and cut red tape. Nascent electronic tools included GIS maps, electronic "universal" program applications for families within the localities, and access to best practices on ways to enhance school readiness. The network model was originally a hub-and-spoke design that brokered assistance from various federal agencies, but eventually evolved to a peer-to-peer network based on community-wide conference calls that linked all participants together. Though participants found value in the network, it disbanded in the early 2000s after federal sponsorship waned.

- **Stewardship Contracting as a Tool:** Cassandra Moseley wrote a 2010 report, *Strategies for Supporting Frontline Collaboration: Lessons from Stewardship Contracting,* on the use of stewardship contracting as a tool to support frontline collaboration, specifically in ecosystem management of forest lands and watersheds.[33] Stewardship contracting involves a set of legal authorities granted to the Forest Service and the Bureau of Land Management (BLM) to contract and partner with outside entities "to perform restoration work and create local community benefit," according to Moseley. The traditional contracting approach was "an adversarial system that rewarded inexpensive rather than high quality work."[34] The new approach allowed timber harvesting in ways that reduced fire hazards, and the revenues from that timber could be reinvested within the local community to pay for other restoration activities developed by the community in conjunction with the Forest Service and BLM. This approach allowed experimentation with new strategies and resulted in bringing "additional financial and technical resources to the collaborative from non-federal entities."

These and other examples of collaborative networks show that, as governance strategies, they were beneficial and made a difference in their respective policy arenas—and that the various supporting tools have lowered barriers to using the network approach. However, in most cases, these networks could not sustain themselves over the long run because of the difficulties with working in a collaborative environment—especially in the context of the traditional and self-sustaining hierarchical model. In the 2010s, efforts were undertaken to address some of the common challenges to creating and sustaining collaboration-based initiatives.

Identifying Challenges to Institutionalization

The wide range of experimentation in multiple policy arenas in the 1990s and early 2000s surfaced institutional, cultural, political, and other challenges to the use of collaborative approaches. These challenges were explored by Janet Popp and her colleagues in a literature review of studies on collaborative networks in their 2014 report discussed earlier. These challenges can be grouped into three categories:
- Institutional, organizational, and governance challenges
- Cultural and staff challenges
- Political, accountability, and measurement challenges

Institutional, Organizational, and Governance Challenges

With government traditionally organized along bureaucratic lines of authority, sharing authority and responsibility across program or organizational boundaries is counter-intuitive. In addition, statutory constraints reinforce agency and program boundaries, thereby discouraging sharing and working collaboratively—and reinforcing organizational autonomy. Furthermore, there are often clashes in culture and "institutional logics." For example, the food safety approach used in the 1990s by the Food and Drug Administration was scientific and pathogen-based, while the Department of Agriculture's traditional approach to meat inspection was based on the use of visual "poke-and-sniff" to detect diseased carcasses.

In addition, bottom-up collaborative efforts are often seen as undermining the authority of a hierarchical system. In addition, the bottom-up efforts can be viewed as lacking the legitimacy to act. Furthermore, bottom-up efforts are administratively difficult for staff to work across boundaries and administrative systems. For example, how are employees' performance to be appraised if they work on-site at another agency? What about paying travel and training expenses? How is accountability defined? Finally, using a collaborative approach is time-consuming and requires patient consensus building to develop a shared commitment to common purposes, goals and approaches.

Cultural and Staff Challenges

Members of a collaborative initiative often lack experience working across organizational boundaries, and leadership within a network requires different styles than in a hierarchical organization. Typically, individual incentives and rewards are recognized in hierarchical, not horizontal, systems. Managers successful in hierarchical systems know how to compete for resources for their own stovepipe. In addition, they are recognized and rewarded within their own professional circles, not across disciplines or organizational cultures. Those involved in a collaborative network can find themselves isolated from their hierarchical peers and feel their career opportunities may be jeopardized by working in a collaborative environment. Yet, some entrepreneurial managers are so committed to a mission that they take these risks. For example, the leadership cadre within the BPHC, described earlier, undertook such an initiative. However, these types of networks are often driven by individual personalities and lack resilience if they lose key network participants—as was the case with the BPHC.

Political, Accountability, and Measurement Challenges

The traditional agency- and program-based hierarchical structure can dictate the distribution of how power, influence, dollars, and accountability is held. Competition is a natural trait in the political sphere; however, it can present a stumbling block in collaborative ventures. Accountability can raise problems in a collaborative network because it is often not clear to whom a network is accountable, especially in an emergent network that forms informally at first and then grows. Also, the diffusion of accountability can lead to "free riders" whose organizations benefit but do not contribute to the work of the network. For example, the early stages of the 2013 cross-agency priority goal for Science, Technology, Engineering and Math—to collaborate around improving educational instruction approaches across about 200 different programs in 13 different agencies—found participants meeting in many subcommittees but with little accountability to accomplish anything. In later years, greater visibility to top-level government leaders and clearer measures of long-term outcomes led to strengthened accountability for action.[35]

These and other challenges combine to make it difficult to sustain the use of a network approach over time, but there have been lessons learned about reducing "coordination fatigue" and costs—mainly by developing an appropriate governance structure, meaningful measures of progress, and a network culture that reinforces good behavior.

INSTITUTIONALIZATION: OVERCOMING CHALLENGES TO THE USE OF NETWORKS

Collaborative networks tend to be institutionally fragile, as seen in some examples presented earlier that were initially successful but disbanded over time. They depend heavily on the development of interpersonal trust between stakeholders, higher-level executive champions to provide a sense of legitimacy, and the availability of network leaders who are skilled in managing across boundaries and can serve as neutral brokers and facilitators rather than as more traditional top-down "strong leaders." Networking is hard work and time-consuming because of the coordination and transaction costs imposed on the network's leaders and participants. In fact, Bryson and his colleagues observe that "collaboration is not an easy answer to hard problems but a hard answer to hard problems.[36]

Still, collaborative networks can effectively address key public issues in a wide range of policy domains. As a result, efforts have been taken to reduce challenges and improve the chances for the sustainability of networked approaches. In recent years, progress has been made in three areas: (1) enhancing organizational capacity to act via the use of networks, (2) enhancing staff capacity to work in networks, and (3) developing a capacity to measure and assess the progress of networked initiatives. Probably the most prominent marker for the move to institutionalize the use of collaborative networks was the passage of the GPRA Modernization Act in 2010, which advanced progress in each of these three areas.

Enhancing Organizational Capabilities to Act

As noted earlier, there are many institutional, organizational, and governance challenges to creating and sustaining the use of collaborative networks to solve public problems. However, in the past decade, a number of new statutory and administrative capabilities have appeared.

New Statutory Authority

When the effectiveness of the Government Performance and Results Act (GPRA) was revisited in 2010 by Congress and the Administration, it expanded to include provisions that encouraged cross-agency collaboration around common priorities. The GPRA Modernization Act provided statutory authority to create a small handful of Cross-Agency Priority (CAP) Goals, designate goal leaders, and publicly report on their progress. In a 2017 study, *Cross-Agency Collaboration: A Case Study of Cross-Agency Priority Goals,* John Kamensky concluded that demonstrable progress occurred across the board: "The actions taken within each of the CAP Goals have resulted in increased performance and results in several areas that, in a number of cases, had previously demonstrated little to no progress. For example, past efforts to coordinate permitting and review processes between agencies lagged until this initiative was designated as a CAP Goal."[37]

The Trump Administration continued this effort by releasing its own set of cross-agency priority goals in March 2018. This was seen as a sign of continuity of commitment to using the process of cross-agency goals to manage multi-agency collaborative efforts. For example, one of the new priority goals involves improved coordination of infrastructure permitting and review processes. This Infrastructure Permitting and Review CAP Goal supports a major Administration priority – increasing investments in public infrastructure – by creating a central coordination point for 35 statutory review and permitting processes across 18 federal agencies.

In addition to the overarching statutory authority for CAP Goals, there are other statutory authorizations for collaborative approaches. For example, the 2014 Workforce Innovation and Opportunity Act requires the federal Departments of Labor, Education, and Health and Human Services to collaborate on an ongoing basis around implementation. The law's requirements involving interagency collaboration include "issuing regulations, developing a common performance system, and overseeing state planning." Interestingly, GAO assessed the progress in implementing this program, using as assessment criteria seven leading practices that can enhance and sustain federal collaborative efforts.[38] Having such assessment criteria is also an encouraging step toward institutionalization.

New Governance Institutions

In addition to statutory authorities provided by the new law, parallel developments contributed to greater institutionalization and sustainability of the use of collaborative networks that involved advances in technology, processes, people, and structures.

For example, a number of organizational structures have evolved over the past decade to support various collaborative initiatives. Over the past two decades, Congress has mandated the establishment of cross-agency councils for the leaders of financial management, technology, personnel, and acquisition. The General Services Administration (GSA) staffs these various councils, in addition to the President's Management Council comprised of the chief operating officers (generally the deputy secretaries) of the major departments and agencies. Together, these councils serve as a "network of networks" of the federal government. Other supportive elements include:

- A federal governmentwide online electronic sharing platform, the MAX Community, engages more than 150,000 federal employees at the operational level so they can work with colleagues in other agencies more readily than through traditional channels.
- GSA's Technology Transformation Service continues efforts to provide facilitation, training, and coordination, and serves as a catalyst for cross-agency collaborative efforts. It shares best practices and helps nascent organic networks navigate legal and other barriers to communities of practice.
- The U.S. Digital Service provides cutting-edge technology support to agencies, often by partnering with agency staffs to jointly develop solutions for high-profile technology challenges.
- Collaborative capacities have evolved and innovated at the agency level, such as the Department of Health and Human Services' innovation office, the IDEA Lab.

New Administrative Routines

The implementation of the GPRA Modernization Act led to a series of new administrative processes being put into place that provided both legitimacy for the use of collaborative networks and a degree of institutional stability. The law mandated the creation of Cross-Agency Priority Goals, led by a designated goal leader. While piloting this new approach before fully implementing it, the Office of Management and Budget (OMB) found greater strength in designating at least two co-goal leaders—one with policy authority, often out of OMB or the White House, and one with agency-level authority, often a deputy secretary. OMB also found that having a small support staff and a small fund to support individual goals was critical to ensuring day-to-day attention to the development and operation of the network of agencies involved in implementing a goal. And, having small amounts of seed funding helped get individual goals off to a quicker start than if goal leaders had to wait for funding to flow from participating agencies via different accounts.

The other important routine was the requirement that cross-agency goal leaders conduct quarterly progress reviews and post their progress and next steps on the performance.gov website. This ensured an ongoing rhythm and focal point for goal teams to continue meeting, and to engage senior government officials in helping address barriers the teams could not solve themselves.

Enhanced Staff Capacity

A second set of developments over the past decade involved building greater capacity for leaders, managers, and participants to operate in networks.

Developing Network Leadership Skills

GAO has forcefully articulated the importance of investing in the development of effective collaborative leadership. GAO noted in a 2010 report on national security threats that "no single federal agency had the ability to address these threats alone" and that there are barriers to agencies collaborating to address threats. GAO observed: "One barrier stems from gaps in the knowledge and skills national security professionals need to work across agency lines" and that interagency training and other professional development may "help bridge such gaps by enhancing mutual trust and understanding among personnel from different organizations."[39]

Two reports examined the competencies needed by senior executives for network leadership. Interestingly, a 2012 survey of federal career executives, *Collaboration Across Boundaries: Insights and Tips from Senior Federal Executives,* by Rosemary O'Leary and Catherine Gerard, found that executives themselves felt the most important attributes for their success were interpersonal and group process skills—not policy or technical expertise.[40] A 2013 report, *Developing Senior Executive Capabilities to Address National Priorities,* by Bruce Barkley, recommends creating "a small, high-level cadre of cross-agency executives," drawn from the existing ranks of career senior executives, to take on large cross-agency priority initiatives. He also offered a set of competencies as key attributes that such executives should have for success in this newly defined role.[41]

In 2014, President Obama committed to a White House leadership development program for a select group of promising career managers that reflected some of the recommendations offered by Barkley. That year-long program launched in 2015 and continues today to provide developmental experiences for a select group working on governmentwide, cross-agency initiatives.

Developing Network Participant Skills

In addition to overall leadership skills, there is a need for a greater understanding of roles and behaviors among lower-level managers and members of networks. Brinton Milward and Keith Provan wrote *A Manager's Guide to Choosing and Using Collaborative Networks* in 2006. They found that managers of a collaborative effort have to rely on trust and reciprocity rather than hierarchical chains of command. They observed that "There are five different tasks that lead to effective network management" and that these include roles where they have dual responsibilities and roles for management *of* a network but also management *in* a network. These include management of:

- accountability, such as determining who is responsible for which outcomes
- legitimacy, such as attracting positive publicity and new members
- conflict, such as development of mechanisms for conflict and dispute resolution

- design (or governance structure), including when a structure should be changed based on participant needs
- commitment, which includes ensuring support of network goals goes beyond a single person in the organization

Having such a framework for understanding roles and responsibilities provides an essential step in developing the right skills and attributes for network leaders.[42]

New Capacities to Measure and Assess Progress

In addition to developing different models for organizing networks, a number of assessment tools have evolved to address accountability and measurement challenges associated with the use of networks. One of the more prominent is the use of a technique called "social network analysis." Evelien Otte and Ronald Rousseau wrote in 2002 that social network analysis is an analytic approach for investigating social structures within organizations, such as who is linked in terms of informal working relationships. Visual maps show the social structures and networks of people or things and the strength of their ties with each other. This form of analysis helps sociologists as well as network managers to identify "nodes" within networks of key individuals.[43]

In addition to the statutory and administrative capabilities to support collaborative networks described above, a number of parallel developments are essential to the longer-term sustainability of networks. These involve developing capacities to both assess the effectiveness of networks and assure their accountability to the public and taxpayers. Traditional evaluation and audit tools are insufficient because of their complexity. Why is this? Barbara Romzek and Jeannette Blackmar, in a 2012 article, write: "Social service networks operate within a tangled web of bilateral and multilateral ties that encompass multiple vertical and horizontal accountability structures reflecting both formal and informal accountability relationships at the organizational and individual levels." They go on to say: "Accountability arrangements in networks present special concerns because of the potential for accountability to get 'lost in the cracks of horizontal and hybrid governance'."[44]

In a specific network case, Christopher Koliba, Asim Zia, and Russell Mills examined the emergency management network response to Hurricane Katrina and concluded that an accountability model for such a network would need to address three sets of relationships:

- democratic (elected representatives, citizens, and the legal system)
- market (owners and consumers)
- administrative (bureaucratic, professional, and collaborative)[45]

This level of complexity in an evaluation has, to date, been beyond what most evaluators and auditors have considered. So, how does one measure performance in networks? Romzek proposes an informal approach: that participants in networks hold each other jointly accountable. This may work in certain circumstances, but in a strongly hierarchical political system such as in the U.S., that answer does not suffice. Chris Silva writes that participants and stakeholders in a network have varying perspectives on and values about what constitutes network effectiveness. These perspectives range from individual participants in a network, the organizations to which they belong and their stakeholders, and external stakeholders—political leaders and the community at large. He says that evaluating the effectiveness of a network needs to take all these perspectives into account, in addition to the specific outcomes intended—such as reducing human trafficking or water pollution.[46]

In undertaking such an evaluation, Koliba, in a 2011 article, suggests the use of three different methodological approaches:[47]

- **Comparative case study analysis** would be "a systematic way to identify and describe performance management systems within complex, interjurisdictional networks." It also discusses the role of federal agencies in building the capacity for such systems (for example, using traffic congestion management efforts in Minnesota, as discussed earlier, as a model).
- **Social network analysis** would be used to "analyze the relationship between the kinds of network configurations" (for example, using emergency management response plans in different regions of the country as a case study).
- **Complex adaptive systems approach** would be used to evaluate network performance (for example, using the deliberative processes developed to improve healthcare delivery networks as a case study).[48]

Developing these approaches and using them will provide assurances to policy makers that sustaining collaborative governance approaches, in parallel to the traditional hierarchical forms of governing, is an appropriate investment of their political capital.

LESSONS LEARNED

Based on observations over the past twenty years, most effective collaborative networks are not mandated by law in a top-down fashion, but emerge from the community affected largely bottom-up. Participants have to work collaboratively, sharing power and authority. Nevertheless, there is a role for legislative involvement. Legislation can create conditions and grant legitimacy for organizations to work in a collaborative manner, as seen in the GPRA Modernization Act's provisions for the creation of Cross-Agency Priority Goals.

In addition to the challenges of forming, managing, and sustaining networks discussed above, several overarching lessons gleaned from two decades of observing a wide range of different collaborative networks include:

- **First, networks can be an effective tool.** When applied in the appropriate situation, with the right conditions in place, collaborative networks can be a powerful tool for solving challenges. These conditions include factors such as common goals, a willingness to share authority, and the ability to be held jointly accountable. As a result, public managers need to exhibit judgement as to when to deploy the use of networks. This was a success factor in developing the watershed collaborative networks discussed earlier.

- **Second, there is no one-size-fits-all approach or design.** Observing models of different networks in different environments is key for learning about how networks work. Networks need to be developed and applied to fit their specific context, and leaders need to build the institutional and organizational processes that can sustain cross-agency actions over time. Fortunately, as noted earlier, the 2013 report *Implementing Cross-Agency Collaboration: A Guide for Federal Managers* by Jane Fountain indicates that guiding principles have been developed, based on the experiences of pioneers in the field, that serve as useful starting points for those beginning or joining a collaborative network.[49]

- **Third, involving the right kind of people is key.** Probably the most important lesson is the role of individuals in a collaborative effort. Individuals have to be willing to bring the right mindset to the table, assume good intent by fellow network members, make activities transparent to the group, and be flexible about the evolution of the network.[50] The 2012 survey of federal senior executives by O'Leary and Gerard found that executives perceived these attributes as critical success factors in their jobs.[51]

- **Fourth, sustainability of networks is problematic.** A consistent observation over time has been that collaborative networks often die, largely because of changes in key players, the lack of legitimacy or authority, or when partners stop contributing resources—either money or people—when priorities change. In some cases, a network is a project with a clear beginning, middle, and end. But increasingly, collaborative networks involve longer-term efforts, such as networks among veteran services or foster children service providers. Further research can determine ways to ensure sustainability for such networks. The new statutory framework may help, at least for selected, top-down networks.

"Dual operating systems" will always exist in government—both hierarchical and networked. Public managers will benefit from the mix because the complexity of governing in today's world demands both.

LOOKING FORWARD

All of government will not suddenly transition to collaborative networks. And this model is not appropriate for everything that government does. As in the private sector, there will continue to be "dual operating systems," with traditional hierarchies and collaborative networks operating side by side.[52]

But, as the prevalence of collaborative governance increases, the use of "collaborative platforms" will grow as part of the broader family of collaborative network models. The platform concept is not new and has been widely adopted in the private sector. Businesses such as Uber, AirBnB, and Facebook all have a platform-based business model. Currently, platform models in the public sector are more prevalent at the state and local levels, and in other countries, than in the U.S. federal government. They seem more sustainable than some other forms of networks.

What is meant by "platform?" Chris Ansell and Allison Gash wrote in 2018: "...collaborative platforms are defined as organizations or programs with dedicated competencies and resources for facilitating the creation, adaptation and success of multiple or ongoing collaborative projects or networks."[53] They also noted that collaborative platforms "specialize in facilitating, enabling, and to some degree regulating 'many-to-many' collaborative relationships." More effective platforms do not mandate participation, but rather catalyze and facilitate voluntary efforts.

Ansell and Gash found that a platform's two key characteristics are to provide "a framework upon which and through which other activities may be organized," and relative stability over time that is easily reconfigured to respond to changes in demand and the broader environment. The use of platforms may mitigate in ensuring the sustainability of networks by capturing information on progress, knowledge, and work products. The use of a platform may also allow networks to scale and more quickly pivot in response to external shocks, such as funding cuts or the loss of a critical stakeholder.

In a 2008 report, *Integrating Service Delivery Across Levels of Government: Case Studies of Canada and Other Countries,* Jeffrey Roy and John Langford describe how other countries have adopted digital platforms to improve the delivery of services to citizens. They wrote that public services are "traditionally delivered by a plethora of government agencies via programs that are not connected to each other." They found a global movement to be more citizen-centric in the design and delivery of services using a network approach that relies on the use of digital platforms. This is being done in countries such as Canada, Belgium, Denmark, and Australia.[54]

At the U.S. federal level, this approach is not yet widely used in citizen interactions. However, the federal government has committed to the use of "enterprise platforms" for internal services, which is more about integrating services onto a common platform than using a voluntary collaborative networking approach. Examples include the move to shared services for human resources and payroll,[55] the creation of the Defense Health Agency that is a new platform for providing healthcare services such as pharmaceutical support across military services,[56] and the Department of Homeland Security's development of a multiagency operations center.[57]

As state and local citizen services platforms multiply and gain experience in delivering integrated services in the coming years, this model will likely be adopted more widely at the federal level as well.

John M. Kamensky is a Senior Fellow with the IBM Center for The Business of Government. He previously served as deputy director of Vice President Gore's National Performance Review (later renamed the National Partnership for Reinventing Government) and a special assistant to the Deputy Director for Management at the U.S. Office of Management and Budget. Before that, he worked at the U.S. Government Accountability Office. He is a Fellow of the National Academy of Public Administration.

Endnotes

1   Donald P. Moynihan, *Leveraging Collaborative Networks in Infrequent Emergency Situations,* IBM Center for The Business of Government, 2005.

2   Donald F. Kettl, *The Next Government of the United States: Why Our Institutions Fail Us and How to Fix Them* (New York: W.W. Norton, 2008), 25.

3   Helen Dickenson, "From New Public Management to New Public Governance: The Implications for a 'New Public Service,'" *The Three Sector Solution: Delivering Public Policy in Collaboration with Not-for-Profits and Business,* ed. John Butcher and David Gilchrist (Canberra, Australia: Australian National University Press, 2016), 42.

4   Charles Hecksher, *The Collaborative Enterprise: Managing Speed and Complexity in Knowledge-Based Business,* (New Haven, CT: Yale University Press, 2007); and John M. Bryson, Barbara C. Crosby, Melissa M. Stone and Emily O. Saunoi-Sandgren, *Designing and Managing Cross-Sector Collaboration: A Case Study in Reducing Traffic Congestion,* IBM Center for The Business of Government, 2009.

5   Rosemary O'Leary, "From Silos to Networks: Hierarchy to Heterarchy," *Public Administration Evolving: From Foundations to the Future,* ed. Mary E. Guy and Marilyn M. Rubin. (Routledge: New York, 2015), 88-89.

6   Barack Obama, "Transparency and Open Government," *Memorandum for the Heads of Executive Departments and Agencies,* The White House, January 21, 2009.

7   John M. Kamensky and Thomas J. Burlin, eds., "Chapter One: Networks and Partnerships: Collaborating to Achieve Results No One Can Achieve Alone," *Collaboration: Using Networks and Partnerships,* (Lanham, MD: Roman & Littlefield Publishers, Inc. 2004), 3-20.

8   Janice Popp, H. Brinton Milward, Gail MacKean, Ann Casebeer, and Ron Lindstrom, *Inter-Organizational Networks: A Review of the Literature to Inform Practice,* IBM Center for The Business of Government, 2014.

9   Robert Agranoff, *Leveraging Networks: A Guide for Public Managers Working Across Organizations,* IBM Center for The Business of Government, 2003, 85.

10 Mark Imperial, *Collaboration and Performance Management in Network Settings: Lessons from Three Watershed Governance Efforts,* IBM Center for The Business of Government, 2004.

11 Mark Imperial, *Collaboration and Performance Management in Network Settings: Lessons from Three Watershed Governance Efforts,* 13.

12 William Waugh, *Leveraging Networks to Meet National Goals: FEMA and the Safe Construction Networks*, IBM Center for The Business of Government, 2002.

13 Waugh, *Leveraging Networks*, 34.

14 John Scanlon, *Extraordinary Results on National Goals: Networks and Partnerships in the Bureau of Primary Health Care's 100%/0 Campaign*, IBM Center for The Business of Government, 2003.

15 Scanlon, *Extraordinary Results*, 46.

16 John M. Kamensky, "Making Big Plans: Bush Expands Use of National Strategies" *PATimes*, October, 2006, 5.

17 U.S. General Accounting Office, *National Preparedness: Integration of Federal, State, Local, and Private Sector Efforts is Critical to an Effective National Strategy for Homeland Security*, GAO-02-621T (Washington, DC, April 11, 2002).

18 U.S. Government Accountability Office, *Food Safety: A National Strategy Is Needed to Address Fragmentation in Federal Oversight*, GAO-17-74 (Washington, DC, January 13, 2017).

19 Donald P. Moynihan, *Leveraging Collaborative Networks in Infrequent Emergency Situations*, IBM Center for The Business of Government, 2005; and Donald P. Moynihan, *From Forest Fires to Hurricane Katrina: Case Studies of Incident Command Systems*, IBM Center for The Business of Government, 2007.

20 John M. Bryson, Barbara C. Crosby, Melissa M. Stone and Emily O. Saunoi-Sandgren, *Designing and Managing Cross-Sector Collaboration: A Case Study in Reducing Traffic Congestion*, IBM Center for The Business of Government, 2009.

21 Hee Soun Jang, Jesus N. Valero, and Kyujin Jung, *Effective Leadership in Network Collaboration: Lessons Learned from Continuum of Care Homeless Programs*, IBM Center for The Business of Government, 2016.

22 Friedman and Foster, *Environmental Collaboration: Lessons Learned About Cross-Boundary Collaborations*, 2011.

23 Friedman and Foster, *Environmental Collaboration: Lessons Learned About Cross-Boundary Collaborations*, 2011: 4.

24 Friedman and Foster, *Environmental Collaboration: Lessons Learned About Cross-Boundary Collaborations*, 2011: 10

25 Noel P. Greis and Monica L. Nogueira, *Food Safety—Emerging Public-Private Approaches: A Perspective for Local, State, and Federal Government Leaders*, IBM Center for The Business of Government, 2010.

26 U.S. Government Accountability Office, *Food Safety: A National Strategy Is Needed to Address Fragmentation in Federal Oversight*, GAO-17-74 (Washington, DC, January 13, 2017).

27 Office of Management and Budget. *Delivering Government Solutions in the 21st Century: Reform Plan and Reorganization Recommendations*. June 21, 2018: 32. Accessed on June 22, 2018, https://www.whitehouse.gov/wp-content/uploads/2018/06/Government-Reform-and-Reorg-Plan.pdf

28 Gregory F. Treverton, *New Tools for Collaboration: The Experience of the U.S. Intelligence Community*, (Lanham, MD: Rowman & Littlefield, Co., 2016), 1.

29 Ines Mergel, *The Social Intranet: Insights on Managing and Sharing Knowledge Internally*, IBM Center for The Business of Government, 2016, 7.

30 Mergel, *The Social Intranet*, 2016, 15.

31 Mergel, *The Social Intranet*, 2016, 16.

32 William Snyder and Xavier Briggs, *Communities of Practice: A New Tool for Government Managers*, IBM Center for The Business of Government, 2003.

33 Cassandra Moseley, *Strategies for Supporting Frontline Collaboration: Lessons from Stewardship Contracting*, IBM Center for The Business of Government, 2010.

34 Cassandra Moseley, *Strategies for Supporting Frontline Collaboration: Lessons from Stewardship Contracting*, 17.

35 John M. Kamensky, *Cross-Agency Collaboration: A Case Study of Cross-Agency Priority Goals*, IBM Center for The Business of Government, 2017, 87.

36 John Bryson, Barbara Crosby, Melissa Stone, and Emily Saunoi-Sandgren, *Designing and Managing Cross-Sector Collaboration: A Case Study in Reducing Traffic Congestion*, IBM Center for The Business of Government, 2009, 14.

37 Kamensky, *Cross-Agency Collaboration: A Case Study of Cross-Agency Priority Goals*, 6.

38 U.S. Government Accountability Office, *Workforce Innovation and Opportunity Act: Federal Agencies' Collaboration Generally Reflected Leading Practices, But Could Be Enhanced*, GAO-18-171 (Washington, DC, February 8, 2018).

39 U.S. Government Accountability Office, *National Security: An Overview of Professional Development Activities Intended to Improve Interagency Collaboration*, GAO-11-108 (Washington, DC, November 15, 2010).

40 Rosemary O'Leary and Catherine Gerard, *Collaboration Across Boundaries: Insights and Tips from Senior Federal Executives*, IBM Center for The Business of Government, 2012.

41 Bruce Barkley, *Developing Senior Executive Capabilities to Address National Priorities*, IBM Center for The Business of Government, 2013.

42 H. Brinton Milward and Keith G. Provan, *A Manager's Guide to Choosing and Using Collaborative Networks*, IBM Center for The Business of Government, 2006.

43 Evelien Otte and Ronald Rousseau, "Social Network Analysis: A Power Strategy, Also for the Information Sciences," *Journal of Information Science* 28, No. 6 (2002) 441-453.

44 Barbara S. Romzek, Kelly LeRoux, and Jeannette M. Blackmar, "A Preliminary Theory of Informal Accountability among Network Organizational Actors," *Public Administration Review* 72, No. 3 (2012): 442-453.

45 Christopher J. Koliba, Russell Mills, and Asim Zia, "Accountability in Governance Networks: An Assessment of Public, Private, and Nonprofit Emergency Management Practices Following Hurricane Katrina," *Public Administration Review* 71, No. 2 (2011): 210-220.

46 Chris Silva, "Evaluating Collaboration: The Solution to One Problem Often Creates Another," *Public Administration Review* 78, No. 3 (2018): 472-478.

47 Christopher Koliba, "Introduction to Performance Management in Governance Networks—Critical Concepts and Practices," *Public Performance & Management Review* 34, No. 4 (2011): 515–519.

48 Koliba, "Introduction to Performance Management."

49 Jane Fountain, *Implementing Cross-Agency Collaboration: A Guide for Federal Managers*, IBM Center for The Business of Government, 2013.

50 Fountain, *Implementing Cross-Agency Collaboration*.

51 O'Leary and Gerard, *Collaboration Across Boundaries*.

52 Hecksher, *The Collaborative Enterprise*.

53 Christopher Ansell and Alison Gash, "Collaborative Platforms as a Governance Strategy," *Journal of Public Administration Research and Theory* 28, No. 1 (2018) 16-32.

54 Jeffrey Roy and John Langford, *Integrating Service Delivery Across Levels of Government: Case Studies of Canada and Other Countries*, IBM Center for The Business of Government. 2008.

55 Office of Management and Budget, M-16-11, *Improving Administrative Functions Through Shared Services*, May 4, 2016.

56 Shannon Collins, "Defense Health Agency Achieves Full Operating Capability," *DoD News* (October 2, 2015).

57 U.S. Government Accountability Office, *DHS Multi-Agency Operation Centers Would Benefit from Taking Further Steps to Enhance Collaboration and Coordination*, GAO-07-686R (Washington, DC, April 5, 2007).

CHAPTER SEVEN

Assessing Risk

Michael J. Keegan

Highlights

- Since the 1990s, the federal government has substantially expanded its focus on managing risks inherent in its programs and activities.

- Over the past twenty years, agencies have evolved from a focus on compliance-based internal operational control and siloed approaches that address specific kinds of risk—such as financial, security, or program-specific risks—to adopt an organization-wide enterprise risk management approach.

- Enterprise risk assessments are increasingly being incorporated into other government processes, such as strategic planning, resource allocation, decision-making, and internal controls. This trend brings processes together to create an integrated governance structure that will improve mission delivery, reduce costs, and mitigate the range of critical risks facing agencies.

ASSESSING RISK

By Michael J. Keegan

In 2004, the U.S. Department of Education's Office of Federal Student Aid (FSA) established an enterprise risk management organization and hired its first chief risk officer, Stan Dore. Its goal was to strengthen FSA's financial integrity and internal controls. This management decision exemplified the agency's commitment to resolving high-risk organizational issues and emphasized the importance of proactively identifying and managing risks, especially at the strategic or enterprise level. In fact, as FSA began to systematically pursue risk management, in 2005, the Government Accountability Office removed FSA from its list of High-Risk programs.

As the first chief risk officer for FSA, Dore led the effort to develop and prioritize activities for establishing and implementing an Enterprise Risk Management (ERM) vision, strategy, and framework. FSA began to implement an international standards-based ERM approach. Most federal agency efforts relating to risk had been limited to financial and internal control activities. Dore, like other ERM champions in federal agencies, faced a limited availability of ERM guidance, best practices, and other strategic approaches to identify, assess, and manage risk in government.

Despite these challenges, FSA moved forward to establish a foundation for implementing its own ERM program. Fourteen years later, this example and experience serves as a guide for other agencies working to respond to requirements from the Office of Management and Budget (OMB) and to realize the benefits of ERM.

INTRODUCTION

This world is fraught with uncertainty, and all activities entail a certain level of risk. The increasing complexity and interconnectedness of today's society only ups the ante on the unknown. What makes a difference for individuals and organizations alike is how well they can handle an uncertain environment, with risks ranging from financial to reputational to operational. The way to manage this uncertainty is to build government's capacity to anticipate and be resilient – to prepare for the future and its effects.

Government agencies are hardly immune to the effects of uncertainty, such as sequestration, budget cuts, or a government shutdown. Along with these threats, each day federal agency leaders face similar, as well as unique, risks associated with fulfilling their respective program missions. Today's headlines are full of stories about troubled website launches, cyber hacks, abuses of power, extravagant spending, and a host of other risk management failures. The U.S. federal government has taken a hit, with the public's trust in government continuing to be low as measured in numerous surveys.[1] This view stems in part from stories about how federal agencies could have improved their operational and mission performance, had leaders taken the time to foresee and mitigate potential risks.

Defining Risk as "Uncertainty that Matters"

The first step in tackling risk is defining it. The conventional view of risk focuses on potentially negative effects. Risk management in this context typically addresses managing threats to objectives. As Thomas Stanton and Douglas Webster describe in their 2014 book, *Managing Risks and Performance: A Guide for Government Decision Makers,*[2] defining risk as merely a threat that objectives will not be achieved leaves unanswered the question of how to actively balance risks that may pose opportunities as well as threats.

Maximizing the opportunity for success requires that threats and opportunities are managed together. As government leaders allocate and invest resources and develop strategic plans for their agencies, it is apparent that not all risks are threats -- some in fact bring opportunities. All future events and the achievement of future results—the heart of strategic planning—are uncertain because they have yet to happen. In identifying, analyzing, and mitigating risk, the methods of Enterprise Risk Management (ERM) can also be a powerful resource for strategic planning and effective decision making. To that end, government leaders should view risk as "uncertainty that matters."

When does risk matter? Webster underscores that this occurs when risk has a material impact on the achievement of an agency's strategic objectives and mission execution.[3]

With uncertainties that face government widening and deepening, external and internal risks pose threats to achieving an organization's goals and objectives. Such risks include strategic, cyber, legal, and reputational, as well as a broad range of operational risks such as information security, human capital, financial control, and business continuity. Risks come from both outside and inside an organization:[4]

External risks. Factors as diverse as an aging workforce, changing social norms, or increased cybersecurity threats impact federal agencies in multiple ways. Changes in the external environment produce numerous risks over which the organization has little to no direct control. Having limited control over external risks, however, does not mean ignoring them. Instead, agencies should assess external risks as part of evaluating the impact on achieving their objectives, and the range of options available to address or mitigate that impact.

Internal risks. In addition to risks caused by events outside the organization's control, internal risks can be affected by organizational actions. These actions include internal processes, such as controls, training, values and culture. They are under the direct influence, if not outright control, of the organization.

Risks come in many different dimensions. The box below provides examples of the types of external and internal risks that organizations face, as described in a 2015 report, *Improving Government Decision Making through Enterprise Risk Management,* by Douglas Webster and Thomas Stanton.[5]

Examples of Types of External and Internal Risks

- **Hazard risks**, such as:
  Liability suits (e.g., operational, products, environmental)
  Fire and other property damage
  Theft and other crime

- **Financial risks**, such as:
  Price (e.g., interest rate, commodity)
  Liquidity (e.g., cash flow, opportunity costs)
  Credit (e.g., default by borrowers)

- **Operational risks**, such as:
  Customer service
  Succession planning
  Cyber security

- **Strategic risks**, such as:
  Demographic and social/cultural trends
  Technology innovations
  Political trends

- **Reputational risks**, such as:
  Procedural and policy mistakes by staff
  Perceptions of misuse of government resources
  Fraud or contract mismanagement

Source: Adapted from Brian Barnler, "Creating and Keeping Your Options Open - It's Fundamental," Chapter 5 In *Managing Risk and Performance: A Guide for Government Decision Makers*, by Thomas H.Stanton and Douglas W.. Webster, eds. Hoboken, NJ: John Wiley & Sons, Inc., 2014, p.123.

Ways of Managing Risks

This chapter explores three approaches to managing risks in government:

- **Use of internal control:** The U.S. Government Accountability Office (GAO) has defined "internal control" as a set of activities that provides reasonable assurance that the objectives of an agency will be achieved—specifically, effectiveness and efficiency of operations, reliability of financial reporting, and compliance with applicable laws and regulations.[6]
- **Use of siloed approaches to risk management:** The International Standards Organization (ISO) defines "risk management" as coordinated activities that direct and control an organization with regard to risk.[7] In 2006, GAO defined this as a continuous process of assessing risks, reducing the potential that an adverse event will occur, and putting steps in place

to deal with any event that does occur.[8] Risk management involves a continuous process of managing—through a series of mitigating actions that permeate an entity's activities—the likelihood of an adverse event and its negative impact. Typically, traditional risk management has been implemented in "silos"—that is, specific functions such as financial management, or specific programs such as flood management.

- **Use of Enterprise Risk Management (ERM):** The international risk management society, RIMS™, defines ERM as "a strategic business discipline that supports the achievement of an organization's objectives by addressing the full spectrum of its risks and managing the combined impact of those risks as an interrelated risk portfolio," rather than addressing risks only within silos.[9] ERM provides an enterprise-wide, strategically aligned portfolio view of organizational challenges that offers improved insight about how to more effectively prioritize and manage risks to mission delivery.

The first two approaches provide the necessary foundations for the effective use of the third. According to OMB: "ERM is viewed as a part of an overall governance process, and internal controls as an integral part of risk management and ERM."[10]

Organization of Chapter

As seen in the chart below, "Evolution of Risk Management: 1998-2018," this chapter describes the evolution of risk management policies in U.S. federal agencies over a twenty-year period. This evolution can be divided into three phases:

- **Early action:** Early efforts in the 1980s and 1990s to manage risk in government focused largely on internal and administrative controls, with some application of traditional risk management principles. Congress passed laws, OMB issued guidance, and the General Accounting Office (since renamed the Government Accountability Office) defined standards—all in an effort to prescribe how federal agencies should manage internal risks (i.e., financial, human resources, systems, compliance, and operations risks). This early emphasis on internal control was part of a burgeoning movement focused on improving accountability in federal programs and operations that addressed fraud, waste, and abuse (see, for example, the box about GAO's High-Risk Government Programs later in this chapter). Federal agencies also began to employ, on an ad hoc and frequently siloed basis, risk management approaches to manage functional risks. Risk management practice also matured generally, with the issuance of a "first of its kind" standard risk management framework and process by the international Committee of Sponsoring Organizations of the Treadway Commission (COSO).

- **Expansion:** Recognizing the benefits of managing risk from an organization-wide enterprise perspective, federal agencies incrementally expanded their use and adoption of formal ERM disciplines and principles beginning in the early 2000s. Lacking a formal federal risk management policy, agencies acted independently to leverage practices with proven track records in the private sector and had access to an increasing number of ERM frameworks and processes. The emergence of chief risk officers began in federal agencies. The coalescing of informal networks of risk management practitioners and thought leaders championed the benefits of ERM as a critical management tool. Revised OMB policy guidance on agency strategic planning and reviews suggested the use of ERM in agency strategic planning, signaling ERM as the way forward for managing risk in federal agencies.

Evolution of Risk Management: 1998—2018

1998

Early Action: Managing Risk in Government Using Internal Controls and Siloed Approaches

- Managing Risk by Internal Controls
- Managing Risk in Silos
2003
- Managing Risk Beyond Internal Control Requirements

2004

Expansion: Broadening Risk Management Approaches Across the Federal Enterprise

- Emergence of Enterprise Risk Management (ERM)
- Emergence of Chief Risk Officers in Federal Agencies
2013
- Creation of ERM Networks Across Agencies

2014

Institutionalization: An Enterprise Approach to Managing Risk in Federal Agencies

- OMB Integrates Internal Control and ERM Guidance
- OMB Guidance Requires Agencies to Create Risk Profiles
- Risk Profiles Incorporated into Agency Annual
2018   Strategic Reviews

- **Institutionalization:** Technological advances have made federal agency systems, infrastructure, processes, and technologies interconnected and interdependent, such that a risk encountered by one area impacts other operations. This interconnected environment makes the managing of risk across the enterprise more necessary than ever. It also precipitates a change in how government leaders view risk, no longer thinking about risk management as largely a compliance exercise or perceiving risks in solely negative terms as something to be avoided. With that as the backdrop, OMB revised its risk management guidance, Circular A-123, setting forth for the first time a formal governmentwide policy for how government leaders should manage risk and internal control in their agencies. Federal agencies must now implement an ERM framework that also integrates their existing internal control process.

The remainder of this chapter discusses each of these phases, highlighting how federal agencies manage risk, describing the evolution of U.S. federal risk management policies, and offering insights and best practices from IBM Center reports. The chapter concludes with lessons learned and observations of what's on the horizon for federal agencies as they implement and use ERM.

EARLY ACTION: MANAGING RISK IN GOVERNMENT USING INTERNAL CONTROLS AND SILOED APPROACHES

Unlike countries such as Canada and Great Britain, during this period the U.S. lacked a governmentwide risk management policy. Agencies complied with a host of laws and requirements that focused on managing risks associated with a specific functional activity, but no overarching governmentwide policy prescribed an approach to risk management in the federal government. This section explores the building blocks of internal control and the use of siloed approaches to traditional risk management that set the future foundation for what followed—a more strategic use of enterprise risk management.

Managing Risk Using Internal Controls

The early efforts of managing risk in government focused on internal and administrative controls. OMB issued Circular A-123 in 1981, prescribing assessment and reporting requirements for internal financial and administrative controls. Subsequently, Congress passed the Federal Managers Financial Integrity Act of 1982 (FMFIA),[11] an important step in the evolution of federal accounting—and the initial step in taking internal control and risk management seriously. In parallel, GAO developed internal control standards with its release of *Standards for Internal Control in the Federal Government* (often called the "Green Book").[12] FMFIA and OMB Circular A-123 have remained at the center of federal requirements to improve accountability in federal programs and operations. Eight years later, passage of the Chief Financial Officers Act of 1990 (CFO Act)[13] compelled the development of an infrastructure for auditable financial statements.

These laws, their accompanying guidance, and the financial management framework they built helped federal agencies arrive at a common definition of internal controls and risk management.[14]

What Are Internal Controls?

Internal controls are a set of activities that provide reasonable assurance that the objectives of an agency will be achieved. For example, the organizational objective for financial reporting is to provide financial statements free of material omission or error. Internal controls focus on operational effectiveness and efficiency, reporting, and compliance with applicable laws and regulations—they are a way to manage internal risk. These controls primarily address traditional financial, compliance, transactional, and operational risks, with a focus on risk reduction through the application of discrete controls. Risk assessments traditionally review past performance and activities and are generally not forward-looking. The risks are identified and managed in a siloed, non-integrated basis (e.g., financial reporting, information technology, or physical assets) and documented through external reporting requirements (e.g., audit reports or identified material weaknesses).

Source: U.S. Government Accountability Office, *Standards for Internal Control in the Federal Government*, 2014 Edition

---

Managing Risk in Silos

After these earlier requirements were established, additional legislation and regulations soon followed, prompting a renewed focus on internal control and the managing of risk. These efforts—largely by Congress—continued, and on some level reinforced, a siloed approach to risk management:

- **Program risk:** GAO established its High-Risk List in 1990 to call attention to agencies and program areas at high risk due to their vulnerabilities to fraud, waste, abuse, and mismanagement, or are most in need of transformation (see accompanying box).
- **Performance risk:** The Government Performance and Results Act of 1993 (GPRA) required agencies to clarify their missions, set strategic and annual performance goals, and measure and report on performance toward those goals.[15]

- **Financial management risk:** The Federal Financial Management Improvement Act of 1996 (FFMIA) identified internal control as an integral part of improving financial management systems.[16]
- **Information security risk:** The Federal Information Security Management Act 2002 (FISMA) required each federal agency to develop, document, and implement an agency-wide program to provide information security for the information and systems that support the agency.[17]
- **Improper payments risk:** The Improper Payments Information Act (IPIA) of 2002 required agencies to annually review their programs and activities to identify those susceptible to significant improper payments.[18]

Almost every one of these legislative mandates required agencies to better manage risk and improve controls in discrete areas. Virtually all of these requirements ultimately focused on a common objective—improved risk management—so that an agency's response to risk provides reasonable assurance that the organization will achieve its strategic objectives. However, these separate requirements were not strategically linked.

To comply with the requirements of each of these new mandates, agencies usually put into place risk management and compliance programs. Karen Hardy's 2010 report, *Managing Risk in Government: An Introduction to Enterprise Risk Management,* says: "This stovepiped approach to compliance is costly and does not optimize value."[19] The dramatic increase in compliance requirements, coupled with the realization that effectively managing risk cannot be achieved simply through discrete risk compliance programs in various business units, has contributed to the movement toward an enterprise-wide risk management approach in the government.

GAO Identifies High-Risk Government Programs

As federal agencies began to focus on internal control, putting the systems and process in place, GAO began identifying high-risk government programs. Since 1990, every two years at the start of a new Congress, GAO calls attention to agencies and program areas that are high risk due to their vulnerabilities to fraud, waste, abuse, and mismanagement, or are most in need of transformation. The value of this work in terms of highlighting risk management cannot be overstated. It has brought much-needed attention to problems impeding effective government and costing billions of dollars each year.

To help improve these high-risk operations, GAO has made hundreds of recommendations. Executive agencies either have addressed or are addressing many of them and, as a result, progress has been made in a number of these areas. GAO uses five criteria to assess progress in addressing high-risk areas: (1) leadership commitment, (2) agency capacity, (3) an action plan, (4) monitoring efforts, and (5) demonstrated progress.[20]

> As Don Kettl points out in his 2016 report, *Managing Risk, Improving Results: Lessons for Improving Government Management from GAO's High-Risk List,* a careful look at the high-risk list reveals useful insights and a roadmap for improving the performance of all government programs. Patterns emerge from the progress that agencies have made in getting off the list. The steps taken to get off the list are the very steps government executives should follow every day. The high-risk list is particularly useful to risk managers, chief risk officers, and agency leadership because it serves as an independent review for flagging risk areas that may be missed by agencies.[21]

Managing Risk Beyond Internal Control Requirements

As Karen Hardy chronicles in her 2015 book, *Enterprise Risk Management: A Guide for Government Professionals,* despite federal agency compliance with a wide range of statutorily required reporting requirements over the years, a volatile environment involving fraud in the financial industry "prompted a reexamination of the existing internal control requirements for federal agencies."[22]

After the passage of the private-sector-oriented Sarbanes-Oxley Act of 2002 to strengthen corporate financial reporting, OMB revised Circular A-123 in 2004 in order to strengthen internal control over internal federal financial reporting. OMB also emphasized the need for agencies to integrate and coordinate these controls with other internal control-related activities. The latter objective, according to Hardy, represented a critical shift that expanded the view of risk in the evaluation of internal controls. This shift was just one small step towards the use of ERM in government.

Risk management and internal control as implemented in the 1990s were important aspects of an organization's governance, management, and operations. However, as Hardy notes, "internal control guarantees neither the success of agency programs nor the absence of waste, fraud, and mismanagement, but is a means of managing the risk associated with federal programs and operations."[23] This is why the early phase begins with a focus on the establishment of internal control policy within the federal government; federal agencies first managed specific types of risks, like those having to do with internal systems and process that could compromise an agency's ability to operate. Starting with how federal agencies manage internal risks via internal control led to key policy and guidance documents such as Circular A-123 and GAO's *Standards for Internal Control in the Federal Government.* Throughout the years, the revisions and updates to these documents chronicle the evolving approach to managing risk in government. In fact, both documents played a role in how the federal government has moved towards adopting ERM.

While federal agencies complied with the requirements surrounding internal control, pockets of activity appeared within the government applying risk management principles to address and manage programmatic challenges. For example, the Department of Labor applied traditional risk management approaches to reduce its level of improper payments.

Department of Labor: Using Risk Management to Reduce Improper Payments

In a 2016 report, *Risk Management and Reducing Improper Payments: A Case Study of the U.S. Department of Labor*,[24] Robert Greer and Justin Bullock provide a case study on how the department developed and implemented risk management strategies to reduce improper payments in the Unemployment Insurance program. Unemployment Insurance is a jointly administered federal-state program that provides benefits to eligible workers unemployed through no fault of their own. This program is a federal-state partnership based on federal law, but administered by state government employees under state law.

In 2010, Congress passed the Improper Payment Elimination and Recovery Act. This statute set a 10 percent improper payment rate as a limit for federal programs. The improper payment rate for Unemployment Insurance had fallen from 2006 to 2009, but began to increase in 2010 and remained in violation of the statute's standard for improper payments.

Improper payments are a type of operational risk. In response, the Department of Labor implemented eight risk management strategies to combat improper payments, thereby minimizing financial and reputation risks to the program. One of the eight strategies was to increase collaboration between the states and the federal government to aid states in lowering improper payments across all of the program's elements.[25]

Limitations to Managing Risks in Silos

The early action phase was characterized by the use of internal controls and siloed approaches to manage risk in government. These efforts served two useful purposes:

- Internal controls focused on internal risks that can compromise the operation of an agency—effectiveness and efficiency, financial accountability, and the ability to comply with all laws and regulations.
- The functional- and program-based siloed risk management approaches in specific areas, such as improper payments, performance, and cyber, helped develop risk management capabilities in pockets around the government.

However, the "[most significant] limitations in traditional risk management practice," note Thomas Stanton and Doug Webster, "is the treating of risks within functional and programmatic silos."[26] This siloed approach to risk management lacked a central point of coordination and provided no basis for ensuring a consistent approach to risk management. In addition, no single organization or person focused on ensuring the development of an integrated view of risks (across all functional or organizational silos) that aligns with an overall enterprise strategy.

The 2015 report, *Improving Government Decision Making through Enterprise Risk Management,* by Doug Webster and Thomas Stanton, details key limitations to the siloed approach to managing risk, including:

- Gaps in the identification, assessment, and treatment of risks between functions, programs, or organizational subdivisions
- Inefficiencies due to overlaps in the treatment of shared risk
- Inconsistencies in the treatment of risks by various functions due to dissimilar risk appetites and approaches to risk management
- Lack of strategic alignment
- Reduced return on investment in the application of limited resources to the delivery of a portfolio of products and services[27]

EXPANSION: BROADENING RISK MANAGEMENT APPROACHES ACROSS THE FEDERAL ENTERPRISE

Recognizing the benefits of managing risk from an enterprise perspective, agencies expanded the use and adoption of the formal discipline of ERM and its principles. As Webster and Stanton note, "Despite the initially slow progress and misunderstanding of the term ERM, concrete progress is now demonstrably underway."[28] This expansion phase describes progress in key aspects of ERM. The discussion below highlights examples of its expanded use among federal agencies, identifies selected benefits and challenges of ERM, and presages the trends toward institutionalization.

What Is Enterprise Risk Management?

The Association for Federal Enterprise Risk Managers (AFERM) defines ERM as "a discipline that addresses the full spectrum of an organization's risks, including challenges and opportunities, and integrates them into an enterprise-wide, strategically-aligned portfolio view."[29] This definition provides leaders a forward-looking view of risk that can better inform strategy and business decisions. It allows for more risk management options through enterprise-level tradeoffs, versus a primary focus on reducing risk through controls. It explicitly addresses risk appetite and tolerance. Effective ERM facilitates improved decision making through a structured understanding of opportunities and threats.

Webster and Stanton sum it up succinctly in their 2015 report: "ERM is more than simply 'good' risk management as traditionally practiced in silos. The AFERM definition references 'the full spectrum of an organization's risks,' which inherently require a top-down, strategically driven approach to risk identification. The problem of 'white space' means that such a comprehensive view of risk will not emerge simply from a bottom-up aggregation of risks identified within functional and programmatic silos."[30] They also note that the need to incorporate risk management into the strategic planning process is an inherent part of any meaningful ERM program, which again requires a comprehensive view of major risks to the agency and its programs.

Examples of Federal Agencies Using Enterprise Risk Management

Implementing an ERM program takes hard work, and often the push to implement comes on the heels of a risk-related failure. The following two examples illustrate the efforts and experiences of pioneering federal agencies that implemented ERM in advance of any failures.

Office of Federal Student Aid: An Early Pioneer in the Use of ERM

The U.S. Department of Education's Office of Federal Student Aid (FSA) put in place the first formalized ERM framework in the federal government, starting in 2004. Some 14 years later, this example and experience serve as a guide for other agencies working to realize the benefits of ERM.

FSA works to ensure that all eligible individuals can benefit from federal financial assistance for education beyond high school.[31] Over time FSA has granted or guaranteed more than $1.2 trillion in student loans, with 40 million borrowers at more than 6,000 universities around the country. Given the size of its loan portfolio, coupled with a high student loan default rate at the time, GAO placed FSA on its High-Risk List of programs in 1990. In 1998, FSA was legislatively designated as a "performance based organization" which allowed it a certain degree of autonomy, and its chief operating officer was appointed by the Secretary of Education on a term contract. Some have noted that being designated a performance-based organization "helped pave the way" for the creation of a risk management function at FSA.[32]

The department's goal of strengthening financial integrity and internal controls was the primary driver behind FSA's decision to establish an ERM organization and hire FSA's first chief risk officer (CRO), Stan Dore.[33] This management decision exemplified the agency's commitment to resolving potentially high-risk organizational issues and emphasized the importance of proactively identifying and managing risks, especially at the strategic or enterprise level. As FSA began to systematically pursue risk management in 2004, the following year GAO removed FSA from its High-Risk list. As the first CRO, Dore led the effort to develop and prioritize activities for establishing and implementing an ERM vision, strategy and framework at FSA. He set out to create an enterprise-wide risk management office, which formally stood up in 2006.

FSA began to implement a COSO-based ERM framework (see box below for a discussion of the COSO framework). Since most federal agency efforts relating to risk had focused primarily on financial controls, Dore had limited ERM guidance, best practices, or other strategic approaches for identifying, assessing and managing risk. Despite these challenges, FSA moved forward with establishing a foundation for implementing its own ERM program.[34] In 2007, the then-chief operating officer and sponsor for the risk management office left FSA. FSA had several acting leaders until a full-time chief operating officer was named in 2009. The new chief operating officer, Bill Taggart, was a former bank executive and a strong supporter of risk management. He appointed a new chief risk officer, Fred Anderson, who raised the profile of the office, expanded the risk management framework, and formalized the role of risk management in FSA's five-year strategic plan.

In addition, Anderson chaired a cross-FSA Risk Management Committee, which includes FSA operational and business leaders. The committee met monthly and Taggart attended all meetings. The committee was "intended to assess and evaluate major strategic risks, establish the organization's risk profile, and set risk tolerances [across the organization]."[35]

Defense Logistics Agency: Top Leadership Support is Key

A key lesson in implementing an ERM program is the importance of top leadership support. In 2009, the then-director of the Defense Logistics Agency (DLA), Vice Admiral Alan Thompson, developed his strategic priorities for the agency, including introducing ERM into the agency.

DLA is the nation's combat logistics support agency that manages the global supply chain—from raw materials to end users to disposition—for the Army, Navy, Air Force, Marine Corps, Coast Guard, 10 combatant commands, and other federal agencies. At the time, VADM Thompson led a global enterprise with operations in 48 states and 28 countries, and fiscal year 2009 sales and services of close to $38 billion, which would place it in the top 65 on the Fortune 500 list of companies.[36]

VADM Thompson identified three key priority areas that framed his strategic direction for DLA: warfighter support, stewardship excellence, and workforce development. The second-priority area involves enhancing the DLA's stewardship of resources, for which managing risk at DLA took on an enterprise approach. In 2009, Thompson established its ERM function, with the goal of bringing together existing risk management activities and strengthening its Stewardship Excellence initiative.[37]

Prior to establishing its ERM function, DLA instituted risk-based pilot programs. These programs showed that one organizational component would sometimes identify a potential risk that another component had already experienced and resolved.[38] ERM seemed like the right solution to reduce this siloed and fragmented approach to risk management. Once implemented, DLA focused on developing a standardized, repeatable process for identifying and assessing risks, making recommendations to leadership for actions on those risks, tracking the actions taken in response, and learning from the process, to make DLA more efficient and effective.[39]

Under the leadership of VADM Thompson, DLA recognized that success would come from embedding a consistent set of risk management principles, concepts, and shared language across the agency. It established a small ERM staff office headed by chief risk officer. To leverage the inherently collaborative nature of other successful ERM programs, DLA established a broad-based ERM community of practice—encouraging robust discussion among a multifunctional management group, to arrive at an enterprise view of risks in the agency.

Expanding the Use of Risk Management Frameworks and Processes

As the use of ERM expanded, so did the use of recognized ERM frameworks, such as the international COSO and ISO 31000 standards, to guide the success of the expansion. The federal agencies profiled above adopted the COSO ERM framework to guide their implementation efforts.

Another use for ERM involved the managing of specific risks related to IT systems and cybersecurity. During this period, the National Institute of

---

Risk Management Framework Standards

Risk management frameworks provide the foundations and organizational arrangements for designing, implementing, monitoring, reviewing, and continually improving risk management throughout the organization.[40] The following two international organizations have established widely used standards:

Committee of Sponsoring Organizations of the Treadway Commission (COSO). Originally issued in 2004, COSO's *Enterprise Risk Management—Integrated Framework,* expands on internal control, providing a more robust and extensive focus on the broader subject of enterprise risk management. It was updated and re-titled in 2017 to *Enterprise Risk Management–Integrating with Strategy and Performance.* It expanded its emphasis on risk in both the strategy-setting process and in driving performance.

ISO 31000: 2009/2018 Risk Management—Principles and Guidelines. First released in 2009 and later updated in 2018, this international standard put greater emphasis on the iterative nature of risk management, principles of risk management, and the integration of risk management into governance of the organization.

Standards and Technology (NIST) released *The Guide for Applying the Risk Management Framework to Federal Information Systems*, NIST 800-37,[41] a risk management framework focused on managing risks associated with the federal information systems. This IT risk framework promotes the concept of near real-time risk management and ongoing information system authorization through the implementation of robust and continuous monitoring processes.

In 2013, Executive Order 13636 called for the creation of a Cybersecurity Framework, a voluntary risk-based strategy—a set of industry standards and best practices to help organizations manage cybersecurity risks. In addition to helping organizations manage and reduce risks, the Cybersecurity Framework fostered risk and cybersecurity management communications among both internal and external organizational stakeholders. In May 2017, Executive Order 13800, *Strengthening the Cybersecurity of Federal Networks and Critical Infrastructure,* required that all federal agencies adopt the Cybersecurity Framework. As of July 2018, an update to this risk management framework was in draft. This update adds an overarching concern for individuals' privacy, helping to ensure that organizations can better identify and respond to these risks, including those associated with using individuals' personally identifiable information.

Applying ERM to Cybersecurity[42]

As government organizations expand operations to include the use of technologies such as social media, the Internet of Things, mobile, and cloud, they inherently extend their cyber exposure. Today more than ever, agencies face an increasing number of cybersecurity risks and threats of data breaches. Cyber risk persists anywhere data exists. This creates a need for cybersecurity risk strategies to protect and manage private and sensitive information.

Government systems continue to have vulnerabilities and to be targets of successful attacks. Examples include the Office of Personnel Management (OPM) and the IRS, as well as Pentagon intrusions and data breaches compromising private information and data. Today's attackers have expanded their reach to not only include anything connected to the internet, but to also work through unaware intermediaries to launch their attacks.

To address these issues, existing ERM plans are expanding to include cyber risk assessment frameworks. The World Economic Forum's *Partnering for Cyber Resilience* report indicates that cyber risk is increasingly viewed as a key component in ERM frameworks. The report quantified cyber risk in a three-fold approach to make sound investment and risk mitigation decisions:

- Understand the key cyber risk drivers required for modeling cyber risks

- Understand the dependences among these risk drivers that can be embedded in a quantification model

---

> • Identify ways to incorporate cyber risk quantification into ERM
>
> ERM has become an integral element in organizational strategy today, and securing data and managing cyber risk must now be viewed as a key component within an organization's ERM framework. Strong IT governance coupled with a rigorous ERM approach is critical to restoring confidence in the security and privacy protections provided by the federal government.
>
> *Note: For more insights on properly addressing cybersecurity and privacy risks, please see Dan Chenok's series of blogs on the IBM Center website: http:// www.businessofgovernment.org/node/2073*

Emergence of Chief Risk Officers in Federal Agencies

Though not mandated, chief risk officers (CRO) continued to emerge in federal agencies. Each agency profiled above established the CRO role. In these and similar cases, CROs champion agency-wide efforts to manage risk within the agency and advise senior leaders on the strategically-aligned portfolio view of risks at the agency. They also serve as strategic advisors to an agency's chief operating officer, as well as other staff, on the integration of risk management practices into day-to-day business operations and decision making. For example:

- The Transportation Security Administration's (TSA) CRO serves as the principal advisor on all risks that could affect TSA's ability to perform its mission, reporting directly to the TSA Administrator.[43]
- The Defense Logistics Agency defined the role of its CRO as akin to an orchestra conductor leading a multifunctional, multitalented, and multi-perspective ensemble through a risk management score.[44]
- Though originally established in 2004, the Federal Student Aid CRO did not become a part of the executive team until after 2009. At that time FSA's chief risk officer began to connect the dots across all key business and risk oversight activities of FSA.

A 2014 revision to OMB Circular A-11, *Preparation, Submission and Execution of the Budget,* includes the first mention of the value of the ERM approach (addressed further in the next section). It also provides a valuable description of what an effective enterprise risk manager does:

- Develops, manages, coordinates, and oversees a system that identifies, prioritizes, monitors, and communicates an organization's enterprise-wide risks
- Establishes and provides oversight of policies that enable consistent use of enterprise risk management; ensures the incorporation and dissemination of enterprise-wide risk management protocols and best practices
- Establishes the procedures for determining the amount of risk an agency will accept or mitigate[45]

Creation of ERM Networks and Policy

As federal agencies began to steadily adopt the ERM approach on an ad hoc basis, an informal network of risk practitioners within government self-organized into a Federal Executive Steering Group for Enterprise Risk Management dedicated to expanding the use of ERM. This small but growing network of interested professionals worked to champion the benefits of approaching risk management at an enterprise level. In 2011, this informal network established a formal organization, the Association of Federal Enterprise Risk Management (AFERM). As the only organization focusing on the advancement of risk management principles and standards in the federal sector, AFERM is dedicated to instructing, training, and informing government managers in the field of ERM.

The work of both informal and formal networks has contributed to expanding the use of ERM in agencies, and subsequently the move to institutionalize ERM across the federal government.[46] GAO's Chris Mihm observed: "In a relatively short amount of time, enormous progress has been made in the area of risk management in government. Due to major efforts of many risk managers in the public and private sectors, risk management both as a discipline and a way of thinking has deepened and expanded significantly."[47] He called on the community to continue to expand the discipline across programs, help managers understand and calculate the risk in the status quo, and find ways to use risk management to help address governance challenges.

During the expansion phase, OMB broadened the scope of its existing risk management policy for federal agencies. This broadening, as envisioned at the time, would include the development of guidelines addressing both agency strategic risk management and governmentwide governance of risk management. In 2014, Dave Mader, then controller at OMB, acknowledged that the federal financial community was beginning to think about risk more broadly than just financial risk: "What we are doing is stepping back and thinking isn't there really a way to take the lessons learned and what we've accomplished with A-11 and A-123, and broaden that perspective across the entire organization, particularly around mission programs."[48] At that time, Mader hinted at a flexible approach, not a one-size-fits-all ERM framework.

Identifying Challenges to Institutionalization

Using ERM approaches brings important benefits, but implementing ERM is an iterative process. These benefits cannot be achieved without overcoming specific implementation challenges, such as:
- Providing the appropriate foundation, assessment, and management platform
- Sustaining support from the top

- Positioning ERM as a strategic management practice and not as an additional task
- Addressing power concentrated in silos
- Making trade-offs between competing priorities—key ERM staff participate in various special projects and initiatives that are risk-related, but do not directly support the implementation of an ERM program
- Balancing federal government regulations and requirements
- Overcoming a lack of understanding about risk management and a culture of caution
- Overcoming a lack of qualified risk management professionals and expertise
- Educating agency staff about ERM[49]

INSTITUTIONALIZATION: AN ENTERPRISE APPROACH TO MANAGING RISK IN FEDERAL AGENCIES

Technological advances have made federal agency systems, infrastructure, processes, and technologies so interconnected, and so interdependent, that a risk encountered in one area increasingly has the potential to affect operations in other areas. This interconnected environment also requires a change of mindset for how government leaders view risk, no longer thinking about risk management as a largely compliance exercise or perceiving risks solely as problems to be avoided. It is about reconceiving risk management as a value-creating activity integral to strategic planning and decision making.

OMB Circular A-11 Signals the Way Forward for an Enterprise Approach

As noted earlier, OMB Circular No. A-11, *Preparation, Submission, and Execution of the Budget*,[50] provides guidance to agencies on preparing and submitting their budget requests for the upcoming year, and instructions on budget execution for the current fiscal year.

In 2014, OMB revised this circular to encourage agencies to institute an ERM approach and leverage such efforts when conducting their annual strategic reviews. Since agency strategic plans focus on long-term objectives, agencies were to incorporate risks and how risks change over time. Considering risk management in the early stages of the strategic planning process can ensure that the agency's management of risk is appropriately aligned with the organization's overall mission, objectives, and priorities. This signaled to agencies that ERM is a valuable management tool in their strategic planning process. Such an approach, found one former federal chief financial officer, "can drive strategy, help with performance and drive budget decisions...If you know the risks, then you can make decisions on how to accept, eliminate, or manage them."[51]

OMB Circular A-123 Requires an Enterprise Approach to Managing Risk

In July 2016, OMB updated Circular No. A-123, retitling it from *Management's Responsibility for Internal Controls,* to *Management's Responsibility for Enterprise Risk Management and Internal Controls.* As the new title indicates, the revised Circular makes two significant policy changes:
* It requires federal agencies to use the ERM approach to manage risks.
* It updates policies on internal control, directing federal agencies to follow the latest standards as detailed in GAO's 2014 edition of its *Standards for Internal Control in the Federal Government.*
Ultimately, the revised Circular incorporates ERM as a part of the overall federal governance process, including internal controls as an integral part.[52]

OMB Circular A-123 is the primary guidance to agencies on risk management. Historically, the Circular focused on traditional risk management approaches—the use of internal control systems and compliance with various statutory requirements. Its revision mandates the use of enterprise-wide approaches to managing risk, citing ERM as a discipline that deals with identifying, assessing, and managing risks. The policy states that ERM is an effective agency-wide approach to addressing the full spectrum of the organization's external and internal risks by understanding the combined impact of risks as an interrelated portfolio, rather than addressing risks only within silos. This provides an enterprise-wide, strategically aligned portfolio view of organizational challenges, and improves insight about how to most effectively prioritize resource allocations to ensure successful mission delivery.[53]

According to the revised Circular A-123, risk management practices must be forward-looking and designed to help leaders make better decisions, alleviate threats, and identify previously unknown opportunities to improve efficiency and effectiveness. Agency management is responsible for establishing and maintaining internal controls to achieve specific objectives related to operations, reporting, and compliance. Agencies must consistently apply these internal control standards to meet the principles and related components outlined in the Circular, and to assess and report on internal control effectiveness at least annually.

Agencies must also develop a risk profile, a prioritized portfolio of the most significant risks identified and assessed through the risk assessment process, with priorities based on the likely impact of an identified risk on strategic and operational objectives and coordinated with annual strategic reviews. Circular A-123 complements Circular A-11 by integrating agency responsibilities for identifying and managing strategic and programmatic risk as part of agency strategic planning, performance management, and performance reporting practices. Taken together, these two circulars now constitute the ERM policy framework for the federal government.

The revised Circular A-123 also prescribes ERM development and implementation deadlines. OMB acknowledges that federal agencies are at different maturity levels in terms of their capacity to fully implement ERM. It calls on agencies to use an iterative approach to refine and improve their efforts at developing risk profiles and implementing ERM each year.[54] In support of this iterative approach, federal agencies have access to resources and tools that can assist them meet the requirements of Circular A-123 and implement ERM, such as:

- The Chief Financial Officers Council's *Playbook: Enterprise Risk Management for the U.S. Federal Government* identifies the objectives of a strong ERM process, laying out seven steps to setting up an ERM model, the so-called "pitfalls" of its implementation, how to determine an agency's risk "appetite" (the level of risk acceptable for an agency to achieve its objective), questions agencies should consider in establishing or reviewing their approaches to ERM, and examples of best practices.[55]
- The Government Accountability Office's *Good Practices in Managing Risk* identified six practices that illustrate ERM's essential elements. The selected good practices represent steps that federal agencies can take to initiate and sustain an effective ERM process, and can apply to more advanced agencies as their ERM processes mature.[56]

Integrating Internal Control and ERM Guidance

As noted earlier, the Federal Managers Financial Integrity Act of 1982 (FMFIA) requires OMB, in consultation with GAO, to establish guidelines for agencies to evaluate their systems of internal control and determine FMFIA compliance. OMB Circular No. A-123 now includes guidance for federal agencies to integrate and coordinate risk management and internal control efforts across the enterprise and between management silos, consistent with the principles for effective internal control in GAO's 2014 edition of its *Standards of Internal Control in the Federal Government*. Internal control can no longer be considered an isolated management tool.

The revised Circular A-123 also requires agencies to establish and maintain internal control to achieve specific objectives related to:

- operations, reporting, and compliance
- assessing and reporting effectiveness
- providing assurances on financial and performance reports that include information regarding identified material weaknesses and corrective actions

Agencies were also directed to develop risk profiles to document their assessments and ensure an appropriate balance between the strength of controls and the relative risk faced by programs and operations. Ultimately, the benefits of controls should outweigh the cost. This shift in policy changes the way government manages risk. To implement these requirements successfully, agencies must incorporate risk awareness into their institutional culture and ways of doing business.

Reflecting Risk in Agencies' 2018 Strategic Review Guidance

In 2018, the Trump administration continued the focus on managing risk more effectively with the issuance of OMB guidance to agencies for conducting annual strategic reviews in accordance to requirements of the GPRA Modernization Act.[57] The 2018 Strategic Reviews built on previous efforts, inclusive of an agency risk assessment that outline significant risks, identified through the development of agency risk profiles, that can impact the achievement of strategic and performance goals.

LESSONS LEARNED

Managing risk in any sector comes with its own unique challenges. Perhaps the greatest challenge for any organization is ensuring that managing risk is a meaningful process that adds value to decisions. Following are some key lessons learned, based on IBM Center reports, research, and experience over the past two decades.[58]

- **First, senior leadership is key.** Effective enterprise risk management begins with establishing the tone at the top of an agency. As illustrated by the Federal Student Aid and Defense Logistics Agency experiences described earlier in this chapter, top leadership support is key in pushing the successful implementation of ERM. Without senior leadership support, getting the necessary buy-in throughout the organization will be unlikely and an ERM effort may be reduced to just another compliance exercise that is not integral to the agency's strategic management discipline. In addition, ERM can improve agency decision making by strengthening both the quantity and quality of the information available, and offering the opportunity for a fact-based information flow that can challenge the leadership team's assumptions.

- **Second, cultivating a risk-aware culture matters.** Agency leadership benefits from embedding systematic risk management into business processes, including strategic planning, policy development, program delivery, and decision making. Doing so goes a long way to developing a positive risk culture that promotes an open and proactive approach that considers threats and opportunities. In turn, this enables effectively communicating and consulting about risk with relevant stakeholders and facilitates transparent, complete, and timely flows of information between decision makers. Building cooperation and collaboration into individual performance standards encourages staff to accept and listen to feedback about risks. Agency leadership needs to nurture risk awareness as a cultural value so that it remains integral to the way people in the agency carry out their activities.

- **Third, recognize that ERM is an iterative process.** Successful ERM is dynamic, iterative, and responsive to change. Its effectiveness depends on maturity, and agency levels of risk management maturity vary. A critical first step is to define key players' roles and responsibilities, while also creating an organization-wide committee to identify, prioritize, and plan to deal with high-priority risks. Governance frameworks are a critical start, but as the agency processes mature, their governance approach will be refined with each subsequent stage informing the preceding one. For example, FSA developed a time-bound, phased plan for implementing its enterprise risk management approach; each phase had defined risk criteria and an accountable owner, who also was responsible for continuous review and updating based on changing conditions. An upfront investment in planning and engaging senior leaders made the eventual implementation easier to act upon. Such an approach lends itself to reviewing and continuously improving the management of risk so it is not a "one-off event," but rather a process of continuous improvement based on internal reviews.

- **Fourth, enhancing data for decision-making processes are a key contribution of ERM.** The ERM discipline can enhance an agency's existing decision-making processes. ERM starts with a focus on events that could potentially happen and their classification into opportunities and risks. Keeping track of these possible events requires good data and data governance, managed at the enterprise level. Improved data management allows the enterprise to take advantage of modern analytical methods in order to quantify the impact of risks. Data analysis also enables the enterprise to gain an overall view of current risks, as well as trends and potential future risks. An accurate, useful ERM process is based on sound analytics. Both the Federal Student Aid and Defense Logistics Agency examples illustrate that implementing ERM yields benefits to an organization in managing risks and informing its decision making.

- **Fifth, managing change and learning are crucial in shifting to an ERM-based discipline.** Moving from traditional risk management, conducted in functional and programmatic silos, to truly collaborative ERM requires significant organizational change management. A complete set of policies and procedures reflecting best practices in ERM will have little value if those called upon to execute the policies and procedures resist the required changes. An effective organization needs to support ERM. To that end, agencies should not work in a vacuum, but can learn from the experience of similar operational functions or missions and benchmark risk management practices using data from ERM-focused organizations. A knowledgeable workforce is the key to successful ERM implementation, so a key lesson learned is to hire and train staff with the right skills.

LOOKING FORWARD

The risks facing government agencies are hardly static. They morph and transform in ways never seen before. It is a leadership imperative for government executives to mitigate the potency of uncertainty by managing the realities of risk. In an increasingly uncertain, complex, and interconnected world, the need for determined and adept risk leaders will be greater than ever.

Many current transformations (i.e., blockchain, artificial intelligence, robotics, and smart technologies) have the potential to make government function more effectively. Each of these advances bring unique risks, as well as their potential application in managing current risks. It is a positive change that OMB has mandated the use of ERM, that an increasing number of federal agencies have recognized the value of ERM, and that they are taking actions to make ERM an important part of their operational model to address emerging transformations beyond simply meeting external requirements.

However, today's digitally disruptive environment continues to usher in new and evolving threats. The immediate future is already taking shape:

- **Increased technological risk.** Technological advances—as represented by artificial intelligence, big data, robotics, the Internet of Things, blockchain technology, and the implications of the share economy—are transforming the risk environment and ushering in new benefits and new risk for government. Though the immediate effects of these changes may appear over time, some if not all will permeate the operations of agencies into the future. As one observer notes, "Technological risk is expected to become increasingly complex with the growth of new technologies beyond those currently recognized."[59]

  Given this reality, agency risk architecture and ERM governance will need to identify suitable ways to prioritize, respond, and ultimately manage new and potentially unknown and unknowable risks. Technological risk leads to greater uncertainty, compelling government leaders to look ahead with strategic foresight. Making strategic foresight an integral discipline within ERM can help agencies anticipate risks and prioritize resources accordingly.

- **Increased interconnectedness of different kinds of risks.** Many federal agencies now collaborate with external parties to achieve mission outcomes. This interconnectedness means these entities share data, systems, and thus a level of risk. Agency leaders must identify innovative ways to manage risk collectively in an increasingly networked and collaborative world. Couple the changing nature of how work is done with the proliferation of new technologies described above, and agency leaders must proactively address the risks associated within an increasingly complex organizational ecosystem.

- **Cultivating agile and adaptive risk leaders.** The perception of risk has evolved over time. Risk is no longer viewed as inherently negative, something to avoid, but as a potential way to create value and enhance performance. Managing risk must become an integral part of an agency's strategic mission. ERM elevates the role of the risk professional from an operational to a strategic level. As a result, risk professionals will need to expand their knowledge and experience while honing essential risk management skills. For example, today's risk leader may have a basic, albeit insufficient, understanding of the components of technological risks. To be ready for the future will require them to become cognizant of technological advances and their implications on how an agency operates. Successful risk leaders in the future must be adaptive, informed, and ready for the impact of inevitable change.

As government operates in a world of increasing speed and complexity, and as citizens expect better, faster, and more cost-effective results, managing risk becomes ever more critical. Government executives need to understand and apply tools and techniques like ERM to their specific operating environment addressing the inherent risks facing the public sector. The promise of ERM, now and into the future, goes to the core of program delivery and mission success.

Michael J. Keegan is the Leadership Fellow at the IBM Center for The Business of Government and Host of The Business of Government Hour. He has interviewed and profiled hundreds of senior government executives and thought leaders who are tackling some of the most significant public management challenges facing government today. He has more than two decades of experience in both the private and public sectors, encompassing strategic planning, business process redesign, strategic communications and marketing, performance management, change management, executive and team coaching, and risk-financing.

Endnotes

1   "Government Gets Lower Ratings for Handling Health Care, Environment, Disaster Response," Pew Research Center, December 14, 2017.

2   Thomas H. Stanton and Douglas Webster, *Managing Risk and Performance: A Guide for Government Decision Makers* (Hoboken: John Wiley & Sons, Inc., 2014).

3   Michael J. Keegan, "Introduction: Pursuing Risk Management in Government—A Leadership Imperative," *The Business of Government Magazine* (Fall 2015): 57, IBM Center for The Business of Government.

4   Daniel J. Chenok, Haynes Cooney, John M. Kamensky, Michael J. Keegan, and Darcie Piechowski, *Seven Drivers Transforming Government,* IBM Center for The Business of Government, 2017, 21.

5   Douglas Webster and Thomas Stanton, *Improving Government Decision Making through Enterprise Risk Management,* IBM Center for The Business of Government, 2015, 6.

6   This definition was first published in GAO/AIMD-00-21.3.1, *Standards for Internal Control in the Federal Government,* November 1999, 4, and slightly updated in GAO-14-704G, 5.

7   International Standards Organization, "ISO 31000:2018 Risk Management – Guidelines," 2018, accessed June 22, 2018, https://www.iso.org/obp/ui/#iso:std:iso:31000:ed-2:v1:en.

8   U.S. Government Accountability Office, *Risk Management: Further Refinements Needed to Assess Risks and Prioritize Protective Measures at Ports and Other Critical Infrastructure,* GAO-06-91 (Washington, DC, 2005): 17.

9   "What is ERM?," RIMS, accessed June 6, 2018, accessed June 22, 2018, https://www.rims.org/resources/ERM/Pages/WhatisERM.aspx.

10   Office of Management and Budget, OMB Circular No. A-123: *Management's Responsibility for Enterprise Risk Management and Internal Control,* July 15, 2016, 7.

11   *Federal Managers Financial Integrity Act of 1982,* Public Law 97-255, 1982.

12   U.S. Government Accountability Office, *Standards for Internal Control in the Federal Government,* GAO-14-704G (Washington, DC, 2014).

13   *Chief Financial Officers Act of 1990,* Public Law 101–576, 1990.

14   William R. Phillips, et al., *Public Dollars Transformation: Common Sense for 21st Century Financial Managers,* IBM Corporation, 2003.

15   *Government Performance and Results Act of 1993,* Public Law 103-62, 1993.

16   *Federal Financial Management Improvement Act of 1996,* Public Law 104-208, 1996.

17   *Federal Information Security Management Act of 2002,* Public Law 107-347 Title III, 2002.

18   *Improper Payments Information Act of 2002,* Public Law 107-300, 2002.

19   Karen Hardy, *Managing Risk in Government: An Introduction to Enterprise Risk Management,* IBM Center for The Business of Government, 2010, 5.

20   Karen Hardy, *Enterprise Risk Management: A Guide for Government Professionals* (Hoboken: John Wiley & Son, 2015): 10.

21   Donald F. Kettl, *Managing Risk, Improving Results: Lessons for Improving Government Management from GAO's High-Risk List,* IBM Center for The Business of Government, 2016.

22   Hardy, *Enterprise Risk Management,* 42.

23   Ibid, 44.

24   Robert Greer and Justin Bullock, *Risk Management and Reducing Improper Payments: A Case Study of the U.S. Department of Labor,* IBM Center for The Business of Government, 2017.

25   *Improper Payments Elimination and Recovery Act of 2010,* Public Law 111-204 (July 22, 2010).

26   Stanton and Webster, *Managing Risk and Performance,* 116.

27   Webster and Stanton, *Improving Government Decision Making,* 12-13.

28   Ibid, 16.

29   Association for Federal Enterprise Risk Managers, *Enterprise Risk Management in the Public Sector: 2015 Survey Results.* 2015, 3.

30   Ibid, 14.

31   Hardy, *Managing Risk in Government,* 33.

32   Stanton and Webster, *Managing Risk and Performance,* 140.

33   Hardy, *Managing Risk in Government,* 35.

34   Ibid.

35   Stanton and Webster, *Managing Risk and Performance*, 143.

36   Alan Thompson, *Managing a Responsive Supply Chain in Support of U.S. Military Operations: Interview with VADM Alan Thompson, Director, U.S. Defense Logistics Agency*, interview by Michael J. Keegan, The Business of Government Hour, *Federal News Radio*, April 2009.

37   Stanton and Webster, *Managing Risk and Performance*, 182.

38   Sara Moore, *Risk and Reward, Loglines*, Defense Logistics Agency, March-April 2010, 4.

39   Ibid, 3.

40   "Enterprise Risk Management—Integrated Framework," Committee of Sponsoring Organizations of the Treadway Commission, accessed June 6, 2018, https://www.coso.org/Pages/erm-integratedframework.aspx and International Standards Organization: ISO 3100:2009 Risk Management – Guidelines," 2009, https://www.iso.org/obp/ui/#iso:std:iso:31000:ed-1:v1:en.

41   U.S. Department of Commerce, *Guide for Applying the Risk Management Framework to Federal Information Systems*, 2010.

42   Rajni Goel, James Haddow, and Anupam Kumar, *A Framework for Managing Cybersecurity Risk*, The IBM Center for The Business of Government, 2018.

43   Transportation Security Administration, *Enterprise Risk Management: ERM Policy Manual*, August 2014, 9.

44   Stanton and Webster, *Managing Risk and Performance*, 164.

45   Office of Management and Budget. *Circular A-11, Preparation, Submission and Execution of the Budget Part 6*, Section 270, 2014.

46   Karen Hardy, *Interview with Karen Hardy, Deputy Chief Risk Management Officer, U.S. Department of Commerce*, interview by Michael J. Keegan, The Business of Government Hour, *Federal News Radio*, August 22, 2016.

47   Karen Hardy, *Enterprise Risk Management* 2015, 5.

48   Jason Miller, "OMB to Require Agencies to Measure Risk at the Enterprise Level", *Federal News Radio*, October 17, 2014.

49   These challenges are gleaned from two IBM Center for The Business of Government reports, *Managing Risk in Government: An Introduction to Enterprise Risk Management*, 2010, and *Improving Government Decision Making through Enterprise Risk Management*, 2015.

50   Office of Management and Budget, *Circular No. A-11: Preparation, Submission, and Execution of the Budget*, August 1, 2017.

51   Charles Clark, "OMB Prepares to Ratchet Up Enterprise Risk Management," *Government Executive*, February 29, 2016.

52   Office of Management and Budget, *Circular No. A-123: Management's Responsibility for Enterprise Risk Management and Internal Control*, July 15, 2016, 7.

53   Office of Management and Budget, *Circular No. A-123*, Section 2, 9.

54   U.S. Chief Financial Officers Council. *Playbook: Enterprise Risk Management for the U.S. Federal Government*, 2016. p.6 and U.S. Government Accountability Office. *Enterprise Risk Management: Selected Agencies' Experiences Illustrate Good Practices in Managing Risk*, GAO-17-63, Dec. 1, 2016.

55   U.S. Chief Financial Officers Council. *Playbook: Enterprise Risk Management for the U.S. Federal Government*, 2016. p.6.

56   U.S. Government Accountability Office. *Enterprise Risk Management: Selected Agencies'Experiences Illustrate Good Practices in Managing Risk*, GAO-17-63, Dec. 1, 2016.

57   Office of Management and Budget, M-18-15: 2018 *Strategic Review Guidance*, April 24, 2018.

58 These lessons are derived from the following IBM Center for The Business of Government reports: *Managing Risk in Government: An Introduction to Enterprise Risk Management,* 2010, *Improving Government Decision Making through Enterprise Risk Management,* 2015, and *Risk Management for Grants Administration: A Case Study of the Department of Education,* 2015.

59 Claire MacRae and John Houston, *Setting the Risk Agenda: Exploring the Future of the Risk Management Profession,* Institute of Risk Management, 2016, 5.

PART II: VISIONS OF GOVERNMENT IN 2040

Perspectives on the Future

CHAPTER EIGHT

A Report from Mars

W. Henry Lambright

"**Dispatch from Mars Exploration Base, Stardate July 20, 2039.**
We have landed on Mars and have established our Mars exploration
base. We landed today, the 70th anniversary of the Apollo 11 Moon
landing by the United States in 1969. Let us tell you how we got to
Mars and how the Mars 2039 mission differed dramatically from
the way the United States reached the Moon in 1969."

A REPORT FROM MARS

By W. Henry Lambright

Dispatch from Mars Exploration Base, Stardate July 20, 2039. We have landed on Mars and have established our Mars exploration base. We landed today, the 70th anniversary of the Apollo 11 Moon landing by the United States in 1969. Let us tell you how we got to Mars and how the Mars 2039 mission differed dramatically from the way the United States reached the Moon in 1969.

Our "Mars Together Project," as it is called, involves space agencies from the United States, Russia, China, Canada, Europe, Japan, Korea, India, and other nations. It is undergirded by hundreds of private sector and university partners, comprising thousands of scientific researchers from all over the world. The private sector partners are not only involved as contractors, but share in the costs of the project, an approach pioneered by Elon Musk's SpaceX earlier in this century. In contrast, the Apollo program was a strictly national project undertaken by the United States and its team of contractors.

A collaborative governance model was used to get us to Mars and to effectively deploy the expertise that was assembled for our Mars mission. The Mars Together Project is a strong contrast to the NASA-dominant Apollo model. Our Mars mission is a logical extension of collaborative programs that began with the International Space Station (ISS) and were succeeded in the late 2020's and 2030's by a global project to build a base on the Moon. Along the way, government and private sector companies found incentives to cooperate to explore the universe. Public interest in Mars was stimulated by unmanned soil-sample returns to Earth indicating strongly that Mars once had or still had life. In the past decade, the 2030s, human spaceflight and robotic technology merged in the interest of exploration.

First Steps on the Road to Mars (1969 to 2018)

What did it take to get to Mars? What made collaboration among nations, and between nations and the private sector, successful? The past was our guide to the present, 2039, and the past showed us examples of false starts, mixed results, and successes.

The first false start—actually a non-start—related to Mars came after the Apollo landing of 1969. NASA pushed for a comprehensive human space flight program that included Mars missions as early as the 1980s. President Nixon rejected this proposal, holding human spaceflight in low-Earth orbit via the space shuttle. A second false start came in 1989. President George H. W. Bush proposed a Space Exploration Initiative to return astronauts to the Moon and then advance to Mars. When the possible cost of such a program leaked, Congress refused to fund the effort. It was aborted.

The road to Mars in 2039 also included projects with mixed results. In 2004, President George W. Bush announced his Vision for Space Exploration plan, along with Project Constellation. Vision for Space Exploration was akin to George H. W. Bush's program. It got underway but, in February 2010, President Barack Obama terminated it. Parts of the program were resurrected by Congress in a presidential-congressional compromise in October 2010. Obama substituted an asteroid mission for Bush's goal of a Moon landing, and called for reaching Mars in the mid-2030s. The Obama Administration emphasized commercial crew and delivery to the International Space Station. The 2010 compromise provided for NASA's development of a rocket (Space Launch System) and spacecraft (Orion) capable of taking astronauts to deep space. In 2018, President Trump ended the asteroid mission, and brought back a mission to the Moon with Mars the ultimate objective.

The road to Mars also included the ExoMars project, which was driven by the European Space Agency (ESA) and had mixed results. This was a robotic program designed in the Obama years to help answer the question of life on Mars. It aimed to return a sample of Mars soil to Earth for scientific examination. The program was initially led by ESA and NASA, and it entailed a sequence of missions. But the United States dropped out of the partnership as a lead funder owing to domestic budget troubles. ESA turned to Russia to keep ExoMars going, although delayed.

The International Space Station was not sold as a Mars mission, but NASA surely saw it as a "next logical step" beyond the shuttle in that direction. Moreover, it was a successful example of international space cooperation. Launched by President Reagan in 1984, ISS achieved "assembly complete" in 2011, and continued in operations during the decade of the 2020s. ISS served as a model of collaborative partnership for us in which the United States served a "managing partner" role of an enterprise embracing five space agencies and fifteen sovereign nations.

ISS was initiated during the Cold War to compete with the Soviet Union's space station, MIR. It was saved in 1993 as a post-Cold War symbol of cooperation between the United States and Russia by President Clinton. ISS partners included the United States, Russia, ESA, Japan, and Canada. Also involved were commercial companies that delivered cargo and later astronauts. Whatever else may be said of ISS, it was a remarkable success as a collaborative project, and helped make the Mars Together Project's mission in 2039 possible.

Another key step to Mars was the "roadmap" to Mars published in 2018 by the International Space Exploration Coordination Group (ISECG). ISECG was initially formed in 2007 after Bush's Moon/Mars decision and was established as a mechanism for sharing ideas and information. Members included the United States and space agencies from 13 other participants, including Australia, Canada, China, ESA, France, India, Italy, Japan, Republic of Korea, Russia, Ukraine, United Arab Emirates, and the United Kingdom. The ISECG's

2018 "Global Exploration Roadmap" was a technical roadmap, not a political or administrative design. The roadmap was consistent with then-US policy that made the Moon—a lunar base in particular—a key interim step.[1]

Becoming More Collaborative (2018-2030)

Following planning, in 2022 a group of nations and private sector companies agreed to create the Mars Together Project with a 2039 landing goal. Crucial to the success of this effort were key decisions on who does what, how, why, and when. The participants assumed (correctly) that NASA and other partners would accompany flight missions to the Moon and Mars with rigorous research and development to create new technologies to speed transport, bring down costs, and increase safety. For example, in-space propulsion technologies, were necessary, along with technologies enabling human stays on the Moon and Mars.

The path to Mars began with the International Space Station providing relevant knowledge about exploration and travel to Mars. Knowledge about the human impact of long-duration spaceflight was crucial. Astronauts on ISS suffered bone weakening and immune system deficiencies. Some astronauts also seemed to have alterations of DNA. Long-duration spaceflight was essential to Mars exploration, and ISS provided us with experience at long durations. It was necessary to learn the impact of space travel on humans, and how to mitigate negative impacts. Research included the psychological impact of being distant from Earth and loved ones. ISS showed us that humans from very different cultures and languages could work together. In addition, missions to the Moon during the 2020s proved a great testbed for our mission to Mars. We also learned how to work together as a team on the ground, as well as in space.

Policy shifts were made in the 2020s. The United States ended its role on the International Space Station and diverted funds to the Moon and beyond. During this decade, NASA relinquished its leadership in low-Earth orbital flights, and begin to move more aggressively toward the Moon and Mars in preparation for the 2030s.

Due to its age, the International Space Station mission ended in the late 2020s. Starting in the 2020s, newer, smaller space stations were launched and run by the private sector and other nations. Russia assembled its own space station in low-Earth orbit. China began a small space station in the 2020s and built and deployed larger space stations in the 2030s. The United States and NASA, in partnership with other nations and the private sector, began a robotic presence on and around the Moon in the late 2020s. The United States and China, previously rivals, furthered mutual exploration goals as partners throughout the late 2020s and early 2030s.

Exploring the Moon in Preparation for Our Trip to Mars (2030-2039)

During the decade of the 2020s, NASA and its partners (other nations and the private sector) built a small space station to go around the Moon as a step between the International Space Station and a Moon base. A space station orbiting the Moon, operating in 2030, enabled communications between Earth and the Moon and served as a vehicle from which international astronauts were able to guide robots and humans in lunar tasks. This outpost continued the International Space Station's function of studying how humans adapted to journeys away from Earth. The lunar outpost was 250,000 miles away, in contrast to the ISS's 250 miles, and astronaut stays exceeded one year. We were breaking the umbilical cord to Earth.

Our next step toward Mars, in the early 2030s, was to land and operate on the lunar surface. Other nations and the private sector also built landers and ascent vehicles. A lunar base was urged by the European Space Agency, which had proposed a "Moon Village" earlier, and it played a significant role in developing the Moon base. ESA, NASA, and their partners developed techniques to turn lunar materials into resources astronauts can use to sustain a presence. "Living off the land" was a requirement for our stay on Mars. Establishing a base on the Moon prepared us for that task on Mars. Given its minimal gravity, the Moon served as an ideal point of embarkation to Mars for humans and supplies. As with the International Space Station, NASA needed to pioneer, develop, and avoid becoming an "operating" organization on the Moon. The Red Planet was our goal.

With the Mars Together Project in place in the early 2030s, full attention was given to landing on Mars. We employed new propulsion and habitat technologies. We advanced techniques demonstrated on the Moon. Our first key success was an orbital outpost around Mars, a small space station around the planet. It helped direct robotic activity on the Martian surface, some of which was geared to establishing habitation and in-situ resource-conversion facilities.

In order to land on Mars in 2039, we required multiple transportation, navigation, communication, and other services. The Mars Together Project partners participated in planning and facilitating our Mars mission. Our achievement of landing on Mars was multi-national and multi-sectoral. In addition, the public participated through social media all along our trip to Mars.

Success Factors in our Trip to Mars

The Mars Together Project, declared in 2022, has reached its goal of landing on Mars. What critical factors brought our mission to its successful landing on Mars?

Success Factor One: Collaborative partnership and leadership. Collaboration embraced many nations and private companies. The overall "managing partner" was the United States and NASA. Senior partner status was based on who invested the most money and personnel in the project, and who took the greatest risks in moving outward towards Mars. Partners made policy mainly through consensus—using a "heads of organizations" committee. The Mars Together Project coalition had decided on roles and authority at the outset of the project. There were disagreements, but partners worked through them.

Success Factor Two: Inclusive partnership. Members of the project included all International Space Station partners plus additional nations and the private sector. It took time to bring China aboard, but China joined at the lunar-landing stage in spite of political opposition in the United States. China was going to go to the Moon and Mars eventually and was already investing more money and talent in doing so than any other nation aside from the United States. It was better for all if China was part of the project team to share costs and risks. NASA, as project catalyst, kept its aim on the goal. It led in developing capabilities, deploying hardware, using that hardware, and then relinquishing control as it advanced to the next step. Others took over operations of each specific milestone.

Success Factor Three: Interdependence. What motivated the partners to stay together was the realization that so ambitious a goal—a Mars landing in 2039—required multi-institutional cooperation. There was no practical alternative given financial realities. This meant a division of labor in which different organizations took the lead in different facets of the project. The partners in the Mars Together Project established goals and division of labor at the outset and sustained both throughout the project. Trust and transparency were observed. The US, as collaborative leader, made choices openly and distributed information to all members of the team as soon as possible whenever possible. It exercised "power with," not "power over."

Success Factor Four: Personal relationships and project cohesion. These factors developed among national and private sector participants. Cooperation involves people. The heads of organizations who served for long periods of time developed personal rapport. Political skills also proved crucial. This domestic-international maneuvering required not only political and managerial skill, but diplomatic talents of a high order.[2] Given the length of the project, a succession of NASA administrators demonstrated such political, managerial, and diplomatic skills. It was necessary to buffer the project from internal and external forces.

The success factors discussed above took the Mars Together Project from a concept to a launch to the Martian surface. The project required nations, government agencies, and private sector companies to think big and "outside the box" about ends and means.

Ben Darius, National Aeronautics and Space Administration, United States

Katie Bryce, Joint-company Representative, Mars Together Project

Chen Ming, China National Space Administration

Yuri Ivanov, Roscosmos, Russia

Otto Wernher, European Space Agency

W. Henry Lambright is Professor of Public Administration and International Affairs, and Political Science at the Maxwell School of Syracuse University. He is author or editor of nine books, including Powering Apollo: James E. Webb of NASA, and Why Mars: NASA and the Politics of Space Exploration. He has also written several studies for the IBM Center, the most recent of which is Leadership, Change, and Public-Private Partnerships: A Case Study of the Transition from Space Shuttle to Commercial Space Flight. He is a Fellow both of the National Academy of Public Administration and American Association for the Advancement of Science.

Endnotes
1   International Space Exploration Coordination Group, NASA, *The Global Exploration Road-map,* (Washington, DC, January 2018).
2   Mark Boyer, "Issue Definition and Two-Level Negotiations: An Application to the American Foreign Policy Process," *Diplomacy & Statecraft* 11, No. 2, (2000).

CHAPTER NINE

Engaged Government:
Five Predictions for 2040

Lora Frecks

"Volunteers will be treasured by government. Volunteerism will provide government with access to expertise not otherwise available. Volunteerism will have a dollar cost but, when organized properly, volunteerism will save government both time and money. However, the most valuable benefit of volunteerism will be increased trust in government."

ENGAGED GOVERNMENT: FIVE PREDICTIONS FOR 2040

By Lora Frecks

By 2040, we will be nearing the end of the Internet Revolution. As the Industrial Revolution altered how we organized labor at the start of the twentieth century, the Internet Revolution changed how we share information and work. Looking to the Post-Internet-Revolution Era, we can make some predictions based on identifiable trends. What will an engaged government look like in 2040? To answer that question, this chapter presents five predictions:

- Prediction One: A more agile government
- Prediction Two: An increased reliance on artificial and augmented intelligence (AI)
- Prediction Three: The ubiquitous need for collaborative skills
- Prediction Four: The rise of volunteerism
- Prediction Five: Increased citizen trust in government

Prediction One: A More Agile Government

Aided by the quality and quantity of data available from artificial and augmented intelligence (Prediction Two) and the support of a more trusting public (Prediction Five), government organizations large and small will embrace an agile approach to problem solving. Government will experiment with small trials of multiple innovative solutions derived from a wide variety of sources. Government will alter its plans in response to evolving data and feedback.

Nearly all problems addressed by government will benefit from a more agile approach. Innovation will become the norm. For example, in its efforts to provide potable water to the public, an agile 2040 government will run dozens of small trials in multiple locations, testing different types of water quality sensors and systems that automatically measure and report water quality. These mini-trials will provide valuable data for deciding which sensors and systems are best used under specific circumstances. With the idea that water conservation leads to less potable water loss, agile governments will run small trials to test which water conservation methods work best, which have the greatest impact in specific areas, which have the most public support, and how best to communicate new conservation policies to residents. At any point, during either the testing or the implementation of plans derived from the testing, an agile government will stop, reassess, and decide to adjust the plan as needed.

A more agile government will also have a different approach to long-term problem solving. Once a solution is chosen and the plan implemented, government will periodically collaborate with the public and other partner organizations to assess how well the solution is working and whether changes are needed. These assessments could be triggered by a preset calendar term, which may be overridden by a predetermined number or severity of concerns from the public, organizations, or government employees. The assessments will be regular events with all parties understanding the norms necessary to productively reach decisions. In 2040, participating in assessments will be viewed as a civic duty similar to voting or jury duty.

In our potable water example, an assessment could be triggered from concerns raised by contractors maintaining water sensors, residents worried about a change in their tap water, a business planning to greatly increase its water consumption, or government employees analyzing data. Notice of a formal assessment and the necessary timeframe will then be issued and the participants (some required and some self-selected) will gather. Collaborative skills (Prediction Three) and more public trust in government (Prediction Five) will be critical to the success of these assessments.

What is Agility?

This prediction on agility is derived from agile software development. The term "agile" has been applied in a wide variety of situations and fields. Agile development was first used to describe an iterative process where, instead of coding a program completely from start to finish, the process stops at several points to reevaluate the goals and progress of the program. During any of these reassessments, a new direction may be chosen for moving forward, if it's deemed appropriate. In other words, agile approaches don't have to stick to the original plan. Instead, plans change and adapt as the original plan is implemented. In 2040, the operations of government will follow a more agile approach and have the ability to swiftly change course when needed. For a more detailed discussion of agility, see Paul Gorans and Philippe Krutchen, *A Guide to Critical Success Factors in Agile Delivery*, IBM Center for The Business of Government, 2014.

Prediction Two: An Increased Reliance on Artificial and Augmented Intelligence (AI)

AI will increase the volume and sources of data collected and decrease the amount of "drudge work" which currently requires lots of human attention, time, and energy. AI will generate two giant leaps forward for government. First, it will provide government with the information necessary to make informed decisions in ways never possible before. Second, it will free employees to focus on data quality and using data to make better decisions.

The rise of AI will be a radical change for government. Executives will have more time to consider and evaluate the work to be done rather than spending all their time overseeing the day-to-day operations of government. There will be multiple databases of information available to government for answering questions surrounding any issue under consideration.

Every field will be impacted. Remote sensors will collect and report information from many sources. Like the water quality sensors discussed earlier, sensors will track metrics relevant to the weather, traffic patterns, community health, criminal activities, economic development, environmental conditions and usage of public resources such as parks, recreational facilities, buildings and roads. Continuing advancements in technologies with increasingly more affordable pricing will make the testing of almost anything possible.

Government will only be limited by its imagination and what society decides to allow government to measure. Such augmented intelligence will enable government to quickly detect disease outbreaks and protect vulnerable populations. Government will be able to better predict when weather conditions and road usages will require extra work to maintain roads. Economically, government will have a host of new tools for predicting when a region or individual household requires access to public assistance programs. AI will enable the government of 2040 to be more predictive than reactive.

Government employees will spend their time in different ways. Thinking through and discussing decisions takes time. These discussions will require new skills to successfully navigate change. Not everyone will have to be an expert in everything, but they will need a basic operating knowledge of data collection, management, analysis, knowledge sharing and the ethics surrounding these processes. They will also need to learn how to work with others who possess the necessary expertise in other policy and technology fields.

By 2040, government will have developed guidelines and general practices for the use of AI. Government and the public will have agreed on standards for protecting confidential information and where to draw the line between an individual's privacy rights and the good of the larger population. Government will have rules and norms on how data is accessed. The public will be comfortable with the flow of information and will benefit greatly from the use of "augmented intelligence," where artificial intelligence supports a human decision. After much testing, routine decisions will benefit greatly when AI supports human decisions.

Prediction Three: The Ubiquitous Need for Collaborative Skills

With the extra time provided by artificial and augmented intelligence, government employees will be able to invest time in new ways to work with each other and to work with the public. Collaboration will be necessary, because problems will become more complex. This rise in complexity will derive from our ability to perceive new levels of intricacy in the problems we face. In 2040, it will be impossible for one person or organization to have all the skills, knowledge, and resources needed to understand or solve a particular problem.

To return to the potable water 2040 example, the sensor selection process will require collaboration between sensor engineers, water system managers, water system maintenance workers, health professionals, politicians, statisticians, and community members. This will involve collaboration across government departments (public works, public health, a data analysis team) as well as with the private sector (water sensor providers) and the public. The expertise of all parties will be valued and used in 2040 for making decisions.

Collaboration will require mastery of a diverse skillset including communication, negotiation, storytelling and project management skills, and competence with the ever-evolving technologies supporting collaborative efforts. Many of these soft skills have seldom been taught in schools. Universities will add collaboration to their curriculums.

Collaborative skills will be used in many different ways. From our potable water example, good communication skills enable participants to clearly be understood and to recognize when accommodations in communication modes or styles are necessary. Training in negotiations sets expectations for making compromises and adopting a standard of amicable behavior during discussions. Storytelling helps each individual and group share their perspective and reasoning in a manner easily comprehended by others. Storytelling is also useful in conveying not only the level of importance of the information being shared, but also why it is so important. Project management skills allow all parties to appreciate the volume of work to be done and the associated expected timeframes.

Prediction Four: A Rise in Volunteerism

By 2040, government employees will regularly produce public services side-by-side with volunteers. Community members will be frequent and active volunteer participants in the work of government. Volunteers will provide both labor and input in the form of ideas, feedback and opinions. Today, there is an ebb and flow of employees between government and the private sector. By 2040, government will have a similar ebb and flow between volunteer and paid employees.

This influx of volunteers will be driven by several forces. First, as the nation's population ages, more people will retire and seek ways to remain actively involved in their communities. Second, the increased use of artificial intelligence and augmented intelligence for routine tasks will give citizens more time to engage with the community on higher-level activities. Third, people will want to contribute to society and help solve the problems facing their communities and the nation.

Volunteers' "nonemployee" status will require management and operational adaptations to avoid problems for either the government or the volunteer. Governments will develop guidelines for identifying the line between volunteer work and paid employment. A spectrum or matrix of employment and volunteering will develop.

Government will also need to develop ways for inventorying volunteers' skills, desires, focus areas, past experiences, availabilities, goals, commitments, needs and expectations. Their expectations should align with organizational needs. Such a system will require frequent updating and AI will assist in maintaining a complex volunteer tracking system. Volunteer managers will become masters at interacting with these tracking systems.

Volunteers will be treasured by government. Volunteerism will provide government with access to expertise not otherwise available. Volunteerism will have a dollar cost but, when organized properly, volunteerism will save government both time and money. However, the most valuable benefit of volunteerism will be increased trust in government.

Prediction Five: Increased Citizen Trust in Government

Trust has a value that societies often don't recognize until it's gone. Trust is also something difficult to regain once lost. Government has been coping with a loss of public trust since the 1960s. When viewed as something that can be gained or lost, it becomes clear that trust is a resource. In 2040, trust will be perceived as a valuable resource.

Trust is also the means by which government will obtain the ability to risk the mistakes that happen when solving problems. National and local problems are far more difficult to address without the public's trust. Additionally, trust will enable governments to make long-term investments. In terms of management and operations, trust buys governments time and goodwill, with the public being well-served.

Three changes in government operations will lead to large increases in public trust in government by 2040.

First, governmant will include volunteers in its work. Government organizations that invite citizens into the work of government will be more open and trusted by the communities they serve. This manifests in the form of engagement and participation when government asks the public for ideas or input regarding what should be done or feedback regarding what government is presently doing or has done in the past. Both engagement and participation are public investments in government. They are also a means by which the public learns about government and its employees. This knowledge demystifies government decisions and actions. In 2040, most government operations will routinely include both public engagement and participation.

Second, governments will devote more time and effort toward making operations and decisions transparent. This transparency will be manifested in communications between government and the public. These communications will include sharing datasets like those described in Prediction Two above. They will also include information about how government operates, what government does, who runs each portion of it, and how the public can contact government. In 2040, it will be unacceptable for anyone to not be able to easily and quickly find answers to their questions about government.

Third, frequent, well-organized, productive, and thoughtful interactions between government and the public will generate trust. Today, trust in government is most visibly demonstrated by votes for public bonds to invest in infrastructure such as roads, educational efforts, or economic development investments. In 2040, there will be new, regular, and visible acts of trust in government. With enough support, community members will be able to petition that specific topics be added to ballots. Moreover, there will be public forums for government issues to be discussed. There will be a means for the public to suggest problems for government to solve and provide feedback for how solutions are progressing.

In 2040, the above three changes will take place via multiple platforms, locations, and times. Government will have determined (likely through small trials) how best to ensure that these options are accessible to all segments of society. In addition to making sure that information is physically or digitally available, governments will make sure it is understandable in terms of language, reading levels and cultural references. Whether working with digital interfaces, physical offices or phone systems, government interactions will be designed and tested to ensure accessibility for all in 2040. Differences in sensory abilities, mobility, comprehension, educational levels or any other areas will not hamper anyone's ability to interact with their government. Governments that listen to and talk with community members and organizations are governments that can be trusted.

Lora Frecks is a public administration doctoral candidate at the University of Nebraska at Omaha. Previously, Ms. Frecks managed a public medical research university's intellectual property portfolio. Continuing her collaborative work with innovators and inventions, she's volunteered with other civic hackers in Nebraska and serves as the treasurer for the American Society of Public Administration's Section for Science & Technology in Government. Her research focuses on the co-production of services and resources by community members, governments and nonprofits.

CHAPTER TEN

Networked Government: Managing Data, Knowledge and Services

Lori Gordon

"...by 2040, the federal government will disband its traditional agency structure and will establish networked teams to perform government work. These teams crowdsource the priority topics or challenges of the moment, then bring cross-disciplinary talent, research, and ideas to develop solutions that they tailor to each individual citizen."

NETWORKED GOVERNMENT: MANAGING DATA, KNOWLEDGE AND SERVICES

By Lori Gordon

By 2040, given rapid advances in technology, the federal government will radically improve its ability to engage and involve more of the American public in its policy and administrative processes. Through a new organizational structure less focused on the institution and more focused on communities of interest and a redistribution of responsibilities, the re-engineered government will be more accountable to, and reflective of, its constituency—and more nimble and able to shift priorities, policies, and programs in strategic directions. These successes result from resolving challenges posed in earlier decades by some of the very technologies that the government was betting on to carry it into the future.

As a result, by 2040, the federal government will disband its traditional agency structure and will establish networked teams to perform government work. These teams crowdsource the priority topics or challenges of the moment, then bring cross-disciplinary talent, research, and ideas to develop solutions that they tailor to each individual citizen. To help lead this effort, the government will recruit non-traditional and less-represented individuals—including newly patriated American citizens and younger Americans.

Establishing a New Managerial Class in Government

To organize this new redistribution of decision making and responsibilities, by 2040 the government will establish a new managerial class that redesigns how data, knowledge, and services flow across digital pathways and provide an evolving variety of service offerings that reflect society's changing needs and requirements.

Data Managers will oversee a virtual government workforce comprised of teams that aggregate data in digital workspaces and process it almost instantaneously via the eighth-generation wireless network. Volumes of local anonymized data on transportation, energy, and municipal services that were once only used by insular Smart City ecosystems to increase their efficiency and reduce costs will be fed across state, regional, and even international networks to public and private organizations, to enhance processes and systems at global scale. Data will be stored in distributed ledgers in countless applications across the homeland security, financial, energy, and healthcare sectors and their supply chains.

Knowledge Integration Managers will bridge knowledge, methods, data, and investigative communities. They will serve as catalysts and conveners, bringing together disciplines and experts from different domains to pursue shared research challenges. They will proactively recruit underrepresented or non-traditional thought networks into government operations. They will train employees on how to interface with their non-human counterparts, determining when artificial intelligence (AI) will lead or augment the human. They will forge stronger ties with universities and other learning centers. They will place students at the cusp of resolving significant national security challenges—often ideated from collage campuses—which will resolve significant workforce pipeline issues and skills gaps in cybersecurity and other STEM fields that were raised in decades prior. From an organizational perspective, Knowledge Integration Managers will also deconflict or synchronize similar or redundant government initiatives.

Customized Services Managers will use the data aggregated by Data Teams and analyzed by Knowledge Integration Teams to provide tailored resources and services to constituents at the community level, which includes everything from prescribing medicine to veterans to providing emergency kits to disaster victims. With the ability to produce tools and resources onsite, the federal government will soft-pedal its role in coordination and logistics, enabling local and state responders an expanded role. The Customized Services Teams will create learning tools in virtual reality and a "in-a-box" so that generalists will be able to do this work—specialists no longer need apply. These virtual cross-discipline networked teams will develop tailored services and solutions that replace government departments and agencies by 2040.

The Data Management Function: Crowdsourcing Citizen Input

After setting up a management system and distributed workforce that bridges disciplines and domains, in 2040 government will focus on data management. It will be clear that new models in societal-government engagement are needed, and that these new collaborations could be based on the handling of these data vaults. Reaching into the technology and scientific communities, Data Managers will peel back how virtual reality, augmented reality, machine learning, and the Internet of Things (IoT) are crunching volumes of unstructured data, and how they can better amass even larger amounts of it. Amidst a world of 'smart' everything that thrives on new ways to analyze data, the government will ask for bold answers to big questions: How can we improve how data is being created, collated, curated, and consumed across the sensing spectrum to do things smarter, faster, better? At what risks? And, as we gather more data, how do we manage the additional questions and unknowns that result?

The Data Network will reimagine and reorganize data sensing and feedback loops so that the government can gain rich insights from citizens to inform knowledge-driven decisions. As citizens place a digital imprint on every commercial and retail purchase that they make, Data Managers will realize that people are also making their values, needs, wants, and ethical and moral demands transparent. Government will recognize the value in capitalizing on this concept as a way to capture constituent input, and so it will develop a variety of crowdsourcing mechanisms to elicit better citizen participation in policy and acquisition processes, creating the ultimate "data lake." Without needing to procure costly studies or to requisition surveys, government will have instantaneous citizen input on issues that range from early childhood services to flood management to space security.

Data Managers will set up two types of crowdsourcing initiatives:

- **In active crowdsourcing,** government will establish a social media app that tees up issues prior to a congressional vote so that constituents can pass their opinion to their congressperson.

- **In passive crowdsourcing,** government will establish thousands of IoT sensors across a city to pulse instantaneous citizen-level input on transportation, healthcare, municipal services, and the environment. Through 'adaptive optics' the government will be able to remove distortion and data noise from high-tech sensing mechanisms and communication tools. These will include gesture-controlled devices, iris recognition systems, and sensor swarms that will enable coordination of their activities and decisions about what to measure—and where—through a self-learning system directing their movements and data collection. Light-emitting drones that sense and follow movement and activity around the city will determine citizen feelings based on how people respond to an 'issue' (e.g., placement of a stoplight or recycling bin). In the future, privacy protection technologies will enable a rich personalized experience to be implemented in a way that protects individual data and gives individuals greater control over their information exchange with government.

These crowdsourcing practices will balloon voter turnout and capture feedback from those who are often underrepresented. Just as people in the 2020s had become increasingly addicted to their personal devices, by 2040 this will translate to them becoming consciously attuned to continuous civic engagement, connecting to their city as they move around town, and owning their rights as a citizen to participate in civic processes.

The Knowledge Integration Management Function: Taking a Cross-Discipline Approach to Analyzing Data

These large governmental data sets will be observed by Knowledge Integration Teams that bridge talent and research in a cross-discipline approach to investigate ever-evolving citizen needs. Using crowdsourced data, they will build heatmaps of high-priority issues. A net assessment will result in local, regional, national, and global issues that affect citizens—from rising cyber dependency, to increasing income and wealth disparity, to the shifting landscape of geopolitical power and international governance. This will trigger government processes to move resources and develop responsive solutions.

To do this well will require entirely new actors—from volunteer groups to nascent organizations which are both passionate about mission—to bring rich ideas and analytical techniques into the process. Because these groups will encourage exploration and a higher tolerance for failure, they will be more iterative, more agile, and more innovative, and will take more risk in predicting, optimizing, and adapting processes. The government will have been conscripting these types of organizations for years, and by 2040 it will have finally structured its acquisition and hiring processes, new contracting categories, and new tax structures to accommodate this dynamic workforce. The government will tap the gig economy, giving it an open door to a global market of specialized communities to obtain sought-after knowledge. Government's more inclusive and diverse workforce—such as starting apprentice-ships for students while in high school—will be a signal to the private sector to do the same.

The Customized Services Management Function: Tailoring Programs to Individuals' Needs

Similar to how design thinking helps to enhance user experience and elicit values and ethics, Customized Service Teams will seek tech-enabled feedback mechanisms as an opportunity to better understand constituents' changing values and ethics that are embedded in their digital fingerprint. They will see it as an opportunity to tailor programs to an individuals' needs, getting them the services and products that matter to them.

Led by Customized Services Managers, these teams will facilitate delib-erative dialogue between technologists and policy makers to ensure they understand the privacy, security, trust, physical and psychological wellbeing, and intellectual property rights they demand from government-produced services. Alongside the Knowledge Integration Teams, they will recommend policies and controls that embed stakeholder values, and they will design out those that are at odds. One significant hurdle they will overcome is a fear that quantum computing's ability to process at astronomical speed would break database encryption, changing the paradigm for privacy and security.

Technologies like blockchain are built with enough modularity that they will withstand decryption, and distributed ledger technologies will be used in synchrony with quantum computing to secure data. This will enable processes that once took months to now take mere seconds. For example, blockchain and artificial intelligence will enable once-belabored and protracted processes such as the U.S. procurement system to instantaneously adjudicate decisions like eligibility requirements and other critical factors in the acquisition process.

Customized Service Teams will provide solutions tailored to the relevant community of interest. For example, new algorithms—benefiting from the growing volume and complexity of data afforded by machine learning and artificial intelligence—will aggregate information in a natural disaster to predict how much response capacity the government and private sector must provide. Teams will recommend ways in which precision medicine can improve prediction and treatment for disease, and how physicians can better tailor a patient's medical treatment to their life expectancy. They will design solutions using 4D printing and create objects that reshape themselves and self-assemble over time. In many cases, the constituents will have a hand in directly creating the services they will receive, as people place higher value on products and services when they have a role in developing and shaping the product or service.

With these technologies, the government will also be better at collecting and disseminating performance data as it responds to natural disasters, ensures the provision of safe food and medicine, and manages the U.S. immigration system. As this data is shared transparently for the first time with the public, the gaps, incongruities, and redundancies, as well as strengths and successes, will rise to the forefront. As examples, by 2040, the resounding gap in cybersecurity jobs and the lagging innovation in digital identity will be resolved with world-class STEM education and digital research.

Operationally, these teams will set a standard for how the rest of government begins to operate. The process will work like this: as Customized Service Teams solve challenges, they will be rewarded with more complex, challenging issues. Once they resolve these challenges, they will become eligible for bonus pay. This will incentivize them to prioritize tackling and resolving the toughest challenges, and to encourage constituent feedback and response. A new era in government-constituent engagement will begin.

2040: A More Accountable Government

By 2040, government will realize that technology is the best lens through which it can understand its constituency. Advances in technology will enable it to not only better aggregate data, but to analyze that data and lay out a compelling picture of everything from what risks society is willing to take to what it chooses to buy. For the first time, government will capture a first-order look—the first accurate look—at how its policies, governance, and structure can be informed by a citizenry that will engage and determine more acutely how the government should spend billions of dollars, from designing future transport hubs to distributing veteran benefits.

Society's allegiance to bytes—regardless of technology booms or busts and even in periods of 'irrational exuberance'—will be the means through which government can connect to its constituency. And so government will reshape its structure, distribution of responsibilities, and technology investment to engage the American public more directly. The newly re-engineered, networked government will be more accountable to and reflective of citizens, and much better able to shift priorities, policies, and programs in strategic directions.

Lori Gordon advises a range of government and nonprofit organizations in foresight and strategic planning, workforce development, and process improvement. She has specialized in cyber and infrastructure security and resilience in the Federally Funded Research and Development Center and private sector communities, and currently serves on technical advisory groups, including ISO's Sustainable Development in Communities, ANSI's Standards Consortium, and the National Institute of Standards and Technology's National Initiative for Cybersecurity Education. Ms. Gordon has an MPA from the University of Massachusetts.

CHAPTER ELEVEN

Citizen-Driven Government: Boundaryless Organizations

Sukumar Rao

"In 2040, the government will complete tax returns for most of its citizens, preparing them by using available data from the networked system. The returns will be updated in real time for each transaction. Once finalized, they will be sent to the citizen's virtual assistant which will verify and validate the data, and file on behalf of the citizen."

CITIZEN-DRIVEN GOVERNMENT: BOUNDARYLESS ORGANIZATIONS

By Sukumar Rao

In 2040, the government will be led by citizens in a network of boundaryless organizations. Citizen leaders will shape and drive government management and operations in a co-creation process that involves public, private and social sector organizations. In this networked world, partners will work together to provide services to fellow citizens and have equal responsibility and accountability for service delivery; boundaries between institutions will be less critical, and institutions will be interdependent on each other.

> *Governments (at each level) will compete to recruit new citizens and residents, offering numerous incentives to attract and retain engaged citizen leaders. People will frequently travel and move residences between and among cities, states, and nations due to the nature of work and their personal choices. Going across borders is seamless— advanced biometric technologies, such as facial recognition, will automatically check people in and out at boundaries and borders.*

Citizen services will be personalized, based on events and activities in a citizen's life journey, and will span all levels of government (federal, state, local and international), making this personalization seamless and transparent to users. A network of teams, organized around citizen lifecycle events or transactions, will provide services.

Government will be a facilitator and enabler of service delivery, and government operations will be lean and leverage advances in technology. In this digital future, automation and artificial intelligence, along with other new and emerging technologies of 2040, will amplify the impact on work. As a result, the workforce of the future will undergo dynamic skill refreshes and constant training.

This chapter describes a future vision for government management and operations in 2040. It is structured around four main ideas:

- the role of the citizen as a leader and co-producer
- a citizen-centric approach to providing government services in a future digital economy
- government services delivered by a network of boundaryless organizations and talent
- a workforce skilled in leading networks through relationships

Citizen as Leader and Co-Producer

In 2040, government will be centered around the engaged citizen. Citizens will shape and drive government management and operations. The citizen leader will be skilled in negotiation, facilitation, and collaboration. More importantly, citizen engagement will be proactive—the design and delivery of government policies and services will not only be considered a great opportunity, but a valuable credential and experience in a personal and professional career.

The level of citizen engagement will vary by the citizen, with different roles based on the level of participation. Disengaged citizens will be incentivized to participate. Building on a citizen's willingness to contribute, the government will create the right incentives, such as reinforcing a citizen's ability to make an impact, providing constant training and skill refreshes, and providing incentives.

Citizens will lead and own the design and delivery of policies and services. They will be assigned to lead specific services based on their skills and expertise, and held accountable for their performance. They will recruit team members from a network and form interdisciplinary teams (composed of the public, private, and social sector). This will involve a fundamental change in the identity of citizens: citizens as value creators in a co-creation process working within a network.[1]

Co-design will involve citizen participation in the design process, and will be a building component of co-production in which multiple organizations or entities come together to produce desired outcomes. Co-production will involve forming new relationships, improving interactions, and thereby the experience for all participants in the ecosystem—the process of co-creation will often lead to a reconfiguration of roles. There are examples of co-production in various governments today.[2] So, what will it look like in practice?

- **Scenario One: Improving education in an underperforming local school district.** Consider a scenario involving the design of a program to improve education in an underperforming local school district. First, active citizen leaders in the community and local education will be chosen. Citizens lead multiple competitive teams, and each group will publish a digital agenda used to recruit organizations from the network. Each team will embark on a co-creation process that involves government (federal, state and local), the private sector (with expertise in training, education, and performance management), academia (best-in-class universities with high-achievement programs), and community associations that understand the pulse of the community.

  Each team will draft their design of the program and associated policies—they will be implemented as multiple pilots, with performance tracked by another set of citizen leaders. During the pilots, citizens will sign up to be part of the teams in areas where they can contribute (we discuss the concept of work in the last section of this chapter). Data and evidence from the pilots will be used to make decisions and design the program—best practices from the various pilots will be incorporated. Once the program is implemented, an innovative competition will be formed to help address any issues that may arise.

- **Scenario Two: Improving road maintenance.** Consider another scenario: the delivery of local government services, such as road maintenance. In 2040, materials that can self-repair will be used to build roads—in this case, however, there is a malfunction. A citizen finds the issue and submits a service request to the government—the citizen request will serve to reinforce data from traffic sensors the government has already received. The citizen will get a message upon completion of the repairs, and citizen volunteers will assess if the problem is fixed. All of the interactions and updates will be transparent to the public. Technology will help to identify the root cause of the issue from previous service requests and sensor data. Citizens will offer ideas and solutions to address problems— they work on the solutions in teams and, as a result, improve services for others.

Personalized, Citizen-Centric Services

Design and delivery of services will focus on finding solutions for citizen problems and needs, based on events and activities in a citizen's life journey. Services will increasingly span all levels of government (federal, state, local, and international) and will become more seamless and transparent to users. Services will be designed in an iterative process using a user-centric approach to understand what citizens need—developing, experimenting, and testing multiple ideas and prototypes.

Services will be designed for different citizen segments and personalized at the individual level using available information about the citizen, without requesting data again—in other words, if the citizen has provided information once to a government entity, that information will persist across all interactions and touchpoints. However, this sharing of information does not happen at the cost of privacy—the citizen will have a choice for different privacy levels.

Government will proactively communicate with and engage with the citizen, using data from all previous interactions with the citizen. Government will use advances in technology, such as deep learning and machine learning, to predict future citizen needs and requests. The government will communicate with the citizen's virtual assistant about transactions and requested services. In turn, a customer champion will be assigned to each citizen and serve as the primary touchpoint for providing a seamless, personalized citizen experience. The customer champion will orchestrate the delivery of services, performed by partners in the network.

In 2040, the government will complete tax returns for most of its citizens, preparing them by using available data from the networked system. The returns will be updated in real time for each transaction. Once finalized, they will be sent to the citizen's virtual assistant which will verify and validate the data for final review, and file on behalf of the citizen. Technology will assist citizens by recommending transactions to obtain the maximum benefit during the taxable year, including the impact of lifecycle events on taxes.

A co-production and user-centric approach will be critical in a future digital economy. Automation and artificial intelligence, along with other new and emerging technologies of 2040, will amplify the new approach's impact on work and continue to cause disruption. As a result, government's role will evolve and enable an ecosystem that allows people and organizations to innovate.

In this digital version of the future, the government could be described as a platform for the production and delivery of a range of services and activities that can be mixed and matched.[3] By opening this platform to citizen co-producers, government will extend its value chain to stakeholders with the goal of reducing public sector costs and increasing stakeholder satisfaction.[4] However, in the future, government will not necessarily build the platform but instead create the conditions to enable it.

Estonia, a small country of 1.3 million people, was widely considered in 2018 as one of the most advanced digital economies in the world. Building on its digital advances, the Estonian government continued to innovate between 2018 and 2040: it adopted blockchain to secure all aspects of financial, healthcare, real estate, and other transactions; it shared digital identities with other countries to make international transactions seamless for its citizens; and it made citizen services available on demand, in addition to predicting what services citizens will need.

A Network of Boundaryless Organizations

In 2040, organizational boundaries will blur.

First, the network will include public, private, and social sectors as partners in the value delivery chain, with equal responsibility and accountability for service delivery. As a baseline, the partners will center around the mission but have varying incentives and motivations. The government will develop and sustain the network to ensure capacity and the best skills.

Second, governments will integrate across different levels (federal, state, local, and international) to form a service delivery chain. As described earlier, the focus will be on providing a seamless citizen experience, with boundaries across governments transparent to the user. Based on the service, this integration will happen between and among governments.

In some governments, many citizen services will be open to competition from either a networked system of domestic partners or partners consisting of other governments. Citizens will choose their service providers, and this will lead to a competitive marketplace of partners and service providers.

Third, the future workforce will have vastly more independent and freelance workers who find work by connecting through peer networks. As a result, far fewer people will work for an organization and, if they do, the type of organization for whom an employee works will not limit their collaboration, resulting in a networked system of boundaryless organizations. Groups of teams and a team of teams, aligned with specific services, will make up the network. The teams will be multi-disciplinary, composed of team members from public, private and non-profit sectors—the best minds brought together to solve the complex problems of 2040.

These networks of teams have specific objectives with clear time-frames—groups disband once they achieve their outcome or purpose. The teams will work in two timeframes:

- Long-term timeframes, where objectives are outcome-oriented for long-term issues, such as reducing poverty or homelessness
- Short-term timeframes, where objectives are smaller problem areas with shorter intervals, which in aggregate help to achieve a long-term objective

Government operations will be mostly virtual. There will be few formal departments or agencies—but rather networks of teams organized around providing citizen services. Government will enable and facilitate service delivery and ensure the efficiency and quality of services delivered. Government operations will be lean, automated, and driven by artificial intelligence. Data and analytics will be a fundamental component to provide and optimize service delivery.

A Relationship-Based Workforce

The role of government and its work will evolve and frequently change due to continued advances in technology. In this digital future, there will be fundamental shifts in jobs due to automation, artificial intelligence, and other technologies—while a few occupations will no longer exist, others will experience significant changes since many work activities will be performed using automation technologies.[5]

As a result, the future workforce will need different, and evolving, skill sets and attributes. The future workforce will have a set of generalists more focused on areas that require the human touch: engaging customers/stakeholders, applying context/expertise to problems, managing people and machines. Of course, a critical skill will be the ability to work alongside computers and advanced technologies.[6] The workforce of the future will need to undergo skill refreshes and training before teaming assignments (to obtain the context of their focus problem/area), and a constant re-training and learning of new skills.

Sukumar Rao *is the president of The Parnin Group, a management consultancy that works with senior leaders in public, private and social sector organizations. He serves as an advisor to C-level and senior executive leaders on performance improvement, digital transformation, and organizational development.*

Endnotes

1   Olli-Pekka Heinonen, "Government as a Source of Public Value: Making Public Services Public Again," *Government with the People: A New Formula for Creating Public Value,* World Economic Forum, 2017, 4–5.

2   Panthea Lee, "What Makes for Successful Open Government Co-Creation?," Open Government Partnership, March 28, 2017.

3   Tim O'Reilly, "Government as a Platform," *Innovations: Technology, Governance, Globalization* 6, No. 1 (Winter 2011): 13-40.

4   Francis Gouillart and Tina Hallett, "Co-Creation in Government," *Stanford Social Innovation Review,* World Economic Forum (Spring 2015): 4–5.

5   James Manyika, et al, "Jobs Lost, Jobs Gained: Workforce Transition In a Time of Automation," McKinsey & Company, December 2017.

6   James Manyika, et al, "Jobs Lost, Jobs Gained: Workforce Transition In a Time of Automation."

CHAPTER TWELVE

Leading the Cities of the Future

Marc Ott, Lee Feldman,
and Tad McGalliard

"The smarter city managers of 2040 will be leading an
interconnected community of sensors, automation, data, IoT, and
artificially intelligent technologies that will enable them to visualize
issues and challenges in ways that today's managers cannot. With
this level of operational intelligence and seamless interconnectivity
comes the parallel risk of systemic failure if cybersecurity is not a
core part of local government administration."

LEADING THE CITIES OF THE FUTURE

Marc Ott, Lee Feldman, and Tad McGalliard

Excerpt from 2040 Edition of ICMA's *Effective Local Government Manager*

Like its predecessor, this edition concentrates on how local government managers continue to lead effectively in a complex and rapidly changing environment. When the 2020 edition was published, managers of local governments were leading the push for what was then known as "smart" cities, counties, and regional governments. This was the dawn of artificial intelligence and machine learning, big data, autonomous vehicles, advanced sensors and more—all of which were promising a new day of technological enhancements for city and county management. Today, 2040, those elements that seemed so futuristic twenty years ago are commonplace.

Local government professionals in 2040 will possess the leadership vision that can peer around corners and see past the event horizon to create organizational cultures that embrace a dizzying pace of change and technology innovation. In an op-ed for *Governing Magazine* in 2015, the former executive director of the International City/County Management Association (ICMA), Robert O'Neill, suggested that "technology + governance" is the formula for "smart" cities, writing:

> ... as the trend towards urbanization increases, the need for smarter communities becomes more imperative. Local government service-delivery responsibilities will continue to expand and diversify. To meet those challenges, local officials will need to seek out the right combination of technology and governance.[1]

In tomorrow's world, we believe that a more effective equation for the future divides the "governance" component into "leadership" and "management," with leadership as the dominant variable.

In this chapter, we describe the key characteristics that local government leaders in 2040 will need to effectively lead the smart cities, counties, and regional government of the future. Before we do that, we offer some thoughts on creating "even smarter cities."

Speech by Marc Ott, Executive Director, ICMA, at the 2024 ICMA Annual Conference

For many local government professionals, the future often feels far more present than the past or any given moment at hand. New challenges and opportunities are always barreling pell-mell from different directions to intersect with local government. Such is the case with the growing movement towards smarter cities and communities. With expanding interest in smart cities, it is clear that local governments are at an innovative moment and many are in an innovative mood. It is also clear that the smart cities movement has not only started, but the pace of change is accelerating with an ever-increasing number of opportunities lurking over the horizon.

BUILDING TOWARD THE "EVEN SMARTER" CITIES OF TOMORROW

With ongoing technology advancements underway in many local governments, it is not hard to imagine that there will be disruptions to the long-held assumptions and practices within local government. Technology has always influenced organizational culture and how professional public administrators lead, manage, and staff their organizations. Since the 1990s, technologies have altered the strategies, approaches, and outputs of local service delivery. For example, access to video information has had a major impact on public safety, including speed monitoring, traffic control, and crime solving. Body-worn camera usage is on the rise in police departments across the United States. Other disrupting technologies are bringing about change on an almost daily basis that will serve as platforms for the cities of tomorrow. Following are examples of disruptive technologies in play.

Leveraging Digital Platforms for E-Commerce

The use of websites to share information about local government administration is now widespread in the United States and other parts of the developed world. Many places have turned their sites into digital platforms for e-commerce, allowing residents and businesses to secure permits for new construction or pay taxes, fines, and fees. Looking forward, blockchain and related technologies of the future will change local-level transactions for property titling, survey plats, legal documents, and other transactions facilitated with support from the local government.

Expanding Sensor-Based Smart Traffic Networks and Autonomous Vehicles

Sensors embedded in, or suspended above, roadways help local government planners and engineers understand the conditions of their transportation networks. Intelligent transportation systems can provide real-time information such as incident detection, adaptive signal control, weather-related conditions, roadway volume information, and useful updates for travelers.

Sensors will be linked to autonomous vehicles—a game-changing approach for transportation and related services, which will raise many practical questions for local leaders:

- Will the roadways of the future be dominated by vehicles with advanced sensors and artificial intelligence, creating conditions where the most dangerous thing on the road is a car driven by an actual human?
- Will public parking evolve so that cities no longer need parking garages and meters?
- Will roadways still require traffic signs and stop lights?

In a near-term future, advanced roadway sensors and counterpart technologies in vehicles will optimize the flow of traffic through an efficient and elegant flow of vehicles that will reduce congestion, minimize idling, slash the number of accidents, and improve air quality.

Managing Local Skyways and Drone-based Transit

One can also imagine a transportation network where local roads are not the only mobility pathway. Drones are already being used by some communities, including Fort Lauderdale, Florida, where the technology has been deployed to help with emergency management situations including distressed swimmers, missing or malfunctioning boat locations, shark sightings, and greater awareness about structural fires.[2] In 2040, local governments will have the sole or shared responsibilities of managing skyways where small as well as larger drones capable of much greater carrying capacity—including passengers—operate in increasingly crowded airspace.

Expanding Use of 3-D Printing

"Tea. Earl Grey. Hot." was a familiar line from character Captain Jean-Luc Picard, made famous by actor Patrick Stewart, on *Star Trek: the Next Generation*. Captain Picard used the ship's "replicator" to satisfy his culinary need for a taste of home. While starships aren't hovering in orbit...yet...3-D printers are now capable of building not only small prototypes and molds, but much larger and diverse products. For example, a non-profit and a technology firm are now using 3-D printing to build affordable housing, currently for under

$4,000 per unit.[3] This disruptive technology will be dramatically expanded in the future to solve the chronic shortage of safe and affordable housing. In addition, a more massively scaled 3-D printing technology will be used to build public infrastructure such as roads, sidewalks, and more.

Artificial Intelligence Replacing Routine Jobs

Artificial intelligence is on the rise in everyday usage through devices like Google Home, Siri, and Alexa, that provide information, product ordering, directions, and much more. Facilities management devices like Nest help to control building conditions by learning a user's preferences for temperature. Already, "chatbots" provide customer services in industries of all kinds, from answering questions about wireless services to purchasing shoes and even the delivery of local government services. Similarly, while not at all in widespread use, some futurists speculate that routine activities may one day be performed by artificially intelligent robotics. If the ultimate innovation is to replace humans doing routine or mundane jobs with artificially intelligent technologies, the city hall of 2040 will be more of a cyber city hall, open 24-7.

THE EFFECTIVE LOCAL GOVERNMENT LEADER OF 2040

Technology advances of the last generation have already disrupted the ways in which local governments are managed and operated. If we expect similar disruption over the next twenty years, what will the future require of its government leaders? It is clear to us that the core competencies of the effective local government leader in 2040 will substantially differ from those of today, and the organizational models in which they work will continue to stray further away from those where only public service organizations serve the public good.

For decades, ICMA has monitored and reported on the core attributes that effective local government leaders need to be successful. As technologies continue to advance and provide benefits—many of which are not yet imagined—we believe that governance elements of the smart city equation will remain equally as important as the technology tools with which they will work. We also believe it is imperative that the evolution in management and administration necessary for the next-generation smart city begin immediately. After all, the leaders of 2040 are graduating from colleges today.

Looking forward, elected and appointed leaders of 2040 will need to be a combination of the following types of managers:

- **Facilitative Leaders** create partnerships with public sector, private sector, and non-profit actors, working to continuously improve communities and serving as an advocate for updating obsolete laws and regulations.
- **Technology Champions** are more technologically aware than today's public administrators.
- **Data-Driven Leaders** are capable of accessing and incorporating data and analytics into decision-making and data-driven performance management.
- **Cyber Generals** are proactive and effective decision makers against the continuing threat of cyber-attacks.

The Facilitative Leader

Private sector and non-profit organizations are now essential partners in meeting the service needs of local government stakeholders. We believe that this trend will indeed continue, because the necessity to do it better, faster, and cheaper is not a hallmark of bureaucracy. The implementation of smart city technologies and approaches will need to keep pace with innovation and change, in creating new products and services designed to meet the treadmill of needs for which local governments are responsible. As a result, we expect that local governments will continue moving away from the procurement of technology and toward the procurement of "smart technologies as a service" that can be more quickly improved, tested, updated, and replicated in partnership with the private sector.

Other sectors of society are also filling in the gaps of local needs and service delivery. Non-profit organizations like Cities of Service work with local governments to organize local resident and business volunteers to help confront community needs.[4] Another nonprofit, PulsePoint, activates community volunteers to respond to cardiac events near their current location, providing potentially life-saving cardiac care in the critical minutes before even first responders can arrive on scene.[5] Airbnb supports local and regional disaster response by activating their community of clients to provide shelter for first responders and others deployed to recovery zones.[6] There is power in the crowd. The smarter cities and communities of 2040 will welcome these kinds of game-changing innovations to augment local service delivery. The effective local government leader must be able to identify and quickly assess the value partnerships that mix the skills and talents of different sectors to achieve community benefit goals.

The facilitative manager will also be active in reexamining the 2040 system of laws, regulations, ordinances, permitting process, and other interventions that federal, state, and local governments will have put in place to respond to disruptive technologies. By 2040, the disruption presented by new technology will run headlong into the rules and values of a community, and require reevaluation of those rules and values. The threat of technology racing ahead of community rules and values will require city managers to be facilitators in resolving any differences that may arise.

The Technology Champion

For most of humanity's existence, it was safe to assume that the world in which you lived would be pretty much the same from birth to death. Today however, the pace of change almost surely guarantees the opposite is true. Will local government leaders directly manage significantly more technology, or will they oversee departments of staff who manage and understand different kinds of technologies?

While we don't expect a collapse of the local government workforce, continued resource pressures coupled with ever-increasing technology deployments will likely do away with some kinds of positions, while creating others that require new types of skills. Given the pace of change, it seems clear that the city and county managers of 2040 will be more widely versed in a wider range of technologies than simply desktop software applications, and these managers will require a human resources system that is flexible and agile enough to respond to the varied talent requirements of "even smarter cities."

The Data-Driven Leader

The big data revolution is starting to make its way into local government. In her book, *A Practical Guide to Data and Analytics,* Marie Lowman suggests that:

> To make the case for analytics—convince government and citizens of the need to change traditional business models, share data, and update IT infrastructures—government leaders must be able to show tangible beneficial evidence. They must be able to explain exactly how and why investment in analytics can save money, improve lives, avoid unnecessary future costs, and enhance operational efficiency and compliance.[7]

Compared to other units of government, local governments lag in the use of data and analytics for decision making. However, as the power of analytics and visualization tools penetrates further into the local government marketplace, local public managers of tomorrow will have far better information to support their decision making. It is safe to say that politics in 2040 will still influence priority setting, decision making, and program implementation, and of course data can be manipulated to justify different arguments. Nevertheless, leaders and managers will need to better understand the "collecting, communicating, and crunching" of far larger pools of data, compared to today's elected and appointed officials.[8]

The Cyber General

In the future, the darker underbelly of smart city optimism will be the ongoing and growing threat of cyber-attacks against local governments. Each new technology connected as an Internet of Things (IoT) product will open a new front for cyber-attacks. Historically, ICMA survey data in 2017 suggested that many local governments were not aware of cyber risks, and were ill-prepared to meet cyber-attacks.[9] ICMA survey data and previous ransomware attacks on local governments found that localities are vulnerable to large-scale cyber-attacks. As ICMA staff suggested in a recent op-ed piece in the *New York Times:*

> We must actively prepare for cyberthreats of the sort that have been demonstrated in places like Atlanta. If smart cities and communities are the brightly lit days of the increasingly connected world of local government technology, cyberattacks are the dark and stormy nights. We don't need to halt technological deployments and evolution, but we do need to recognize that cybersecurity is an essential counterpart.[10]

The smarter city managers of 2040 will lead an interconnected community of sensors, automation, data, IoT, and artificially intelligent technologies that will enable them to visualize issues and challenges in ways that today's managers cannot. With this level of operational intelligence and seamless interconnectivity comes the parallel risk of systemic failure if cybersecurity is not a core part of local government administration. The cyber-terrorist would just as easily disrupt local government services to make a political statement as to demand a ransom. The manager of tomorrow will need to lead from the front to ensure the safety and security of the underlying smart city systems.

A 2040 interview with former city manager Lee Feldman

When I look back at how local government leadership evolved, I am struck by how many things we predicted that came true, and honestly how many things we feared that fortunately never materialized. It was an exciting time to be sure but, as a result of advances over the last quarter of a century, local government management today is better than it has ever been.

FINAL THOUGHT

By 2040, the co-authors of this article will hopefully be enjoying retirement after long careers in city and county management (whether we will have genetically- or technology-strengthened organs and longer life spans is the subject of another article for which we claim no expertise). We are each hopeful for the future, while recognizing the challenges that future local government leaders, managers, staff, and stakeholders will face to realize the promise of smarter communities. We expect the next twenty years to be an exciting time for the next generation of local government professionals, where effective governance and leadership, coupled with the right technology solutions, continue to create increasingly smarter cities, counties, and regional governments across the United States.

Marc Ott *is the Executive Director of the International City/County Management Association (ICMA);* **Lee Feldman** *is the City Manager of Fort Lauderdale, Florida; and* **Tad McGalliard** *is the Research Director for ICMA.*

Endnotes
1   Robert J. O'Neill, Jr., "Public Services and the Wonders of the Third Week of August," *Governing*, June 9, 2015.

2   Gregory May, "Fort Lauderdale Places Drone in Service to Help Save Lives and Property," *First Responder Broadcast Network*, accessed June 8, 2018, http://www.1strespondernews. com/webpages/news/displaynews.aspx?ID=a588eeaf-3200-4539-beba-270cd3cd8ce7.

3   Adele Peters, "This House Can Be 3D-Printed for $4,000," *Fast Company*, March 12, 2018.

4   "How We Work," Cities of Service, accessed June 8, 2018, https://citiesofservice.org/how-we-work/.

5   "Pulse Point" home page, accessed June 8, 2018, http://www.pulsepoint.org/.

6   "Disaster Resonse & Relief," Airbnb, accessed June 8, 2018, https://www.airbnbcitizen. com/disaster-response/.

7   Marie Lowman, ed., *A Practical Guide to Analytics for Governments* (San Francisco: John Wiley & Sons, Inc., 2017), 3.

8   Smart Cities Council, *Smart Cities Readiness Guide*, 2014.

9   International City/County Management Association, *Cybersecurity: Protecting Local Government Digital Resources Report*, October 25, 2017, https://icma.org/cyber-report.

10 Tad McGalliard, "How Local Governments Can Prevent Cyberattacks," *New York Times*, March 30, 2018.

PART II: VISIONS OF GOVERNMENT IN 2040

Envisioning the Road Ahead

CHAPTER THIRTEEN

The Future of Work

Darrell M. West

"Flatter, more open, and more collaborative organizations reduce the number of mid-level managers, empower front-level bureaucrats, and give upper echelons the tools to hold service providers accountable for their actions. This approach makes it possible to operate a lean team that still delivers on key objectives. Temporary workers are used when specialized job skills are needed for specific tasks."

THE FUTURE OF WORK

By Darrell M. West

In recent years, there have been numerous efforts to innovate in the public sector. Some government agencies have used Challenge.gov contests to encourage innovation through public competitions that generate new ideas for the public sector.[1] Others have suggested "crowdsourcing" as a means to test proposals. By subjecting possible initiatives to the wisdom of the crowd, they hoped to broaden the range of ideas and help decision makers think outside of traditional patterns.[2]

While these ideas have created some successes, they pale in comparison to the management and technical innovations likely to happen in the next two decades. Taking advantage of initiatives in both the public and private sectors, the U.S. federal government workforce is likely to evolve in several ways that follow best practices for improving performance.

In this chapter, I discuss new management and technology initiatives and how they might affect the future of the federal workforce. I break down the possibilities into the near-term future (2020-2025), the medium-term future (2025-2030), and the long-term future (2030-2040), and argue there are several developments with the potential to transform the public sector.

Near-Term Future (2020-2025)

The near-term future includes several options to change the federal workforce: the increased use of artificial intelligence and data analytics, greater deployment of personal digital assistants, and new employee performance rating systems. These tools would enable greater labor productivity and enhanced accountability.

Increased Use of Artificial Intelligence (AI) and Data Analytics. Artificial intelligence algorithms are designed to improve decision making, often by using real-time data. They are unlike passive machines that are capable only of mechanical or predetermined responses. Using sensors, digital data, or remote inputs, AI systems can combine information from a variety of different sources, analyze the material instantly, and act on the insights derived from those data. With massive improvements in data storage systems, processing speeds, and analytic techniques, they are capable of tremendous sophistication in analysis and decision making.[3]

AI system development generally is undertaken in conjunction with machine learning and data analytics.[4] Machine learning analyzes data for underlying trends. If it spots something relevant for a practical problem, software designers can take that knowledge and use it to analyze specific issues. If data are sufficiently robust, algorithms can often discern useful patterns.

Data can come in the form of digital information, satellite imagery, visual information, text, or other structured and unstructured data.[5]

AI systems have the ability to learn and adapt as they make decisions. In the transportation area, for example, semi-autonomous vehicles have tools that let drivers and vehicles know about upcoming congestion, potholes, highway construction, or other possible traffic impediments. Vehicles can take advantage of the experience of other vehicles on the road, without human involvement, and the entire corpus of their achieved "experience" is immediately and fully transferable to other similarly configured vehicles.

Through advanced sensors and algorithms, AI systems can incorporate their experiences into their current operations and use dashboards and visual displays to present real-time information that helps users make smart decisions. These systems represent a way to take the latest information and incorporate it into policymaking.

There are many ways that AI and data analytics systems can improve government decision making. They can help supervisors track performance, manage resources, and deploy agency assets. These systems can assist in federal efforts to drive energy efficiencies, promote national defense, and improve healthcare.[6] In addition, AI has the potential to augment the work of civil servants by assisting the review of client eligibility determinations in agencies such as the Veterans Benefit Administration and the Social Security Administration. Anti-fraud software can scan financial transactions and service delivery across large organizations and identify unusual patterns or clear outliers in terms of normal procedures and decisions. Transactions that seem out of the ordinary can be flagged for more intensive personal analysis, and this can help managers do a better job of keeping employees directed towards appropriate ends and performing at a high level of activity.

Increased Use of Personal Digital Assistants. Digital assistants are becoming more common in the consumer market. Examples include Apple Siri, Amazon Alexa, Google Assistant, Microsoft Cortana, and Samsung Bixby to help people find information, answer basic questions, and perform common tasks.[7] In the commercial sector, individual digital assistants are geared to improving business processes, such as travel, personnel selection, and acquisition.

These digital assistants also can be used in the public sector to help federal employees complete various activities. For example, they can help workers keep track of leave time, file reimbursement requests, request time off, and undertake routine tasks that used to take employees hours. Through voice-activated commands, workers will be able to navigate mundane tasks quickly and efficiently. The electronic system will free workers from the mountain of paperwork currently required.

One of the stultifying aspects of modern bureaucracy is outdated administrative processes. These processes, often requiring multiple approvals, were initially put in place to safeguard integrity and make sure employees do what they are supposed to be doing. They are part of the "command and control" mentality common in large organizations.

However, form often interferes with function in large organizations and therefore has negative consequences. Rather than making organizations operate more effectively, paperwork requirements take considerable time, demand a lot of emotional energy, and slow agency operations down to a snail's pace. Having digital assistants that administer routine tasks represents a way to overcome these deficiencies and achieve better results in the process.

Increased Use of New Employee Performance Rating Systems. In the new digital world that is emerging, technology will make federal employees much more accountable. Policymakers could borrow a tool currently deployed in China to improve public sector performance. At the Beijing International Airport, airport authorities use digital devices that allow visitors to rate the individual performance of passport officers on a one-to-five scale. After each encounter, visitors can provide numeric feedback on their experience and thereby provide actionable information to agency supervisors. The reams of data gathered by these devices enable Chinese authorities to discipline poor performers and make sure foreign visitors see a friendly and competent face at the airport.

In one respect, this approach would build on the notion of online surveys currently undertaken for U.S. federal agencies by the ForeSee company. The firm regularly polls users about website functionality to gauge online experiences. This approach allows analysts to rank e-government satisfaction for various agencies. In 2016, for example, ForeSee Results collected data from over 220,000 responses and found a citizen satisfaction level of 75.5, up from 63.9 in 2015. Among the top-performing sites were those of the Social Security Administration and the Departments of Treasury, Health and Human Services, and Homeland Security.[8]

Adoption of a broad-based accountability tool would allow many parts of the federal government to become more decentralized and provide employees with greater authority to make decisions. Since the federal organizations are subject to digital ratings, they are accountable and responsive to customers. Also, supervisors can track performance without personally monitoring every interaction.

If deployed broadly throughout the bureaucracy, this technology would strengthen management operations and processes. Employees would know how they were doing throughout the year—not just at evaluation time. In addition, supervisors would have a more detailed and accurate means of determining who is doing their job. Such a mechanism would help them separate high from low performers, and reward those who are doing the best job.

Medium-Term Future (2025-2030)

Between 2025 and 2030, there likely will be movements toward a flattening of agency organizations and greater use of biometric security systems. These shifts are designed to improve agency operations and protect public information systems.

Use of Flattened, More Collaborative Organizations. The sharing economy represents an example of an idea that has revolutionized the private-sector workforce. Through firms such as Uber, AirBnB, and WeWork, companies have flattened their organizations, introduced digital technology, improved collaboration, and moved to temporary workers or outside contractors to fulfill key parts of the business mission.[9]

Over the next 20 years, this collaborative concept likely will be deployed extensively within the federal workforce. The days when government employees were subject to a centrally directed Office of Personnel and Management and filled with permanent, full-time workers sitting in downtown office buildings may morph into flatter organizational structures with greater decentralization, more technology, and increased employee autonomy.

Flatter, more open, and more collaborative organizations reduce the number of mid-level managers, empower front-line workers, and give upper echelons the tools to hold service providers accountable for their actions. This approach makes it possible to operate a lean team that still delivers on key objectives. Temporary workers are used when specialized job skills are needed for specific tasks. That could include drivers, food workers, security personnel, data management experts, routine service deliverers, and information management teams, among others.

Political leaders have long preached the virtue of running government like a business, and the success of flatter and more collaborative private firms will encourage policymakers to bring such models to the federal government. These efforts will build on past approaches such as out-sourcing, contracting, and privatization, but go much further than any of those models.[10]

Of course, permanent civil service workers still will be needed for positions requiring special skills. Strategic planning, crisis management, and high-level policy-making will necessitate well-trained workers with the ability to synthesize and manage information from a variety of areas. They will be vital in setting the overall tone within an agency and making sure temporary or contract workers are performing their jobs.

But long-term employees may no longer form the bulk of the workforce. One of the hallmarks of the contemporary period is "megachange," whereby local, national, or international circumstances can alter quickly and require very different responses from the federal government.[11] Reliance upon short-term workers will produce greater agility in responding to public needs, reduce the cost of government, promote efficiency in the public sector, and speed up government responses.

Use of Biometric-Based Security. Security is currently handled poorly in most federal agencies. A number of organizations rely upon outmoded password systems that are hard to remember and susceptible to external hacking. The result is that public IT systems get compromised on a regular basis and sensitive information flows into outside hands.

The most prominent example of this occurred in 2013 when hackers stole millions of individual records from the U.S. Office of Personnel and Management. This included sensitive background checks and detailed personnel information.[12] This incursion represented one of the most widespread cyberattacks in the history of the federal government.

A better way to handle security is through biometrics and facial recognition software. Employees no longer need alphanumeric passwords that have to be changed every few months. Their mobile devices scan their faces, fingerprints, and irises, and thereby provide safe access to digital files and collaboration tools. Under this kind of system, security is improved dramatically and external adversaries have a much tougher time stealing personnel records, financial data, or email correspondence.

Of course, it is vital to protect personal privacy. No employee would want his or her fingerprints or eye scans to be compromised or used by malevolent intruders. There would need to be safe and reliable protections designed to ensure people's privacy was not harmed.

Long-Term Future (2030-2040)

For 2030 and beyond, there are "farther out" ideas for altering the government workforce. By this time, automation will be fully advancing and workforce disruptions quite substantial. The results could be a 30-hour work week, and scenarios such as dramatic changes in the social contract or a dystopian government to quell a restive population are possible.

Estimates vary considerably regarding the workforce impact from robots, AI, and automation. At the low end, researchers at the Organization for Economic Cooperation and Development (OECD) focused on "tasks" as opposed to "jobs" and found few job losses. Using task-related data from 32 OECD countries, they estimated that 14 percent of jobs are highly automatable.[13] At the high end, though, a Bruegel analysis found that "54% of EU jobs [are] at risk of computerization."[14]

Regardless of whether the disruption is high, medium, or low, the fact that all the major studies report significant workforce disruptions should be taken seriously. Relatively small workforce impacts can have outsized political consequences.

One way to deal with a situation where there are more workers than jobs is to reduce the mandatory hours for full-time positions for everyone, and therefore free up additional jobs for other people. That would enable more people to be able to gain employment and help society cope with a scenario where fewer workers are needed.

Darrell M. West is vice president of governance studies and director of the Center for Technology Innovation at the Brookings Institution and author of the Brookings book, The Future of Work: Robots, AI, and Automation.

Alternative Scenarios for the Future

While "Long-Term" futures are difficult to predict, it is possible to set forth two alternative scenarios:

Scenario One: A Rosy View—Reimagining the Social Contract

In addition to the 30-hour work week, other workforce reform in a new social contract would include increased worker eligible for paid family leave, periodic sabbaticals, and time to perform hobbies or community service projects, while those without jobs receive support through an earned income tax credit that covers their minimal needs.

Providing better work benefits is the route taken by a number of technology firms who face a competitive worker recruitment environment and a substantial need for Millennial workers who prefer a balance between vocations and avocations. Surveys of young workers often find they want time to better their communities and pursue outside interests in the arts, music, culture, and theater. Redefining the nature of work and providing time to satisfy outside interests could be attractive during a time of serious workforce disruption.

Scenario Two: A Pessimistic View—A Dystopian Government

It also is possible to envision a scenario where weakened governance institutions will prevent policymakers from shortening workweeks, reimagining the social contract, retraining workers, or helping with lifetime learning. As job losses accelerate due to automation and income inequality rises, democratic nations could become dystopian to deal with unhappy populations, high youth unemployment, and a loss of economic mobility. Rather than arriving at utopia, the United States could descend into dystopia due to its government's inability to handle the transition to a digital economy.

Weakened governance institutions would obviously have profound consequences for federal workers. For example, their employment might not have the kinds of civil servant protections common today. They might also not be free to perform their duties in a fair, professional, and non-partisan manner, but instead would suffer from lack of clarity in agency missions and lack of direction from the top. This would represent a drastically different workplace than typical today.

Endnotes

1   Kevin Desouza, *Challenge.gov: Using Competitions and Awards to Spur Innovation*, IBM Center for The Business of Government, 2012.

2   Daren Brabham, *Using Crowdsourcing in Government*, IBM Center for The Business of Government, 2013.

3   Darrell M. West and John R. Allen, "How AI is Transforming the World," Brookings Institution, April, 2018.

4   Andrew McAfee and Erik Brynjolfsson, *Machine Platform Crowd: Harnessing Our Digital Future* (New York: Norton, 2017).

5   Alfred Ho and Bo McCall, *Ten Actions to Implement Big Data Initiatives: A Study of 65 Cities*, IBM Center for The Business of Government, 2016.

6   Greg Allen and Taniel Chan, "Artificial Intelligence and National Security," Harvard University Belfer Center, July, 2017, and "How AI Is Transforming Healthcare and Solving Problems in 2017," *Healthcare IT News*, November 9, 2017.

7   David Nield, "We Pitted Digital Assistants Against Each Other to Find the Most Useful AI," *Popular Science*, January 25, 2018.

8   Dave Lewan, "The ForeSee E-Government Satisfaction Index," ForeSee, Q3 2016, http://www.foresee.com/assets/Q3_2016_eGov_Commentary.pdf.

9   Darrell M. West, *The Future of Work: Robots, AI, and Automation* (Washington, D.C.: Brookings Institution Press, 2018).

10 Gerard Roland, ed., *Privatization: Successes and Failures* (New York: Columbia University Press, 2008).

11 Darrell M. West, Megachange: *Economic Disruption, Political Upheaval, and Social Strife in the 21st Century* (Washington, D.C.: Brookings Institution Press, 2016).

12 Brendan Koerner, "Inside the Cyberattack That Shocked the US Government," *Wired*, October 23, 2016.

13 Melanie Arntz, Terry Gregory, and Ulrich Zierahn, "The Risk of Automation for Jobs in OECD Countries," Working Paper 189, Organization for Economic Cooperation and Development, 2016.

14 Jeremy Bowles, "Chart of the Week: 54% of EU Jobs at Risk of Computerisation," *Bruegel*, July 14, 2014.

CHAPTER FOURTEEN

The Future of Artificial Intelligence

David A. Bray

"AI can match humans into different ad-hoc teams…to fit a specific public service goal or problem set. If an emergent event or crisis occurs, AI can help identify who is available to assist with what activities—and even help coordinate swarming activities of both humans and machines to assist with the response to the event. AI can learn which humans work better on specific tasks with other humans…"

THE FUTURE OF ARTIFICIAL INTELLIGENCE

By David A. Bray

Imagine being able to visit a disability claims office in a digital environment. Imagine a patent examiner equipped with digital assistants that could do the bulk of administrative work behind processing patents. Artificial intelligence (AI) may make both of these scenarios a reality. This chapter addresses the question of how advances in and adoption of AI will transform public service over the next twenty years. AI has dual meanings:

- artificial intelligence
- augmented intelligence, specifically how human capabilities can be improved by pairing them with machines to collectively work smarter

Most of the benefits to government will come from a people-centered approach of pairing humans with machine learning to amplify human strengths via augmented intelligence. Such a people-centered approach means that the success of public service in the future depends on identifying beneficial ways to augment the extant human abilities of networked, cross-sector teams— who want to improve the delivery of public service—with digital assistants and learning machines to amplify the team's strengths, mitigate any possible blind spots, and increase the capabilities of the team as a whole.

This chapter breaks down the possibilities into the near-term future (2020-2025), the medium-term future (2025-2030), and the long-term future (2030-2040), and then focuses on specific initiatives that are likely to be launched to employ AI to transform the public sector.

The Near-Term Future (2020-2025)

The near-term future includes using AI in specialized applications to support the information and logistics functions traditionally performed by government to provide government services. It is important to note that when deciding where to use AI, public servants determine to what degree the machines providing this assistance operate autonomously vs. semi-autonomously.[1] For the near future, most machines will probably provide support that still requires a human to act or make a decision.

For all the near-term future possibilities discussed below, government should implement "public review boards" that look at the diversity, consistency, and appropriateness of the data used. Without diverse or consistent data, the AI trained by the data may make decisions that erode public trust. Without appropriate use of data, public trust may also erode. For representative government, using "public review boards" in a form akin to a random jury selection process may be one way to ensure improved oversight. Such activities would also involve outreach efforts by public service organizations, to increase digital literacy and the understanding of AI and what it can do. Following are some examples of how AI will be deployed in the near future.

Increased Use of AI-Supported Assistance for Individuals Seeking Government Information. Several cities already have "311" telephone lines and mobile apps to assist individuals with non-emergency city services as well as to provide information on programs, events, and activities in the city. Such public-facing services will employ AI to help individuals with their questions. Humans would still need to be in the loop for new questions where the AI does not know the answer, or instances where the AI is uncertain about the question being asked. Such AI assistance will also help government employees with questions about onboarding, starting a new role, help with an existing role, retiring, and other internal service queries.

Increased Use of AI-Supported Assistance for Talent Management and Skills Matching. AI will help community members find new jobs and tailor training to hone and improve their skills for upward mobility in their jobs. Unemployment and career assistance services will provide an AI assistant via phone or at a physical career support center. The AI assistant will serve as a personal scout for new jobs based on questions answered by the individual about their skills, abilities, and desired work. The AI assistant will also help with tailored training opportunities accessible through in-person community colleges or online. Such AI assistance for talent management and skills matching will also be employed internally to government itself, to help the existing government workforce find new work opportunities and tailor individual training to further develop skills and abilities.

Increased Use of AI-Supported Review of Public Applications and Filings. Current government functions often entail detailed forms and processes to either prove or approve services to the public. Such functions include licenses, land and jurisdictional approvals, individual claims, payment processing, and travel-related documents. The current linear process of such applications is outdated, usually requiring a human to identify the right form, fill it out, and submit it—only to find that another form was needed or more information was required. Instead, AI assistants will provide more tailored support to individuals, to better understand what they are applying for and pre-review a public application or filing prior to human approval.

Increased Use of AI-Supported Legal, Financial and Ethics Reviews. Legal, financial, and ethics reviews often entail a rules-based approach of reviewing information submitted to ensure it comports with specified requirements. Such reviews fit well with how AI can assist humans. An AI assistant will do the initial review, let an individual know if more information is required, and provide a preliminary result for final review by a human.

Increased Use of AI-Supported Detection of Fake Images, Videos, and Audio Files. It currently is possible to "clone" someone's face to an image or video of someone else's body. Voices also can be "cloned" to produce audio recordings that sound like someone saying something they did not say.

Detecting such fake files requires detailed analysis and pattern matching, looking for inconsistences. An AI can support a human in detecting such irregularities.

Increased Use of AI-Supported Biometrics for Boarding Planes, Crossing Borders. Machines are also good at identifying the biometrics that make one individual different from another. Within sufficient training, an AI application will identify a person based on their face—and possibly other factors, such as their fingerprints or the sound of their voice. Such biometrics would allow individuals to board planes and cross borders without having to carry a physical identification card.

A Brief History of Artificial Intelligence

In 1943, a young academic by the name of Herbert A. Simon received his PhD from University of Chicago with a doctoral thesis focused on administrative behavior within organizations. He wrote his thesis after co-authoring an earlier study in 1939, entitled *Measuring Municipal Activities*, with Clarence Ridley.[2] From research into administration behaviors and municipal administration, Simon would later contribute to the first wave in the field of artificial intelligence, specifically *problem-solving algorithms*. In 1957, he partnered with Allen Newell to develop a General Problem Solver that separated information about a problem from the strategy required to solve a problem.[3] For his contributions to the fields of artificial intelligence, information processing, decision making, and problem solving, both he and Allen Newell received the Turing Award from the Association for Computing Machinery in 1975.[4]

Since then, the field of AI has experienced two more waves of innovation. Starting in the mid-1960s, the second wave of AI innovation included *expert systems* represented mainly as "if-then" statements instead of procedural code. The goal of such systems was to perform tasks that expert humans also could do, such as evaluate geological sites or perform medical diagnoses.[5] In parallel, advances taught machines to solve problems, specifically to intelligently play human games, including IBM Deep Blue playing against chess masters in the late 1990s. Later, IBM Watson won against two *Jeopardy!* Champions in 2011. Google DeepMind's AlphaGo won against a top-ranked world Go player in 2016.[6] A Carnegie Mellon University poker AI won a 20-day tournament in 2017.[7]

Approximately fifteen years into the start of the 21st century, cumulative advances in the speed, size, and scale of microprocessors and computer memory reached a tipping point that triggered a third wave of AI innovation. Some of the algorithms originally envisioned by AI pioneers, such as the backpropagation algorithm that allows neural networks to solve problems far faster than earlier approaches to machine learning, could now be run at sufficient speeds to make the algorithms valuable to solve real-world problems.[8] Machine learning is a branch of AI that employs large data sets to statistically train a machine to make accurate categorizations of what something is or is not; e.g., training a machine to identify images accurately of different objects, places, or entities.[9]

Increased Use of AI-Supported Assistance for Analyzing Geospatial Data. In the next few years, an explosion of geospatial data will become available from drones for civilian purposes, private cube satellites, and sensors associated with the "internet of things." AI can assist in making sense of all that information—as well as identifying patterns of importance to improve the delivery of public services. To do this appropriately, the public will need to have conversations and greater insights into what information is being collected and for what purposes.

The Medium-Term Future (2025-2030)

The medium-term future includes AI moving from specialized applications to embedding AI in all operations to support both the operations of government and the interpretation and decision-related functions traditionally done by government to improve public services. AI will become an essential component of all government operations in this time period.

For all the medium-term future possibilities discussed below, public service will need to solve growing cybersecurity challenges.[10] If more public service functions are supported by AI, then any activity to alter an AI algorithm—or worse, the data used to train the AI—could cause the AI to make decisions that hurt people, harm property, or erode trust. A new science of understanding the resiliency, and by extension the brittleness, of AI apps to disruption by false data or other exploits will need to be developed if both the public and the public service workforce is to trust interactions with AI. Following are some examples of AI-enabled public services.

Use of AI-Enabled Delivery of Materials and Provision of Transportation. By 2025, engineers probably will have solved the limitation of autonomous vehicles to intelligently navigate in heavy rain or snowy conditions. This would allow public services to be paired with AI-enabled autonomous vehicles to include fire and emergency services.

Use of AI-Enabled Robots to Offset Repetitive and Manually-Intensive Work. One of the current limitations of robots today is that most cannot grip objects as well as a human. By 2025, engineers will probably have solved this limitation, making robots paired with AI a beneficial mechanism for the delivery of materials to support public service. This will include using AI for civil construction efforts, disaster response, healthcare, or other public functions.

Use of AI-Enabled "Tipping and Cueing" of Areas to Focus On. In a world in which more and more data is being produced by sensors connected to the "internet of everything," by 2025 AI will have advanced to the point where it will be monitoring different data streams for patterns of interest—or irregularities—that can then cue a human expert to look at something further. The human will then take an action that would further educate the AI for additional patterns to seek. This will include helping public service experts monitoring agricultural and health conditions in a geographic area.

Use of AI-Enabled Digital Assistants to Detect and Help Understand Biases. We all have implicit biases. Each of us have biases that we accumulate from our past experiences, including our early childhood. Some of these biases are discriminatory, such as an implicit preference for people who look like us or a favoritism to people who are taller and exhibit other physical traits. For public service, such implicit biases should not discourage a diverse workforce that seeks to serve the public. By 2025, AI will help hold up a "digital mirror" to compare our decisions and other interactions with those of others. This can help each of us understand where our biases are and what to do so that we may become less biased. Such an activity will also start to probe the boundary between the tacit, implicit knowledge a public service expert accumulates and the explicit knowledge they can articulate and share.

Use of AI-Enabled "Digital Twins" of Real-World Dynamics. Through extending the data collected from the future "internet of everything," by 2025 AI will allow public service organizations to build models of real-world dynamics—either of actual physical assets or social interactions. Such models will create highly accurate "digital twins" that would allow individuals in public service to experiment with certain scenarios in a digital environment. Individuals will also do training for crisis response and other high-intensity environments in a "digital twin" scenario, with AI providing recommendations on how to improve based on performance in the digital environment.

The Long-Term Future (2030-2040)

In 2030 and beyond, there are "farther out" ideas for the future of AI in public service. While predicting the specific future capabilities of AI is difficult, we assume advances will continue in the speed, size, and scale of microprocessors and computer memory to enable faster delivery of all the assisting and enabling functions of public service referenced earlier in this chapter. We can anticipate that the adoption of quantum computing, sophisticated augmented reality, and other techniques will be used to fundamentally transform the role of government to a more personalized approach in which government can respond to the unique needs of each citizen. The job of government will be radically changed.

The ability for AI to work with and help humans better act, respond, and provide public services should be fairly robust by this point. At this point, we could imagine a future where "krewes" of humans augmented with machines perform the work of public service, perhaps on a part-time basis if other predictions associated with the future of work also occur by 2030.

By 2030, functions that used to be provided solely by government agencies may now be provided either through a part-time workforce or a "Public Service Corps" willing to spend some hours a week on efforts assigned to them by a coordinating public service AI. This "Public Service Corps" would embody what science-fiction author Bruce Sterling once dubbed a "krewe."[11]

For a krewe, the entity of importance is not an individual per se. Rather, it is the combined abilities of a team of human individuals augmented with intelligent assistants and relevant information streams to do the work they need to do. A diverse krewe brings many different perspectives to a scenario, ideally overcoming any specific individual biases.

In such a futuristic scenario, several of the rote and repetitive functions currently performed by government would be performed by AI in a semi-automated fashion such that applications associated with civil society activities are pre-screened and feedback provided to human applicants prior to a final human determination. Humans will still be involved for the more creative and final decision roles. The need for clerical workers or administrative workers to process applications will have gone down significantly.

Individuals can work part-time because the machines will do much of the work in the background. In such a civil society, choosing to work in public service is seen as a true service. Individuals may be able to work in the private sector in areas that AI assistants determine do not create conflict with their public service assignments. For humans working with AIs in krewes, it also would be important to identify mechanisms to reward a whole-of-team outcome and performance instead of solely individual actions. By working together, humans and machines, the krewe would be collectively more intelligent and capable than any one individual alone.

AI can match humans into different ad-hoc teams or krewes to fit a specific public service goal or problem set. If an emergent event or crisis occurs, AI can help identify who is available to assist with what activities—and even help coordinate swarming activities of both humans and machines to assist with the response to the event. AI can learn which humans work better on specific tasks with other humans, and AI may even be able to identify which robots or parts of the AI hardware might be faulty or near-failing and thus need repair.

Such a future would represent a major disruption to how government and public service currently function. This disruption would impact the workforce, policies, budgetary allocations, and administrative processes associated with current civil society functions. Such a future might impact military and intelligence functions in similar ways, with individuals who had already signed-up to serve being "called up" by an AI if an urgent need matching their skill set arose, for example responding to a cyber event or helping with some other national security event.

Alternative Scenarios for the Future

While "long-term" futures are difficult to envision, it is possible to set forth two contrasting scenarios for the future of AI in public service.

Scenario One: An Optimistic View of the Future

In order to achieve the vision of "A Public Service 'Of the People, By the People, For the People,'" government workers will need to overcome budgetary challenges, potentially restrictive policies, ossifying processes, aging legacy IT systems, and skepticism to the point of strong distrust of the activities of government. With strong support, both from the public and elected political leaders, our representative government will be able to cross the chasm between how government currently operates and the ways in which public service could be dramatically transformed and deliver vastly better services and results to the public in 2040.

While this chapter presents potential milestones for where AI in public service could go, there will need to be experiments to gain expertise on the best way to align policies, people, processes, and technology to achieve desired goals. Unlike the venture capital community in the private sector, public service operates with money from taxpayers who have a right to expect that their money is spent wisely. This can create an environment in which maintaining the status quo, instead of attempting to embrace AI, may slow or prevent a government from achieving the benefits of AI.

The public will also rightfully need to be informed about what AI and algorithms do and how they are being used. Transparency in these activities will be key to engender public trust. Public discussions on what data should be used to train and inform AI activities will need to occur. A workforce savvy enough to keep up with both the technologies associated with AI—and more importantly the civil, legal, and people-centered impacts of such technologies in public service—will need to be recruited and retained.

Safe spaces to learn and explore how AI can improve public service—and then to translate these activities into public service-wide scaled activities—will need to be put in place.[12] Without safe spaces and possibly high-priority goals, anything that appears to have gone wrong or not worked on the first try may be politicized and prevent representative governments from being able to adapt to the rapidly accelerating age of AI. For public service to become more agile and resilient, the barriers will come not from technology. Rather, the barriers will be human-centered, coming from a risk-averse political culture unwilling to make mistakes in areas where it is okay to make mistakes (i.e., the mistakes do not harm people or property), learning, adapting, and improving.

Scenario Two: A Pessimistic View of the Future

An alternative, cautionary note for the future of AI and public service is one in which AI is used by government, well-intended or not, to monitor the activities of individuals. Instead of empowering individuals, AI is used to sort and filter behaviors that the government does not permit. No insight into what AI and its algorithms are doing for the government is shared with the public, and the public does not know that they each have different risk, credit, and behavioral scores that influence what they can and cannot do in society.

Such a scenario would be a pessimistic one in which people are dehumanized and disconnected from engaging in civil society. Distrust in public service is heightened and no one feels like they can help make a difference. While the foreseen uses of AI discussed in this chapter seek to prevent such a scenario, the cautionary note that it could occur is worth remembering – if only to emphasize why a more people-centered "better way forward" is needed for the future of AI and public service ahead.

As we embrace the future of AI in public service, we must recognize that AI technologies will reflect the choices we humans make about how to use it, whom to include, and how to ensure the diversity, consistency, and appropriateness of AI's activities within civil societies. Since we are human, not all decisions made initially will be perfect. However, with an environment that encourages informed experimentation and appropriate safeguards to protect the public, we can course-correct and over time improve how civil society operates for the future ahead.

David A. Bray *is executive director for the People-Centered internet coalition, Chief Strategy Officer at the geospatial company MapLarge, and gives guest lectures at Singularity and Harvard Universities on leadership in a networked world and how we might encourage a more people-centered internet for the future.*

Endnotes

1   Partnership for Public Service, *The Future Has Begun: Using Artificial Intelligence to Transform Government*, IBM Center for The Business of Government, 2017.

2   C. E. Ridley and H. A. Simon, *Measuring Municipal Activities* (Chicago: International City Managers' Association, 1938).

3   H. A. Simon and A. Newell, "Human problem solving: The state of the theory in 1970," *American Psychologist* 26, No. 2 (1971).

4   "Herbert ("Herb") Alexander Simon," A.M. Turing Award, accessed May 10, 2018, https://amturing.acm.org/award_winners/simon_1031467.cfm

5   "Expert Systems," accessed May 10, 2018, https://people.cs.clemson.edu/~goddard/texts/cpsc8100/chapA7.pdf

6   "Human vs Machine: Five epic fights against AI," *New Scientist*, accessed May 10, 2018, https://www.newscientist.com/article/2133146-human-vs-machine-five-epic-fights-against-ai/

7   "AI just won a poker tournament against professional players," *New Scientist*, accessed May 10, 2018, https://www.newscientist.com/article/2119815-ai-just-won-a-poker-tour-nament-against-professional-players/

8   "How the backpropagation algorithm works," *Neural Networks and Deep Learning*, accessed May 10, 2018, http://neuralnetworksanddeeplearning.com/chap2.html

9   N.M. Nasrabadi, "Pattern Recognition and Machine Learning," *Journal of Electronic Imaging*, 16, No. 4, (2007).

10 U.S. Government Accountability Office, *Artificial Intelligence: Emerging Opportunities, Challenges, and Implications*, GAO-18-142SP, (2018).

11 B. Sterling, *Distraction* (New York City: Spectra, 1999).

12 "Do We Need A "Civilian ARPA" for AI?," *Trajectory*, accessed May 10, 2018, http://trajec-torymagazine.com/do-we-need-a-civilian-arpa-for-ai/

CHAPTER FIFTEEN

The Future of Civic Engagement

Hollie Russon Gilman

"The longer-term future presents an opportunity to set up institutionalized structures for engagement across local, state, and federal levels of government—creating a "civic layer." ...its precise form will evolve, but the basic concept is to establish a centralized interface within a community to engage residents in governance decision making that interweaves digital and in-person engagement."

THE FUTURE OF CIVIC ENGAGEMENT

Hollie Russon Gilman

What is the future of civic engagement for governance that focuses primarily on the interactions between citizens and public policy? While the focus of civic engagement is often on government, the realm of public policy is not constricted to one sector; rather, as public administration scholar Don Kettl notes, it involves the interweaving of the public and private sectors.[1] More specifically, civic engagement scholar Harry Boyte finds that it includes "an emphasis on the interactions among governments, civil society, and business groups."[2]

In the last few decades, the conversation around public administration, public sector reform, and designing innovated institutional structures that are more adaptive, responsive, and accountable has focused on "innovating government." But, there has not been enough focus on how to build structures, models, and opportunities for proactively engaging citizens with meaningful opportunities to participate in decision-making.[3]

Citizen trust in government institutions remains alarmingly low in democracies across the globe.[4] Leveraging transformations in technology and accelerating the current promising models from experiments in civic engagement allows us to imagine a more responsive, participatory, collaborative, and adaptive future for civic engagement in governance decision making. This can start by creating a civic layer.

What is a civic layer? Its precise form will continue to take shape, but the basic concept is to create a centralized interface to involve citizens in governance decision making that interweaves digital and in-person engagement. People will earn "civic points" for engagement every time they sign a petition, report a pothole, or volunteer in their local community.

Without reimagining how to engage citizens with governance institutions, innovations themselves will not enhance trust, legitimacy, or engagement with public sector institutions. This chapter identifies the potential societal contributions of creating a "civic layer." It also identifies examples of the possible components of a civic layer, and the opportunity of emerging technologies to support meaningful, large-scale engagement via this civic layer.

THE NEAR-TERM FUTURE: UNDERTAKING EXPERIMENTATION AT THE LOCAL LEVEL TO CREATE THE FOUNDATION FOR A CIVIC LAYER

In the near term, an opportunity exists to tap energy and excitement at the local level to re-engage citizens in governance, solve public problems, and combine local engagement with new institutional structures and digital tools to deepen civic engagement. People are often inspired by their ability to affect change on the local level and spend more of their time in local communities actively participating in civic, social, and communal life. This points to an opportunity to focus on effective civic engagement, moving beyond initiatives that deliver time and resource efficiencies. In the near term, merely opening access to public data can be an important step in increasing the effectiveness of citizen engagement. The next step is using these data to innovate new ways of engagement.

So, how can government tap into citizens' expertise in the 21st century? This will require creative thinking about how to equip people with the resources and information they need.

Why Begin at the Local Level?

Building the civic layer should begin at the local level because outdated federal statutory citizen participation mechanisms stymie robust civic engagement at the national level. National legislation should be revisited, revised, and adapted to reflect the way citizens interact in the 21st century. There are currently limited opportunities for people to engage in governance decision making at the federal level. Pre-internet statutory mechanisms for citizen engagement, such as the Freedom of Information Act, the Federal Advisory Committee Act, and the Paperwork Reduction Act, are antiquated and have the effect of limiting rather than expanding opportunities for citizen engagement. As Beth Noveck contends, a "new legal framework is needed" to tap into citizens' individual expertise—a framework "that encourages people to contribute their highest and best skills, experiences, and know-how to public service; and that cultivates ongoing communities of practice where citizen experts can convene and disband as needed and can engage with each other and with government."[5]

The First Step: Opening Data

The first step in creating the foundation for a civic layer is to provide government information through a forward-leaning Open Data policy. Only then can citizen expertise be developed that is anchored in fact and data. However, the next generation of open data initiatives needs to not only release data, but also proactively engage communities in how that data is released and shared to make it useful. For example, some communities model the use of Civic User Testing Groups.[6] Miami, Florida, and Chicago, Illinois, partner with community members to empower traditionally marginalized voices in identifying which types and forms of data would be most useful. Several philanthropies, including the Knight Foundation, have supported this model.

This model of civic engagement involves people—with no tech literacy necessary and paid for their time with a gift card—in providing their feedback on apps the city wants to release. This model also involves in-person engagement throughout communities, including in community centers, with little investment in tech literacy or training.[7] Finally, this model puts a premium on engaging people with diverse expertise to create a civic layer in a community.

Brenna Berman, in her role as Chicago Chief Information Officer, explained how the city executes on its open data strategy: "At the Department of Innovation and Technology, our clients are the residents and businesses of Chicago. We're driven by what they need, and how we can serve them."[8] Data is an asset that cannot be released in a vacuum. Data must be coupled with a strategy around engagement that brings marginalized voices to the table, sampling everyone who can effectively use data and relevant applications.

Traditionally, the more information released, the better. In practice, this often included government passively releasing information to the public to engender greater transparency, accountability, and participation. However, this also led to serious limitations for engagement involving a broad cross-section of the public.

Through systems such as the federal e-petitions site "We the People" or e-Rulemaking for comments and notice, the federal government provides opportunities for empowered communities or informed interest groups.[9] For example, after the release of financial spending data with the Recovery Act via the Recovery.gov website, the majority of data users were the traditional "elites" (e.g., journalists or non-profits).[10] In fact, evidence demonstrates that the majority of content produced on blogs and Wikipedia comes from a small subset of informed groups and people.[11] Even the movement to democratize data or information is often dominated by a growing cadre of civic technology enthusiasts with technical or professional expertise.

The Second Step: Promoting Innovative Uses of Data

In the near-term future, the second step will involve the innovative use of information that communities can use to empower more diverse and inclusive viewpoints. The focus here is not just on information, but on targeting the *right type of* information with *proactive outreach* to local communities.

An example of this broader local-level engagement is provided in New York's Public Engagement Unit (PEU), created by New York Mayor Bill de

Blasio in 2015. The concept of the unit is simple yet powerful. Instead of the usual engagement model, where city officials wait for residents to reach out to them, staff from the PEU use neighborhood-level data to identify and reach out to vulnerable populations. In this way, the staff members build face-to-face relationships to engender trust and sign people up for vital services. Some of the programs they connect people to include health insurance, anti-eviction legal counsel, homelessness financial assistance, workforce training, and rent freeze programs.

PEU both generates new cases and works directly with people in their neighborhoods to resolve their disconnects with their communities and city government. As Regina Schwartz, who served as PEU's director, puts it:

> "We serve as a connector and a case manager. If we meet you at your door, or at an elected official's office hours and you're about to be evicted, we'll connect you with a legal service provider to help you fight your case in court. If you need health insurance, we'll schedule an in-person appointment with a certified enroller and help you go through the process of collecting the paperwork and scheduling a wellness visit."[12]

THE LONGER-TERM FUTURE: INSTITUTIONALIZING A CIVIC LAYER

The longer-term future presents an opportunity to set up institutionalized structures for engagement across local, state, and federal levels of government—creating a "civic layer." As noted earlier, its precise form will evolve, but the basic concept is to establish a centralized interface within a community to engage residents in governance decision making that interweaves digital and in-person engagement. People will earn "civic points" for engagement across a variety of activities—including every time they sign a petition, report a pot hole, or volunteer in their local community.

While creating a civic layer will require new institutional approaches, emerging technologies such as the Internet of Things (IoT), artificial intelligence (AI), and distributed ledger (e.g., blockchain) will also play a critical enabling role. These technologies will allow new institutional models to expand the concept of citizen coproduction of services in building a more responsive, connected, and engaged citizenry.[13] Within the civic layer, government will need to acknowledge citizens' time, data, and trust. For this model to be effective, government will genuinely empower people with decision-making authority to move engagement beyond a public relations campaign.

The following examples show different collaborative governance and technology components that will comprise the civic layer. Each could be expanded and become interwoven into the fabric of civic life.

The institutional design of these pilots drives their outcomes. Each example involves potentially serious privacy, ethical, and normative challenges and design considerations to ensure that the creation of "civic points" does not amount to a social score card, such as the one China's government is developing to influence citizens' behaviors and rights. The proposed civic layer would need to incorporate a universal identifier—e.g., a digital identity for each citizen. A challenge with tying civic engagement to a digital identity is to preserve civil rights, civil liberties, and privacy protections.

While technology represents a critical component for deepening civic engagement with governance, institutional structures are essential to facilitate effective engagement processes. Civic engagement scholar Tina Nabatchi argues for more deliberative, collaborative structures within public administration.[14] Models of collaborative policymaking exist where citizens serve as co-producers of policy that can be scaled in the near-term future. Other exciting initiatives are emerging to more actively empower citizens in decision-making.[15]

Increasing the Use of Collaborative Policymaking Models to Build a Civic Layer

While we currently think of elections as a primary mode of citizen engagement with government, in the medium- to long-range future we could see collaborative policy models that become the de facto way people engage to supplement elections. Several of these engagement models are on the local level. However, with the formation of a civic layer these forms of engagement could become integrated into a federated structure enabling more scale, scope, and impact. Following are two promising models.

Participatory Budgeting lets community residents allocate a portion of taxpayer dollars to public projects.[16] Originating from the Brazilian city of Porto Alegre in 1989, participatory budgeting can be broadly defined as the participation of citizens in the decision-making process of how to allocate their community's budget among different priorities and in the monitoring of public spending. The process first came to the United States in 2009 through the work of the nonprofit Participatory Budgeting Project.[17] Unlike traditional budget consultations held by some governments—which often amount to "selective listening" exercises—with participatory budgeting, citizens have an actual say in how a portion of a government's investment budget is spent, with more money often allocated to poorer communities. Experts estimate that up to 2,500 local governments around the world have implemented participatory budgeting, from major cities such as New York, Paris, Seville, and Lima, to small and medium cities in countries as diverse as Poland, South Korea, India, Bangladesh and nation-wide in Portugal.[18] While this process has currently been used on a small portion of public budgets, it could be scaled to included sizable portions of public monies in communities across the globe.

Another promising collaborative policymaking engagement model is the **Citizens' Jury** method, pioneered in the 1980s and currently advocated by the nonprofit Jefferson Center in Minnesota.[19] Three counties in rural Minnesota use this method as a foundation for Rural Climate Dialogues—regular gatherings where local residents hear from rural experts, work directly with their neighbors to design actionable community and policy recommendations, and share their feedback with public officials at a statewide meeting of rural Minnesota citizens, state agency representatives, and nonprofit organizations.[20] Participants also pledge to undertake local action to mitigate climate change. As one participant said, "Before I was a part of these events, I really didn't think there was anything I could do about [climate change]. I was always just one of those who thought, 'It's too big of an issue. It's happening. My hands are tied.' [By participating in] these events, I realize that there are things we can do, even me personally, in my community." While this method has proven successful on a range of topics, it has yet to become integrated into the *core* process of engagement that provide an opportunity for civic engagement in the medium-range future.

Increasing Applications of Emerging Technologies to Build a Civic Layer

In addition to institutional collaborative governance and policymaking models for engagement, the application of digital technologies to decision making creates the potential for a dramatically more connected, distributed, and empowered civic life in the future. The following are some promising technologies to incorporate into a civic layer:

- **Distributed ledger technology to connect citizens with government services.** Austin, Texas is already experimenting with the use of blockchain technology to provide a digital ID for homeless residents, and to use this ID for accessing city services. This project has been named a Champion City semi-finalist for the 2018 Bloomberg Philanthropies Mayors Challenge Award.[21] Distributed ledger technology could be used for a variety of other public service activities, including public comment, public voting, and civic record keeping.
- **Smart phone data to inform public policy.** Governments will increasingly engage citizens through their smart phones. This will include informing decisions through the data acquired from smart phones (with explicit user consent), conducting real-time user feedback, leveraging information through sensors, and communicating to citizens via their phones.
- **Digital one-stop interfaces for engaging.** Governments around the globe will build one-stop interfaces for engaging with government across all levels (national, state, and local). Estonia has been a leader in creating streamlined digital engagement with government. Think of the way e-commerce companies have centralized services for customers. This

will include the ability to report non-emergency 311 issues, participate in collaborative policy making, access open data, co-create policy, and give real-time feedback.

- **Virtual reality for civic engagement.** By 2030 there will be more opportunities for civic engagement using virtual and augmented reality (VR/AR). VR is already contributing to decision making. For example, the Moreton Bay Regional Council in Queensland, Australia, offered several VR experiences for a major development scheme. Through VR, community members and various stakeholders could experience the proposals up close before giving feedback via an online submission form. Moreton Bay even printed customized Google Cardboard Goggles to generate awareness about the project. This pilot example offers just the tip of the iceberg for how VR could give citizens access to inform policy *before* development occurs.
- **Sensors and networks of physical devices which comprise the Internet of Things (IoT) to inform public assets distribution.** Sensors placed throughout communities can be used to report real-time information on a variety of issues, from solar trash cans to water, energy, and transportability.[22] One challenge with sensors and other IoT Smart Cities initiatives involves their vulnerability to hackers and unchecked data, which citizens are handing over to government without regulation. More connected devices with sensitive information (including household devices such as thermostats, fridges, and personal assistances) mean greater potential cyber risk for public services.[23]
- **Artificial intelligence (AI) to directly communicate between public administrators and residents.** AI can help reduce the burden of paperwork and other redundant tasks for public administrators, and free up capacity to more deeply engage with community members. AI faces the challenge of ensuring authenticity and fairness with engagement. For example, fake bots can pose as public commenters. During the Federal Communications Commission public comments period around their net neutrality regulation, more than 1 million out of 22 million comments came from bots that used natural language generation to artificially amplify positions.[24]

By 2040, these technologies will become integrated into the core fabric of government at all levels to ensure more seamless interactions between our online and offline selves. This will result in a more responsive government that pulsates with vibrancy and information from its citizens. In this structure, government must ensure that people do not simply become data points, but are also genuinely empowered in decision-making. These models only work if public administrators can give people authentic decision-making power. Transparency in data collection methods and algorithmic decision processes will be essential. Direct civic oversight by community groups, non-profits, academics, and residents will strengthen these decisions. Another important concern will be to empower traditionally marginalized groups and ensure that not only those with more resources or digital literacy can participate.

FINAL THOUGHTS: BUILDING A TOOLKIT FOR TWENTY-FIRST CENTURY GOVERNANCE

The rapid pace of technological change will outpace public sector progress in civic engagement unless precautions are taken to ensure that government has enough capacity, skilled personnel, and training to leverage technology effectively. Each of the examples offered above could become essential components of a civic layer or civic toolkit to develop civic engagement with twenty-first century governance.

As pilots expand to become institutionalized processes, several normative and ethical questions arise for ensuring democratic and equitable access and use. Authoritarian countries will continue to use technology (e.g., facial recognition and digital identity) for control. The question is precisely if and how democracies can ensure more (not fewer) opportunities for genuine civic engagement that moves beyond public relations campaigns, while addressing concerns around privacy and equity front and center.

In 2040, proposals for civic engagement will be contingent upon trust in public institutions, reducing levels of inequality, adequate public resources, and addressing the privacy and ethical considerations at the intersection of digital technology, equity, and civil rights. While specific nation-state geopolitics will vary considerably, regaining civic legitimacy and trust in public sector institutions across democracies will be essential.

Hollie Russon Gilman is a Lecturer and Postdoctoral Research Scholar at Columbia University's School of International and Public Affairs, and a Fellow at New America and Georgetown's Beeck Center for Social Impact and Innovation. In the Obama Administration, she served as Open Government and Innovation Advisor in the White House Office of Science and Technology Policy. Her first book is Democracy Reinvented: Participatory Budgeting and Civic Innovation in America, *as part of the Kennedy School's series on governance innovation; she has co-authored a forthcoming book on the current state of democratic crisis and opportunities for building civic power in an era of inequality.*

Endnotes

1   Donald F. Kettl, "The Job of Government: Interweaving Public Functions and Private Hands," *Public Administration Review* 75, No. 2 (2015): 219-229.

2   Harry C. Boyte, "Reframing Democracy: Governance, Civic Agency, and Politics," *Public Administration Review* 65, No. 5 (2005): 536.

3   The term "Citizen," as used here, denotes their status in a democratic republic, not their legal status.

4   "2018 Edelman Trust Barometer," Edelman, accessed June 8,2018, https://www.edelman.com/trust-barometer.

5   Beth S. Noveck, *Smart Citizens, Smarter State: The Technologies of Expertise and the Future of Governing* (Cambridge, MA: Harvard University Press, 2015), 237.

6   "Civic User Testing Group," Smart Chicago Collaborative, accessed June 8, 2018, http://www.cutgroup.org/; and "Miami Civic User Testing Group," Knight Foundation, accessed June 8, 2018, https://www.knightfoundation.org/grants/201652509.

7   http://www.knightfoundation.org/grants/201652509 accessed on June 22, 2018.

8   Sean Thornton, *Chicago Launches OpenGride to Democratize Open Data*, Harvard Data-Smart Solutions, January 20, 2016.

9   "Petition the White House on Issues that Matter to You," We the People, accessed June 8, 2018, https://petitions.whitehouse.gov/; and "eRulemaking," Wikipedia, accessed June 8, 2018, https://en.wikipedia.org/wiki/ERulemaking.

10 Francisca M. Rojas, *Recovery Act Transparency: Learning from States' Experiences*, IBM Center for the Business of Government, 2012.

11 Matthew Scott Hindman, *The Myth of Digital Democracy* (Princeton, NJ: Princeton University Press, 2009).

12 Hollie Russon Gilman and K. Sabeel Rahman, *Building Civic Capacity in an Era of Democratic Crisis*, New America, 2017.

13 Kettl, "The Job of Government."

14 Tina Nabatchi, "Addressing the Citizenship and Democratic Deficits: The Potential of Deliberative Democracy for Public Administration," *The American Review of Public Administration* 40 (2010): 376

15 Tina Nabatchi and Matt Leighninger, *Public Participation for 21st Century Democracy* (San Francisco: Jossey-Bass Publishers, 2015).

16 Josh Lerner, "The People's Budget," *Stanford Social Innovation Review* (2016). https://ssir.org/book_reviews/entry/the_peoples_budget.

17 Participatory Budgeting Project, accessed June 8, 2018, http://www.participatorybudgeting.org/.

18 Brian Wampler, Stephanie McNulty, and Michael Touchton, "Participatory Budgeting Spreading Across the Globe," *University of Miami, Boise State University, Franklin and Marshall College* (2018); and Pauline Véron, "Why Paris is Building the World's Biggest Participatory Budget," *New Cities*, accessed June 8, 2018, https://newcities.org/why-paris-is-building-the-worlds-biggest-participatory-budget/.

19 Jefferson Center, accessed June 8, 2018, https://jefferson-center.org/.

20 "Rural Climate Dialogues," Rural Climate Network, accessed June 8, 2018, http://www.ruralclimatenetwork.org/content/rural-climate-dialogues.

21 "2018 Champion City," Bloomberg Philanthropies Mayors Challenge, https://mayorschallenge.bloomberg.org/ideas/austin/.

22 The Internet of Things includes networks of physical devices which enable objects to connect and exchange data (e.g. sensors, software, electronics, etc.)

23 "Cyber risk in an Internet of Things world," Deloitte, accessed June 8, 2018, https://www2.deloitte.com/us/en/pages/technology-media-and-telecommunications/articles/cyber-risk-in-an-internet-of-things-world-emerging-trends.html.

24 Issie Lapowsky, "How Bots Broke the FCC's Public Comment System," *Wired*, (November 2017).

CHAPTER SIXTEEN

The Future of Data and Analytics

Shelley H. Metzenbaum

"For common processes that governments perform—such as benefits and permit processing, fleet management, and cybersecurity—governments will have created and shared default suites of metrics and analytics that all governments adopt, adapting as needed. This will help them improve outcomes and communicate more meaningfully with citizens."

THE FUTURE OF DATA AND ANALYTICS

By Shelley H. Metzenbaum

How should federal, state, and local governments use and communicate data and analytics in the future to improve government performance across multiple dimensions—including impact, return on spending, fairness, interaction quality, trust and understanding? What needs to be done to get from where we are now to where we want to be?

Data and Analytics Are Key to Better Government Performance and Community Outcomes

Government needs to collect data and use analytics to enable policy makers, policy implementers, and citizens to answer a common set of questions:
- What problems need attention, how important are they relative to other problems, and what causes them?

  – Which causal factors can government influence?

  – What characteristics might affect how quickly, successfully, cost-effectively, and fairly the problems can be addressed?

- Are there promising practices for addressing the problems that seem to work well, and can they be successfully replicated?

  – Do they work well for everyone, and, if so, how can they be refined to work better and at a lower cost—and how can broader adoption be effectively and quickly promoted?

  – If not, where do they work well and where don't they? What else should be tried and assessed?

  – Are unwanted side effects associated with the practices, and how can they be prevented or reduced?

- How can we best pursue opportunities for discovery and growth?

- What future risks and advances should government anticipate and plan for?

Government has long collected and shared data, or mandated its collection, starting with the Constitution's requirement for a decennial census. Congress quickly called for the collection of additional categories of data as well, such as censuses of manufacturers and agriculture, and counts of schools, and other groups of interest (which at the time included the insane, mentally retarded, and illiterates).[1] Despite this long history of data collection, federal agencies unfortunately too often failed to collect "policy relevant data," or they published relevant data with "excruciating delays,"[2] impeding governments' and others' ability to use data to inform action.

Other times, however, as with traffic fatalities and morbidity and mortality data, government got it right. It put in place administrative frameworks and governance processes that regularly collect, analyze, and share data, resulting in continuous outcome improvements over decades,[3] albeit not without occasional problems.[4]

Dramatic technology advances over the last few decades in business analytics and visualization software now make it possible for federal, state, and local governments, and those they fund or otherwise influence to collect, analyze, and share data in increasingly relevant and timely ways. These technology advances enable far greater functionality and significantly lower cost for data collection, analyses, and sharing. An increasing number of governments in the U.S. and around the world have opened government data sets and invited others to analyze their content and apply the insights of those analyses as they choose.[5] Some also routinely share performance and spending data and their analyses,[6] visualize problems and progress or enable their visualization,[7] and support the generation and dissemination of the findings of well-designed measured trials.[8] In addition, government and others, such as Code for America and the Bloomberg Foundation, have begun boosting the analytic capacity of people working in or with government[9] and strengthening networks to enable government employees to learn and apply insights from their own and others' data-informed decision-making experience.[10]

Despite government's long history and recent progress with using and communicating data and analytics, as well as technological developments that have increased data processing power and cut data handling costs, current government data and analytic practices are nowhere near as sophisticated as they could and should be. Many government data systems remain clunky and hard to use, while government's analytic and evaluation capacity is woefully scarce.

A VISION FOR 2040

It is tempting to project how new technologies, such as remote sensing and mobile access, and new techniques, such as machine learning and blockchain, will strengthen government data handling and analytics in the future. However, much of what needs to happen twenty years from now could come to fruition with today's technology with the right governance structures and incentive systems, as suggested by the following vignettes about two data-savvy private sector companies, UPS and Amazon.com. Both companies routinely integrate data, analytics, and measured trials into their strategic decisions, daily operations, and internal and external communications today.

To achieve greater beneficial impact, operational efficiency, fairness, understanding, and trust, government should learn from and adapt the data-handling and analytic lessons that these two cases offer. Governments of the future should also learn from past government efforts, both successful and unsuccessful, when using and communicating data.

Specifically, by 2040, all levels of government should:

- Fuel the front line with timely user-tailored analytics and research findings
- Obsess on mission, continuously innovating to improve critical processes
- Use visualization and other communication tools to show problems, progress, causal factors, and likely effects of corrective action in context
- Count and characterize events and conditions to inform continual improvement

FUEL THE FRONT LINE WITH TIMELY USER-TAILORED ANALYTICS AND RESEARCH FINDINGS

UPS, a delivery company, uses and communicates data, analytics, and measured trials in ways that enable front-line drivers to deliver packages quickly, affordably, courteously, and in good condition. Data and analytics teams translate data gathered from every aspect of the delivery process into actionable insights that front-line drivers can use to know when and where to deliver a package; decide the order and routing of deliveries; and avoid dangerous dogs and other risks along the way.

UPS mobile devices collect and transmit data *from* drivers and analytical insights *to* drivers in timely and easily applied ways. Analytics help truck loaders decide which packages to place where. Measured trials test door designs and key fobs to find ones that work faster, easier, and more safely at a reasonable and lower cost. Drivers go to safety school to learn techniques and rules such as "right turn only, no left turns" based on analyses of the costs and causes of past problems. In short, UPS intensely collects, analyzes, and communicates data to enable front-line UPS workers to do their jobs better, in addition to asking and answering central office questions about issues such as revenues, costs, and market conditions.

Who does the equivalent in government? Certainly, the military supports front-line soldiers, sailors, marines, and airmen, but how many non-military agencies support the front line in their own operations and that of their delivery partners with user-tailored insights gleaned from data, analytics, and well-designed measured trials? For example:

- How are analytic and research findings packaged to make it easy for front-line educators, comprising nearly 11 million state and local employees, 8 million of them in elementary and secondary education,[11] to understand how to help the next generation grow, learn, and thrive?

- Who reviews and packages analytics, and the findings of well-designed pilots, so the second largest group of government workers—those working in hospitals and health care—can learn from their own and others' experience how to improve health and reduce health-system-acquired illness and injury?
- Who helps front-line Social Security, Veterans Administration, and social workers in every level of government learn from data, analytics, and measured trials so that they can provide continually better services and benefits?

A 2018 article in *Analytics Magazine* underscored the importance of using data to support workers on the front line:

> Who is the ultimate stakeholder? In most enterprises, there are many proximate stakeholders: analytics leaders, company executives, IT group, etc. However, the ultimate stakeholder—the front-line manager—is often discounted. Ideally, your front-line managers must be the loudest voice in key conversations. But in reality, in most cases they don't even have a seat at the table. Effective synergy among analytics, executives, IT and front-line managers is the cornerstone of outcome mindset.[12]

Twenty years from now, governments should routinely support their front line with relevant information packaged and delivered in a timely way that helps the front line deliver more successfully, courteously, efficiently, and fairly while simultaneously facilitating the front line's ability to share and learn from their own and others' experience.

What Will It Look Like in 2040?

Government will have identified the front-line workers focusing on the government's priority mission objectives, and given them ready access to the information they need to do their jobs well and continue to improve. If these workers need more or different information, government will be working with them to figure out what they need to know and the best way to provide that information on a timely basis.[13] Government will also proactively determine how burdensome field-based reporting is and, if needed, work on ways to reduce the burden and enhance the value.

OBSESS ON MISSION, CONTINUOUSLY INNOVATING TO IMPROVE CRITICAL PROCESSES

Amazon.com, also a delivery company when it started in 1994, quickly expanded beyond its initial focus on books to deliver, or broker the delivery of, approximately the same number of physical items (5 billion annually) just to its Prime members that UPS, started ninety years earlier, delivers to all of its customers today.[14] In addition, Amazon delivers a vast array of electronic services.

How did Amazon accomplish its astounding rate of growth in just over twenty years? It did it by obsessing on its mission: "to be Earth's most customer-centric company."[15] In addition, as Amazon CEO Jeff Bezos wrote in his 2017 annual letter, Amazon pairs its "unrelenting customer obsession" with "ingenuity and commitment to operational excellence".[16] To woo, win, and keep its customers, Amazon continually works to find better ways to support its customers in product search, order placement, fulfillment, delivery, and returns, whether through its website or with new tools such as Alexa and Echo.

Amazon's commitment to operational excellence led it, almost accidentally, to accelerate lagging application development time.[17] "Everyone was building their own resources for an individual project, with no thought to scale or reuse." To tackle this problem, Amazon decided to build "common infrastructure services everyone could access without reinventing the wheel every time." Because of its commitment to ingenuity and operational excellence, Amazon solved its own problem, simultaneously creating a product it realized others would find useful.

In addition to using data and analytics to advance its mission and improve its creation processes, Amazon communicates data and analytics in ways that help the interested public make better-informed decisions and, sometimes, even resolve product-related problems. Crowd-sourced, curated online customer ratings, comments, and FAQs help customers find products best-suited to personal needs and tastes, get answers before and after they buy, and find "workarounds" that minimize product weaknesses.

Government similarly needs to obsess on mission while innovating to master delivery processes owned by multiple lines of business, tap external expertise and effort, and inform individual choice. It is not unusual for government agencies to innovate, but this is usually done by individual agencies at the project and program level. It is seldom done at the agency, and even less frequently at the cross-agency, level. In May 2018, for example, the Transportation Security Agency (TSA) put out a call for smarter luggage scanners,[18] while the Internal Revenue Service (IRS) requested analytic services to detect tax fraud across all levels of government.[19] Government seldom, however, seeks synergies and opportunities to scale and reuse innovations across programs.

By 2040, government must figure out how to:

- support continuous learning and improvement, discovery, and testing to improve critical government processes undertaken by multiple programs. These processes might include, for example: benefits processing; regulatory permissions and compliance; harmful incident prevention, response, recovery, and remediation; and research and development.[20]
- support continuous learning and improvement, discovery, and testing across organizations and levels of government with shared missions.
- communicate data and analytics to inform individual and organizational choices about priorities, strategies, and tactics, and to enlist external expertise and effort to solve public problems and advance opportunities at the local, state, and national level.

What Will It Look Like in 2040?

Government will extensively use analytic and visualization tools that support, enlist, and motivate local action. It will do this while providing context for local priority-setting, problem-solving, opportunity advancement, and precision treatment design. Government will also have enhanced its use of analytic and visualization tools to support learning from and cooperation with others, inform individual and organizational choice, and enlist external expertise and effort.

USE VISUALIZATION AND OTHER COMMUNICATION TOOLS TO SHOW PROBLEMS, PROGRESS, AND CAUSAL FACTORS IN CONTEXT

The public and not-for-profit sectors also offer examples that suggest a vision for powerful data and analytics in the future. Consider, for example, Hans Rosling's brilliant visualization of life expectancy, child mortality, and economic trends across time, across countries, and within countries.[21] Rosling's not-to-be-missed TED talk (on video) debunks myths about presumed problems that no longer exist, and reveals overlooked progress that has been made. In addition, he spotlights areas still in need of attention, as well as variations in historic paths to progress that can inform future action.

Rosling's video animation provides a vivid vision for the way every government should analyze and communicate data in 2040. This analytic approach—using scatter diagrams and bubbles linked to country size to display performance trends for multiple outcome indicators over time in multiple locations, together with drill-downs showing who is faring well and who is not, and easy identification of positive and negative outliers—supports priority-setting, learning, motivation, continual improvement, understanding, and trust.

Rosling appreciated that he was able to undertake his stunning analyses because a government agency, the U.S. Agency for International Development (USAID), launched the international Demographic Health Survey and chose to make the data both public and free.[22] In so doing, USAID embraced practices the public health field, with its remarkable progress,[23] considers critical: "special methods of information gathering" and "corporate arrangements to act upon significant findings and put them into practice."[24]

While recent technological developments undoubtedly enable faster, broader, and more accurate interpretation and application of analytic insights, the will and skill to analyze outcomes in context is far more essential to progress than technology, as Dr. John Snow dramatically demonstrated in London a century and a half ago when he mapped the location of houses with cholera and drinking water wells. His analytic approach allowed discovery of the contaminating pump and removal of its handle, slashing the number of cholera cases.[25]

What Will It Look Like in 2040?

Government will have made it easier to find and see governments' objectives (within and across governments), trends on those objectives, where progress is being made, and where it is not. At the federal level, government will have created visualization tools that agencies and cross-agency teams routinely use to present mission-focused goals and objectives in the context of national and sub-national goals, historic data trends, relevant international comparisons, and other contextual information that enable causal factor identification and fair comparison. In addition, in 2040, governments will routinely collect and broadly share timely outcome data in easy-to-access affordable formats, as USAID did in the 2010s. Governments will have also made it easier for front-line practitioners and the many who support them to find relevant research findings in easily understood and accurately interpreted formats, in locations that successfully catch their attention when they need the information, and not locked behind proprietary firewalls.

COUNT AND CHARACTERIZE EVENTS AND CONDITIONS TO INFORM CONTINUAL IMPROVEMENT

William Haddon, the first leader of what became the National Highway Traffic Safety Administration, appreciated what the public health field understood: the need for special methods for information-gathering and governance

structures that assure ongoing data analyses and translation of analytic findings into effective action. Using an injury epidemiology framework, Haddon
created a matrix that still guides collection of traffic fatality data today. For
every traffic fatality, twelve categories of information are collected: operator,
equipment, environmental, and socio-political characteristics (the columns in
Haddon's matrix) before, during, and after each event (the matrix rows).

These data points enable policy makers in Washington D.C., in state-
houses, and at the local level to understand fatality trends, the riskiest and
safest drivers, the riskiest and safest vehicles and equipment, and the most
dangerous locations. Policy makers use this knowledge to design increasingly
precise, effective, and cost-effective actions that have successfully reduced
traffic fatalities for decades, until the past few years. Analytics of routinely collected data are paired with well-designed measured trials to discover effective
ways to address emerging or still intractable problems, such as drivers[26] and
pedestrians distracted by their smart phones. In the words of Ralph Nader,
Haddon brought the subject of traffic safety "from one of hunch and surmise
to one of rigorous safety analyses."[27]

By 2040, all parts of government similarly need to evolve from "hunch
and surmise" to rigorous analyses. They need to figure out the "special methods" they will use to gather information that helps them understand changes
in outcomes and other dimensions of performance they seek to influence.
They also need to put in place governance structures that ensure continued
analysis and application of analytic insights.

New technologies make it more possible and affordable than ever to
collect data that points to likely causes or enables more informed action or
investigation. By time-stamping and geo-coding our whereabouts as gleaned
from our smart phones, for example, Google can tell us which times of the
day and days of the week state departments of motor vehicles and Social
Security offices are likely to be less crowded, allowing individuals to adjust
when they want to visit. Similarly, by time stamping its violation data, a Coast
Guard office was able to see that most of its violations happened in the wee
hours of the morning while all of its inspections took place during the day.
Changing inspections to the hours when violations occurred sliced the number
of violations.

Most government agencies should time-stamp and geo-code data. In
addition, as Haddon did for traffic fatalities, they need to figure out how to
count and characterize key attributes of the information they collect about
outcomes and other dimensions of performance and process, causal factors,
and unwanted side effects to improve on multiple dimensions.

What Will It Look Like in 2040?

For common processes that governments perform—such as benefits and permit processing, fleet management, and cybersecurity—governments will have created and shared default suites of metrics and analytics that all governments adopt, adapting as needed. This will help them improve outcomes and communicate more meaningfully with citizens. In addition, organizations that try to advance the same or similar outcome objectives will create continuous-learning-and-improvement communities to develop common outcome and other indicators, analytic methods, and data standards, share platforms and principles, and learn from their own and others' experience

---

Steps to Achieve the Vision of 2040

What follows are specific steps to speed the journey to get to where we want to be in 2040.

- **Support Front Line Use of Data:** Identify front-line workers for each government agency and cross-agency priority mission-focused goal. Work with the front line to determine if they have ready access to the information they need, and, if not, figure out how to get it to them on a timely, easily used, accurately understood basis. At the same time, reduce the burden and enhance the value of data sharing.

- **Create analytic and visualization capacity:** Launch Presidential (and Governor/Mayor/County Executive) Analytic Fellows programs to beef up government's analytic and visualization capacity. Create analytic personnel exchanges with data-savvy private sector companies for the same purpose. Build online educational tools to beef up government capacity in these areas.

- **Build process mastery and innovation teams:** Identify three problematic government processes that would benefit from "common infrastructure services everyone could access without reinventing the wheel every time," as Amazon did to speed application development. Launch operational excellence scrums in these areas to learn how to speed process improvements. Support these process improvements with the governance structures they need to sustain continued progress. Based on lessons learned, expand to other critical processes. In the federal government, strategically manage common processes such as credit, benefits, grants, and fleet management by identifying and establishing common infrastructures that advance operational excellence and speed cross-program learning and innovation.

- **Identify priority areas for improvement:** Publish, annually, trends for key outcome indicators in ways that are easy to find and accurately interpret, with peer comparisons providing context when fair comparisons are feasible. Spotlight trends moving in the wrong direction previously trending in the right direction, and pockets of excellence or weakness compared to peers. Use this information to inform priority goal and strategy selection—and build intergovernmental and intersectoral governance alliances to advance the goals. The U.S. federal government, specifically, should pilot at least three mission-focused Cross-Agency Priority Goals in areas where federal trends have been moving in the wrong direction (e.g., mortality and morbidity, traffic fatalities) and two where the U.S. does significantly worse than peers (e.g., infant mortality, life expectancy), naming goal leaders and establishing a cross-agency, intergovernmental, inter-sectoral governance structure and teams that work to close these performance gaps.

- **Invest in cross-boundary information collection, sharing, and use:** Figure out the "special methods" needed to gather useful information that informs the design of effective actions. Geo-code, time-stamp, and tag causal factors linked to outcome indicators. Identify and adopt other data standards to facilitate user-centered, place-based problem-solving and opportunity advancement, with appropriate privacy and security protections. Two good places to start are:

  - government programs that try to prevent bad things from happening and keep costs low when they do. Variations on the Haddon Matrix, for example, could be adapted to learn from harmful past incidents, not just for outcomes such as transportation accidents and oil spills, but also for process problems such as fraud and significant processing delays and errors.

  - benefits/permits/loans/insurance. Government programs that receive applications and confirm continuing eligibility are all likely to benefit, for example, from tracking not just the number of incoming, outgoing, and pending applications, but also by comparing to the same period in prior years and by tallying total time in the system, sorted by complexity.

  Standard-setting organizations such as the Governmental Accounting Standards Board or the Federal Accounting Standards Advisory Board, or intergovernmental networks such as the International City/County Management Association, could develop some of these standards, as could intergovernmental communities of practice such as the What Works Cities network[28] and Mid-Atlantic StatNet. So could federal agencies working with their state and local delivery partners or networks of front-line providers.[29] Complementing this effort, governments and others should experiment with development of shared data warehousing platforms to find ways to cut the costs and facilitate learning and cooperation across programs, while providing needed privacy and security protections.[30]

- **Establish standards for data governance, provenance, and ethics:** Establish one or more intergovernmental bodies to sort out and establish standards for data governance (e.g., who owns, who gets access), data provenance, and ethical issues related to data generation and use. Develop standards that ensure proprietary interests do not interfere with government's ability to learn from experience and undertake iterative trials to discover ways to improve on multiple dimensions.

Shelley Metzenbaum works on variety of projects to encourage a better world through better government. She is also a Senior Fellow at the Volcker Alliance and formerly served as Associate Director for Performance and Personnel Management at the Office of Management and Budget. She was the founding president of The Volcker Alliance and has held positions at the U.S. Environmental Protection Agency, the Commonwealth of Massachusetts, the City of Boston, the State of Arkansas, the University of Massachusetts, the University of Maryland, and the Harvard Kennedy School.

Endnotes

1   Steven Kelman, "The Political Foundations of American Statistical Policy," in William Alonso and Paul Starr, ed., *The Politics of Numbers* (New York: Russell Sage Foundation, 1987), 275-276.

2   Janet A. Weiss and Judith E. Gruber, "The Managed Irrelevance of Federal Education Statistics" in William Alonso and Paul Starr, ed., *The Politics of Numbers* (New York: Russell Sage Foundation, 1987) 367.

3   Shelley H. Metzenbaum, "From Oversight to Insight: Federal Agencies as Learning Leaders in the Information Age," in Timothy J. Conlan and Paul J. Posner, ed., *Intergovernmental Management for the Twenty-First Century* (Washington, DC: Brookings Institution, 2008), 209-242.

4   Metzenbaum, Shelley. "Good Government: Persistent Challenges, Smart Practices, and Needed Knowledge" forthcoming in James L. Perry (ed.), *Building a Government and Public Service for the 21st Century.*

5   "Washington, DC: Open Data," Data.gov, accessed June 3, 2018, https://dc.gov/page/open-data; "Open Data Resources," UK Data Service, accessed June 3, 2018, https://www.ukdataservice.ac.uk/get-data/other-providers/open-data.

6   "Driving Federal Performance," Performance.gov, accessed June 3, 2018, https://obamaadministration.archives.performance.gov/; "USA Spending," Datalab, accessed June 3, 2018, https://datalab.usaspending.gov/; "Performance Dashboard," Transforming India MyGov, accessed June 3, 2018, https://transformingindia.mygov.in/performance-dashboard/; Healthypeople.gov, accessed June 3, 2018, https://www.healthypeople.gov/; "Montgomery County Priority Objectives," CountyStat, accessed June 3, 2018, https://reports.data.montgomerycountymd.gov/countystat.

7   "Code Enforcement," City of Cincinnati, accessed June 3, 2018, https://insights.cincinnati-oh.gov/stories/s/Code-Enforcement/eb9h-rrpu/; Hans Rosling, "Let my dataset change your mindset," filmed June 2009 at U.S. Department of State, TED Video, 19:50, accessed June 3, 2018, https://www.ted.com/talks/hans_rosling_at_state.

8   "What Works Clearinghouse," IES, accessed June 3, 2018, https://ies.ed.gov/ncee/wwc/; Abdul Latif Jameel Poverty Action Lab, accessed June 3, 2018, https://www.povertyactionlab.org/; "Results First Clearinghouse Database," Pew Trusts, accessed June 3, 2018, http://www.pewtrusts.org/en/research-and-analysis/data-visualizations/2015/results-first-clearinghouse-database.

9   Code for America, accessed June 3, 2018, https://www.codeforamerica.org/; "Local Government Fellows," Results for America, accessed June 3, 2018, https://results4america.org/our-work/local-government-fellows/; Presidential Innovation Fellows, accessed June 3, 2018, https://presidentialinnovationfellows.gov/.

10   "What Works Cities," Bloomberg Philanthropies, accessed June 3, 2018, https://whatworkscities.bloomberg.org/; "Mid-Atlantic StatNet: Fostering Peer Collaboration in Performance Management," Socrata, accessed June 3, 2018, https://socrata.com/blog/peer-collaboration-in-performance-management-midatlantic-statnet/.

11   U.S. Census Bureau, "2013 Annual Survey and Public Employment and Payroll," Economics and Statistics Administration, 2013.

12 Shashank Dubey, "Return on Investment: Turbocharging analytics project adoption," *Analytics Magazine* (May 1, 2018).

13 The Annie E. Casey Foundation and its spin-off, Case Commons, provide an intriguing example of this sort of field-supporting, technology-developing effort. "Casebook Gaining Recognition as Game Changer in Child Welfare Technology," December 31, 2015, http://www.aecf.org/blog/casebook-gaining-recognition-as-game-changer-in-child-welfare-technology; Also see Case Commons, accessed June 2, 2018, https://www.casecommons.org/

14 "Amazon Annual Report 2017," Amazon, accessed June 3, 2018, http://phx.corporate-ir.net/phoenix.zhtml?c=97664&p=irol-reportsannual; "UPS Annual Report 2017," UPS, accessed June 3, 2018, https://pressroom.ups.com/assets/pdf/2017_UPS_Annual_Report.pdf ; "Annual Reports," UPS, accessed June 3, 2018, http://www.investors.ups.com/phoenix.zhtml?c=62900&p=irol-reportsannual_pf.

15 "Amazon Annual Report 2017," Amazon.

16 "Amazon letter to shareholders 2017," Amazon, accessed June 3, 2018, http://phx.corporate-ir.net/phoenix.zhtml?c=97664&p=irol-govletter_pf.

17 Ron Miller, "How AWS Came to Be," *Tech Crunch,* July 2, 2016.

18 Mark Rockwell, "TSA Seeks Smarter Luggage Scanners," *Federal Computer Week,* May 3, 2018.

19 Derek B. Johnson, "IRS closes in on industry-based fraud squad" *Federal Computer Week,* May 3, 2018.

20 Recreation.gov is a good example of government working across agencies to organize and share data in a more people-focused way.

21 Rosling, "Let my dataset change your mindset."

22 Rosling, "Let my dataset change your mindset," 11:02.

23 Aaron E. Carroll and Austin Frakt, "It Saves Lives. It Can Save Money. So Why Aren't We Spending More on Public Health?" *New York Times,* May 28, 2018.

24 Philip Rhodes and John H. Bryant, "Public Health" *Encyclopedia Britannica,* accessed May 28, 2018, https://www.britannica.com/topic/public-health.

25 Kathleen Tuthill, "John Snow and the Broad Street Pump: On the Trail of an Epidemic," *Cricket* 31(3), pp. 23-31, Nov. 2003.

26 U.S. Department of Transportation, "U.S. DOT Launches First-Ever National Distracted Driving Enforcement and Advertising Campaign" April 3, 2014, https://www.transportation.gov/briefing-room/us-dot-launches-first-ever-national-distracted-driving-enforcement-and-advertising.

27 William Haddon Obituary, *The Washington Post,* accessed June 3, 2018, https://www.washingtonpost.com/archive/local/1985/03/05/william-haddon-dies/e7b8bd4c-a1b7-4cfb-a0fc-8564fbee5c3f/?utm_term=.11155b2eb627.

28 "What Works Cities," Bloomberg Philanthropies. Accessed June 25, 2018, https://whatworkscities.bloomberg.org

29 See, for example, "Data Design Initiative," National Head Start Association, accessed June 3, 2018, https://www.nhsa.org/our-work/initiative/data-design-initiative.

30 See, for example, "Open Standards Principles," GOV.UK, accessed June 3, 2018, https://www.gov.uk/government/publications/open-standards-principles/open-standards-principles.

ACKNOWLEDGMENTS

The content of this book was twenty years in the making and draws on the work of hundreds of IBM Center for The Business of Government report authors, radio show guests, and colleagues. While we cannot acknowledge each individual for their inspiration, support, and ideas, we would like to thank everyone who has collaborated with the IBM Center and contributed to the ideas presented in this book.

We would first like to thank all those who participated in our envisioning sessions. We found their insights to be highly valuable in developing chapters in Part II. In addition, we would like to thank our colleagues in the public management community who took the time to review draft chapters and provide us with their thoughtful comments: Mark Forman, Jane Fountain, Sally Ann Harper, Donald Kettl, David McClure, Ines Mergel, and Shelley Metzenbaum.

A crucial component to the success of this book was the collective contribution of visions for the year 2040. We would like to acknowledge the thoughtful contributions of our authors: David A. Bray, Lee Feldman, Lora Frecks, Hollie Russon Gilman, Lori Gordon, W. Henry Lambright, Shelley H. Metzenbaum, Marc Ott, Tad McGalliard, Sukumar Rao, and Darrell M. West.

We would also like to thank a number of our IBM colleagues, starting with Lisa Mascolo, Managing Director, U.S. Public Service, and Sreeram Visvanathan, Global Managing Director, Government Services, for their strong support of this project. Other IBM colleagues reviewed drafts and participated in the "envisioning" sessions that contributed to the content of several chapters. Specifically, we would like to thank Marquis Cabrera, Emily Craig, Leanne Haselden, Adam Jelic, Darcie Piechowski, Michael Preis, Jason Prow, Erica Webber, Susan Wedge, and Claude Yusti.

IBM consulting staff provided valuable assistance throughout the project. Khris Jore played a major role in designing and conducting our survey on major management initiatives. Caroline Briseli, Susan Kann, Rishi Setia, and Jackson Viccora provided great assistance by undertaking literature reviews, conducting interviews, and assisting us in reviewing the manuscript. A Humphrey Fellowship Program participant from India, Kiran Kabtta Somvanshi, assisted in editing chapters.

Two key individuals on the IBM Center staff provided valuable contributions to the book: Ruth M. Gordon and Michael J. Keegan. Ruth managed the Challenge Grant review process and assisted us in many ways throughout the process of putting this book together. Michael wrote Chapter Seven and provided us with many of the insights he gained from conducting Business of

Government Hour radio interviews.

Finally, we would like to thank Dan Muggeo, Frank Coffy, Anthony Hanna, and Ryan Bertrand, all with Daniels+Roberts, Inc., for superb editing and production—and for their patience with our seemingly endless revisions to get the manuscript "just right." We would also like to thank Jon Sisk and Kate Powers, with Rowman & Littlefield Publishers, for their support and encouragement.

Mark A. Abramson
Daniel J. Chenok
John M. Kamensky

ABOUT THE IBM CENTER FOR THE BUSINESS OF GOVERNMENT

Founded in 1998, the IBM Center for The Business of Government helps public sector executives improve the effectiveness of government with practical ideas and original thinking. The IBM Center sponsors independent research by top minds in the academic and nonprofit communities. It focuses on the future of the operation and management of the public sector. Since its creation, the IBM Center has published 23 books and nearly 350 reports. All reports and other material are available free of charge at the IBM Center website: www.businessofgovernment.org.

Over the past 20 years, the IBM Center has provided government leaders with instructive ideas that inform actions. Based on this guidance, the IBM Center has earned a reputation for addressing public management issues with a deep understanding—rooted in both theory and practice.

The IBM Center competitively awards stipends to outstanding researchers across the United States and the world. Each award winner is expected to produce a research report on an important management topic.

In addition to its reports and books, the IBM Center publishes *The Business of Government* magazine. The Center also produces *The Business of Government Hour* - an interview program with with government executive who are changing the way government does business.

To find out more about the IBM Center and its research stipend program, to review a full list of publications, or to download a report, visit www.businessofgovernment.org.